SPAIN
NORTH

First Edition
1991

TABLE OF CONTENTS

HISTORY AND CULTURE

TRAVELING IN NORTHERN SPAIN

THE PYRENEES
- by M. Reyes Agudo

COSTA VERDE - THE GREEN COAST
- by Gabriel Calvo

THE PILGRIMS' PATH TO SANTIAGO
- by Sabine Tzschaschel

FROM GALICIA TO MADRID
- by José Manuel Riancho

ANCHA CASTILLA - THE DUERO BASIN
- by José Manuel Rincho

MADRID

THE MOUNTAIN VALLEYS OF NEW CASTILE
- by José Ramón Monleón

FEATURES

GUIDELINES

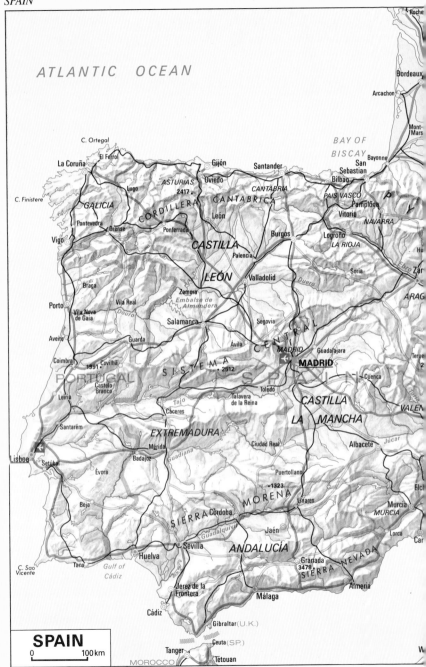

LIST OF MAPS

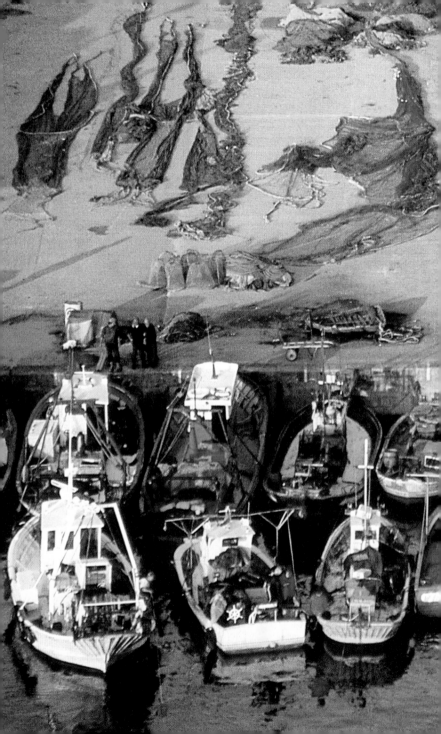

HISTORY
AND CULTURE

The cave of Altamira was discovered in 1868 by a hunter whose dog had become trapped and had to be rescued. It was by no means unusual to find caves in the karstic area of Santillana del Mar. By chance the hunter was the servant of a scholar from Santander who was interested in a new positivistic science, the study of prehistory, which built its knowledge on ancient weapon and tool fragments. When the servant returned home and told his master Don Marcelino about the cave, the latter decided to take a trip there with his eleven-year-old daughter to look for flints. They entered the cave with a carbide lamp. The child crawled through a passage which was too low for adults. And suddenly her father heard her shout: Look, papa, bulls! And there they were, the famous bisons of Altamira. But when Don Marcelino told the world about his discovery, no one believed him. Even the new science could not imagine that 20.000 years ago in the middle of the Paleolithic Age human beings had been able to paint with such amazing beauty and esthetic perfection. About one hundred animals are depicted on the walls of the cave. The artist used the contours of the rocks when forming their outlines and stances. And it is almost as if the rocks were made for them, as if the artist only had to look carefully at the rocks to read the shapes of the bison from their stone disguises. Sculptors including Michelangelo and Picasso have done exactly the same thing as

Preceding pages: A Spanish emblem. Fortress in Iscar (Valladolid). El Barco de Ávila. Barcelona fishermen. Toledo skyline. Left: Cántiga by Alfonso the Wise. The Virgin Mary taming the wild bull.

these ancient artists, finding the shape that is already hidden in a piece of marble or other object.

Don Marcelino died with the sad reputation of being a swindler, of falsifying prehistoric research. The discovery of the cave at Lascaux in France brought increased recognition to Altamira. But within half a century the breath of innumerable visitors began to harm what had been preserved for more than twenty thousand years. Today, anyone hoping to visit the cave has to submit a formal application at least six months in advance. In front of the Archeological Museum in Madrid, German technicians built an exact copy to give visitors an idea of the culture from which the paintings originate. Scientists think that the humans of the time had already made considerable technical progress: they were hunters who made axehandles, harpoons and fishing rods from bone or horn. Pictures of this kind are found all over the mountains and hills in the north of Spain: Puente Viesgo (Santander) and El Pindal (Asturias) are the most important. This culture began declining as of the 7th millennium when devastating climatic changes transformed whole regions into deserts. Their populations fled to the Mediterranean coast where conditions were better. In the Iberian mountains in the south of Aragon and Catalonia there are other paintings. They are not inside caves, but have been painted on rock faces. They show hunting scenes and ritual dances and use only one color. You will find the most interesting paintings of this kind at Cogull (Lérida), El Navazo and Albarracín (Teruel).

The Northern Ethnic Groups

Before the great migration of Indo-European peoples took place during the Neolithic Age, the peninsula was inhabited by Iberians and Basques. Very little is known of the origins of these

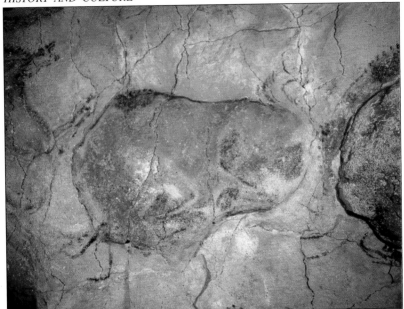

peoples. Some experts believe they came from Asia Minor via North Africa in the 5th millennium B.C. At any rate groups of people settled in the Levant, on the Mediterranean coast, and later came into contact with the cultures colonizing the Mediterranean: the Tyreans, the Phoenicians, Greeks and Carthaginians. The zenith of their culture was reached in the 6th century B.C. At an unknown point in time these Iberian peoples penetrated the interior of the region and mixed with the Celts. They put up little resistance to the Romanization of the area which began during the 2nd century B.C. The peninsula and its most inportant river, the Ebro (Ibero), were both named after these Iberians.

There is much speculation amongst experts regarding the origins of the Basque people. They are thought to be an early Indo-European group of people, and

some claim their language has Caucasian or African roots. They came to the peninsula during the Bronze Age and seem to be descended from Cro-Magnon man. Their territory was in the Pyrenees and finally they retreated back to the mountains, that are present-day Basque country. There the people and their language survived all invasions, even those of the Celts, who left their mark on everything else on the peninsula.

The Celts began crossing into the peninsula in the 8th century B.C. The individual waves of immigration lasted until the 6th century B.C. Their culture, less sophisticated than that of the Iberians – they had no written language or coins –, gradually spread throughout the north. Cantabria and Asturias are names of Celtic origin: *Kent-Aber* means corner of waves, and *As-Thor* means high mountains. The remains of Celtic villages, *castros,* have been found all over the area. Thirty to forty families lived in such villages, in circular houses *(pallozas)* made of slate, humans and animals shar-

Above: An Altamira bull (Early stoneage period). Right: Country folk dance with Celtic pallozas in background.

ing the same thatched roof. The villages had neither roads nor squares. The most important castros are to be found on the Sta. Tecla mountain in the Miño delta (Pontevedra), in Coaña (Asturias) and in the Ancares (Lugo). The Romanization changed the character of these villages, but many retained their cultural independence.

In some areas the different groups of peoples mixed and founded a Celtic-Iberian tribe. Their most important settlement was Numancia. Little is left of this town near present-day Garray (Soria), but it is known that the streets were built at right angles to each other, that the upper parts of the houses were made of adobe and the lower parts of stone, and that the roofs were made of twigs and clay. Many of the buildings in this region are still built in this way today. Numancia was surrounded by a double stone wall and a moat. It also had square towers. The strange stone bulls which can be seen all over the area of Avila and Segovia (El Tiemblo, Avila) date back to this period.

Roman Colonization

In the 3rd century B.C. the Romans gradually began to extend their colonization to Spain. The Punic Wars, in which Romans and Carthaginians fought for the domination of the Mediterranean region, at first affected only the Spanish coast. In the year 205 Scipio finally put an end to the empire of the Carthaginians in the Mediterranean.

But even before the Carthaginians had been forced from the Iberian peninsula the Roman senate had decided to organize the conquered territories into provinces: *Hispania Citerior* on the Mediterranean coast, and *Hispania Ulterior* in Andalusia. A praetor was appointed to govern each province. Initially the Roman policy was to exploit the conquered areas' natural resources. They employed the relatively simple strategy of stirring up anger between the native populations. However, this strategy proved unsuccessful when the natives joined forces and attacked the invader to-

17

gether. Rome sent M. Porcius Cato to occupy the rebellious areas. From 197 B.C. onwards the political strategy in Hispania was changed. Having restricted themselves thus far to military action, the Romans now began to colonize the country which Rome hoped would provide the raw materials for its expansionist politics. Cultural penetration was carried out fairly easily in the coastal regions. But the further the Roman troops went into the interior of the country, the greater the resistance they encountered amongst the tribes of the Meseta.

It was the Lusitanians of Portugal and the Celtic-Iberians of Numancia who put up the greatest resistance to the Romans, and it was not until 153 B.C. that they were able to set up shop in Numancia. Before this they conquered the surrounding settlements (Palencia, Coca) but were then distracted from this front for seven years by fighting in Lusitania. It was there that the shepherd Viriato became famous for developing the art of guerrilla warfare. He incited a rebellion throughout western Spain as far as the Guadalquivir. He stalled the Romans on many occasions through surprise attacks, but was ultimately murdered in his sleep. After that the Romans attacked Numancia again, but the 20.000 Romans were forced to surrender to 4.000 Numancians. A Roman consul was bound naked to the town gate. Finally Scipio Aemilianus arrived with an army, including all the African troops. 60.000 soldiers besieged the town to starve it out. Cervantes dramatized the tragic resistance of the town in one of his plays. Within the walls of the town the people must have resorted to cannibalism, and when the Romans finally entered they found only ruins and corpses.

From the year 133 B.C. onwards Sertorius tried a strategy of understanding

Right: The Roman aqueduct in Segovia, 1800 years old and still intact.

towards the Lusitanians, offering them friendship instead of trying to keep them down by force. They surrendered happily, but Rome was suspicious of this policy of cooperation. Further troops were sent and they finally conquered Sertorius. But peace was not restored to the Iberian peninsula until the year 19 B.C., under Augustus, two hundred years after colonization first began.

Romanization and Christianization

In the region around the Mediterranean and in Andalusia Latin soon replaced the native languages. On the Meseta and in the north, however, Romanization took somewhat longer to complete. An excellent network of roads was gradually built to gain access to the interior of the country and its wealth of natural ressources; many of today's roads were in fact built on these ancient Roman routes. Slaves from the south were sent to work in the mining areas of Galicia and León (the goldmines of Las Medulas), whilst the locals were conscripted to serve in the army and then later sent home to further the cause of Romanization themselves. The Duero and Ebro basins became rich, partly through the development of agriculture.

On the Castilian Meseta the remains of Roman settlements can be seen at Tiermes and Uxama (Soria), Clunia (Burgos) and La Olmeda near Saldaña (Palencia). The most important historical monument to have been preserved is Segovia's Roman aqueduct. There have been Roman walls at Lugo, León and Coca since the 2nd century.

The Spanish people's first contact with Christianity must have come in the year 58. At least it is known that Paul intended to travel to Hispania at this time. Missionaries went first to Betica (western Andalusia) and to the towns on the Mediterranean coast. Under Theodosius I (3rd century), the Christian Church was given

immunity from taxation and as a result became a powerful force in the country. At this time the migration of Germanic peoples to Spain began, ending with the invasion of the Goths.

The Barbarians from the North

In the 4th century the Huns from Central Asia began to arrive in Central Europe, expelling as they did so the tribes living on the borders of the Roman Empire. These Germanic tribes then moved further west and finally reached the Iberian peninsula. The first to settle there were the Suevi (Swabians), the Vandals and the Alani. They quickly occupied the sparsely populated Meseta. Very little is known of their settlements and their way of life. The Suevi moved to the northeast of the peninsula, the Alani, who came from the Caucasus, occupied Lusitania, and the Vandals moved on to Andalusia and North Africa, where they finally settled in Tunisia. But the Visigoths, confederates of the Romans, occupied Aqui-

tania, and then moved to the peninsula to oust the other barbarian tribes. They maintained their kingdom in Gaul almost throughout the 5th century. Their capital was in Toulouse. Under Eurich they ruled from the Loire to the Sierra Morena. In the year 507, following a Frankish attack, the Visigoths retreated to the Iberian Peninsula.

The Visigoths in Toledo

Because the Visigoths were so few in number, they confined their settlements to the Valleys of the Tajo and Duero. They established a court at Toledo and ruled the rest of the country from there. The Basque country was the last region to offer them any resistance. It was brought under Visigoth control in 624, but was never completely conquered. In order to achieve unity in the Visigoth kingdom, the abyss had to be bridged between the minority occupiers, who had all the political and military power, and the Hispano-Roman majority who were domi-

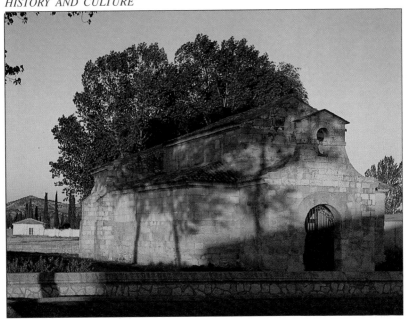

nant culturally and economically. Religion was the greatest obstacle to the achievement of unity. Mixed marriages were forbidden, for the Visigoths followed Arius' doctrine, while the Hispano-Romans followed the Latin rites. In the 6th century Leovigildo attempted to convert the entire peninsula to Aianism. But his son Hermenegildo, under the influence of his wife, a Frankish princess, and the Bishop of Seville, San Leandro, converted to Catholicism. Eventually father and son fought a battle, in which Hermenegildo was defeated and killed, and thus became a martyr and a saint. His brother Recaredo, the heir to the throne, was also converted by San Leandro. Under him the Council of Toledo (587) officially established the Roman Catholic religion in Spain. From that point on the Church had a decisive influence on Visigoth politics.

Above: The 7th century west Gothic San Juan de Baños church (Baños de Cerrato, Palencia).

The weakest part of the Visigoth political system was its way of choosing rulers. According to ancient Gothic traditions, military generals gathered together whenever a king died and chose his successor. These meetings soon lost their significance and many kings came to power by the simple strategy of killing off their predecessors. After religious unification the advisory meetings for the heir to the throne were held in Councils. The 4th Toledan Council of 632 established the rule that no king could come to the throne through regicide or by deposing his predecessor. From now on the bishops were to take part in electing the new king. It also laid down the rule that no one with a tonsure (that is to say no priest) was allowed to become king. But the Councils were unable to keep control of the events. The history of the 18 Gothic kings who reigned over a period of one hundred and fifty years consists of a succession of murders and poisonings, the inventiveness of which would outdo any horror story. Chindasvinto had five hundred noblemen murdered in order to secure the succession to the throne for his own family. One of the most curious cases is that of King Wamba, who was drugged and given a tonsure so that he could no longer continue his rule. His successor was confirmed by the 12th Toledan Council.

At the beginning of the eighth century the fragile structure of Visigoth rule was close to breaking point. The Arab threat was beginning to loom. The last Gothic king, Don Rodrigo (Roderic), had been chosen in a contested vote which left his opponents dissatisfied. For help, they turned to the Arabs, who had already reached North Africa at this stage. In 711 they crossed to Spain. The folklore version of this story gives a more melodramatic account: At the end of the 7th century the Visigoth nobleman Don Julián of Toledo was sent to Tangiers by the king as an observer. His daughter Florinda remained in Toledo. Don Rodrigo saw her bathing in the river one day and took her by force. The daughter told her father of her humiliation and he brought about the invasion as an act of revenge. Don Rodrigo was defeated and the rest of his army fled to northern Spain.

Visigothic Art and Culture

The Visigoths founded their kingdom in a Romanized country, and brought a less developed culture to it themselves. The prime representatives of Gothic Hispania were the Hispano-Romans, who wrote Latin. There were schools and libraries in the many convents and monasteries, and in some of the Bishop's residences as well. San Isidoro of Seville, who wore the miter for 40 years, was the author of *Etymologies*, an encyclopedia containing all the knowledge available at the time and which formed the basis of medieval culture.

Hardly any buildings have survived from the Visigoth era, but four churches

have been preserved. They were built of quarried rocks and were decorated with carvings. They have barrel vaulting and horseshoe arches. These four relics are found in the area often referred to as the "Gothic fields" in the north of Spain between Burgos and Portugal. Only the ground plan and the apse have survived from the church near Quintanilla de las Viñas (Burgos). The apse is decorated outside and inside with bas-reliefs and has angels on the abutment stones, holding symbols of the sun and the moon. San Juan de Baños near Palencia is the most important architectural example from this time. It has three aisles which are separated by arches with Corinthian columns, three apse chapels, a square ground plan and barrel vaulting. San Pedro de la Nave (Zamora) was moved to Campillo in 1930 to prevent it from being flooded by the Ricobayo reservoir. Of the four Visigoth churches this one has the most ornamentation. The symmetry and light of the capitals, made by two different masters or workshops, are extremely expressive. Their themes are the sacrifice of Isaac and Daniel in the lions' den. The church of Santa Comba de Bande (Orense) has a ground plan in the shape of a Greek cross and is hidden away amongst tobacco fields and *hórreos*. The churches are all tiny with unique esthetic harmony and simple architecture.

Moorish Rule

After only one hundred years the religious movement founded by Mohammed in the 7th century already dominated all the former Roman provinces of North Africa, and was moving towards the Atlantic coast. The Umayyads, the ruling dynasty representing the Prophet on earth, had also defeated the Berber tribes of Mauretania, the Moors. The latter joined to form a further force in the political and religious movement. In 711 a delegation from a faction of Visigoths

LITEL SON IOI SANTOS E NON MEN QUE EL XREYER IOVER

went to Islamic Africa to ask the governor of Damascus, Musa Ben Musayr, for help with their domestic political problems. Musa sent the Berber Tariq with 7000 men via Gibraltar (Jebel al- Tariq = mount of Tariq), and he defeated Don Rodrigo at Cádiz. It was almost the only resistance which the Moors encountered before arriving four years later in northern Spain. Tariq decided to place his victorious forces in the services of his own master, the Caliph of Damascus.

Tariq's strategy was swift and intelligent. It combined strength with diplomacy, sometimes attacking towns, at other times making pacts with them and forcing them to pay tribute. In many cases he found important allies amongst the Jews, who were discriminated against by the Visigoth policy of religious unity. Tariq marched north without occupying the land, but he had already demonstrated

Above: Description of a massacre between Christians and Moors (Gothic images, Mondoñedo Cathedral, Lugo).

his superiority. He stopped at Toledo, the former Visigoth capital. Musa followed him with an army of 18.000 men and secured the territories which Tariq had conquered. From Toledo they launched another campaign together to the north, reaching Zaragoza and the foothills of the Pyrenees. They never demanded religious subordination of the people they conquered. Christians were allowed to retain their belief as long as they paid their tribute. These Christians were called *mustarib*, which soon became Mozarab. Many Hispano- Roman noblemen converted to Islam so as to avoid taxes; this was the case with Conde Casius of Tudela (Navarre), who Arabized his name to Banu Qasí. He founded a powerful dynasty and made an alliance with the untamable Basques who led an isolated existence in the Navarrese mountains, struggling against Charlemagne. By the year 718 the whole of Spain was part of the Caliphat of Damascus, ruled by Valís.

In 756 Abd ar-Rahman I made Spain an independent emirate and began the

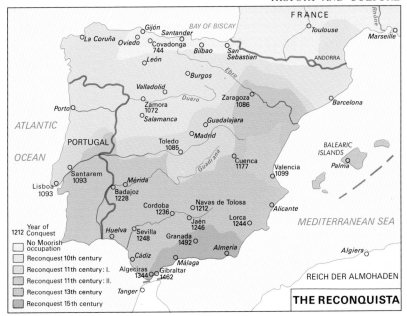

THE RECONQUISTA

process of securing its borders. The Arab governor of Zaragoza was not prepared to obey him and called upon Charlemagne for help in 778. Charlemagne proved to be a threat, not only to the Arabs but also to the Basques. He arrived with 400.000 men and decided to take Zaragoza, but the siege lasted so long that he was forced to retreat again to put down insurgent Saxons on the other frontier of his empire. On his retreat he crossed the Pyrenees at Roncesvalles and left a rearguard of 20.000 men, together with his twelve best noblemen including Roland, Duke of Brittany. They were ambushed by the Basques and, according to legend, no one survived. The legendary battle has been immortalized in one of the most moving European heroic epic poems, the famous *Chanson de Roland*.

Pre-Romanesque Art in Asturias

In 718 only a small strip in the north of the Cantabrian mountains of Spain was free of the Arab presence. It is to this region that Don Pelayo, Don Rodrigo's former guard, had retreated. He refused to be subjugated and faced the Arabs in the legendary battle of Covadonga. They were busy with their expansion in south France and hardly took any notice of this small pocket of resistance. Still following Visigothic protocol, Don Pelayo was chosen as leader of the northern tribes scattered around the region. His son-in-law later became King Alfonso I. What is now referred to as Asturian art dates from this period. This esthetic style is defined by a series of small churches which all date from the 9th century, and which served the first Asturian kings before they spread their empire to León. The legend of Santiago the Moor-killer, or *matamoros*, grew up during the time of Alfonso I, the Chaste (846). Santiago was seen as a patron saint who legitimized the expansion of the empire. The town of Oviedo was founded at this time and became the capital of Asturias. The Camara Santa of the cathedral, the churches of San Tirso, of which only the apse has sur-

23

vived, and the church of San Julián de Prados (812) in Santullano, with an illusionist wall decoration strongly reminiscent of Byzantine predecessors, all date from this period. Under Ramiro I (850) Asturian architecture reached its peak. Santa María del Naranco is the most beautiful building from this time. It is both a two-storied church and a palace. Its lower floor is reminiscent of the Camara Santa, its upper floor has a barrel vault extended by two balconies. Via these balconies the natural world seems to blend into the wide perspectives in the interior. Close by you will find San Miguel de Lillo from the same epoch.

King Alfonso III (910) expanded the Asturian empire to the south of the mountains, pursuing a policy of re-settlement which entailed enormous building projects, partly already influenced by the Mozarabs, who had begun to leave the Arabic regions in the south. Almost everything which was built during his rule was later destroyed by Almansur. But San Adrián in Tuñón has survived, as has San Salvador de Valdedios, consecrated by seven bishops in 893. The church is decorated with Mozarabian stylistic elements and the design of internal space already heralds the Romanesque era. The victory cross, a jewel with national symbolic significance kept in the Camara Santa in Oviedo, also dates from this time.

The son of Alfonso III was Ordoño II. He settled in León at the crossroads on the way to Galicia, Asturias and the front regions on the Duero and Ebro. From there he fought battles with Abd ar-Rahman and encouraged the re-settlement *(repoblación)* of the newly-conquered Duero bank through the awarding of generous privileges to those prepared to live there. Old towns were revitalized and new ones were built, such as Astorga,

Toro or Zamora, founded by Mozarabs from Toledo.

The Caliphs of Córdoba – Almansur

In the 10th century Christian Spain was divided: the Asturian- León Empire, expansionist, strong and large, extended as far as the upper reaches of the Duero, where it bordered on Castile. The influence of the Basque kingdom of Navarre, which was allied with the Arabized Visigoth dynasty of Qasim of Tudela, extended to the Pyrenees, where small independent states had formed. These included Ribagorza, Sobrarbe and the Spanish March, conquered from Charlemagne, which stretched from Urgell to Barcelona. The mountain states were so isolated that the Franks and the Arabs left them alone. As a consequence they were able to retain their independence until the 12th century.

In the Arab south Abd ar-Rahman III had founded the Caliphate of Córdoba. He made renewed attempts to advance to the north, but the Christians were now fighting on a wider front, and both parties inflamed their people with religious slogans: "Santiago!" and "Mohammed!" were the battle cries of the day. The idea of the Reconquista was born. From their legendary Palace of Medina Azahara the Caliphs of Córdoba delegated military power to caudillos. One of these, Ibn Abi Amir al-Mansur (940-1022), advanced so far that he was able to take Barcelona, León and Zamora. With a small army of mercenaries, which also included Christian soldiers, he reached Galicia, destroyed the cathedral of Santiago in 997, and took the bells to Córdoba as symbols of his triumph. His great victories pushed the ruling dynasty of the Umayyads in Córdoba into the shade. He dethroned the eleven-year-old Caliph Hixem II himself. But because he was unable to build on the stability of a ruling dynasty, after his death (1002) his empire broke up into

Right: The 11th century Mozarab chapel San Baudelio de Berlanga (Soria).

various *taífas,* or tribal realms, such as Toledo or Seville. Almansur, as he was called by the Christians, made various pacts left and right, sowing disunity and discord amongst the destroyed and collapsing Christian kingdoms. In León the problems regarding the succession to the throne were solved by violent means, when Ramiro II simply killed all his rivals. In Navarre Doña Toda ruled as regent for her son García Sánchez, who was later murdered. Castile declared its independence under Fernán González.

Mozarabian Pre-Romanesque Art and Architecture

Mozarabs are those Christians who lived under Moorish rulers, but who continued to practise their religion. By the 9th century many Christians had integrated into Muslim society, in order not to have to pay the tax levied on Christians. Islam was experiencing a cultural Golden Age at the time. A religious movement which developed amongst the Mozarabs in Córdoba soon resulted in conflict and disputes, and produced martyrs such as San Eulogio, bishop and initiator of the movement. The conflicts spawned in increased Mozarabian emigration to the Christian regions to the north. Mozarabian towns were founded from Galicia to Catalonia in the 10th century. But the Mozarabian people had many misunderstandings with their religious brothers. They still followed the Visigoth religion, but they had also introduced their own Arab development into the language and religious rites, which were on a higher intellectual level than those of the descendents of Asturian peasants. This sophistication is also reflected in their buildings and literature, and in their love songs *(jarchas),* which are regarded as the precursors of Spanish poetry. Mozarabian Churches still stand in the north, and are unique constructions indeed. The horseshoe arch integrated into the church building is common to all of them. It is more rounded than that of the Visigoth church, with an opening at

25

the most of the radius at two-thirds, and it has no central stone. These buildings have little about them reminiscent of the simple basilica. Inside there are small separate rooms for the monks, and the exterior is, despite its minimal dimensions, a playful mix of building elements, recalling of the Byzantine architectural tradition. The most important of all these churches are to be found in León: San Miguel de la Escalada was founded in 913 by monks from Córdoba and reformed in 1126; the church of Sto. Tomás de las Ollas is in Ponferrada, and that of Santiago de Peñalba is in the "Valley of Silence"; Santa María de Lebeña stands in Santander against the backdrop of the Picos de Europa. Another important church is San Miguel de Celanova in Orense. San Baudilio de Berlanga in Soria has a large central column from which the horseshoe arches branch like

Above: The legendary oath of Alfonso VI in St. Agueda before El Cid (Hiraldez Acosta). Right: El Cid monument in Burgos.

the fronds of a palm tree. There is a secret chamber in the wall, where a monk might once have hidden. San Juan de la Peña in Huesca and the higher of the two monasteries in San Millán de la Cogolla (La Rioja) were both built into the rock at the foot of a cliff. In the 10th century San Millán became quite rich because of the income from its extremely productive agricultural pursuits. A codex with the first written words in the pre-Castilian and Basque languages was discovered in this monastery.

The Time of the Heroic Epic

In contemporary epic poems the Castilian Reconquista was given particular significance. The heroes were portrayed as personalities of flawless moral character, ornamented with poetic attributes and heaped with glorious deeds which made them famous throughout the world. The original function of the heroic epic was to spread news. Although written a hundred years after the events they

describe, the poems were often composed at the time of the events and passed on orally. Mozarabian culture was decisive in the development of this custom; it would have been unthinkable in Asturias two hundred years earlier. El Cid, the epic hero of four *cantares* (heroic songs), was a nobleman of Mozarabian descent. The history of Castile can be traced through such epics.

In the 11th century the county of Castile was no more than a deserted area in the northeast corner of Burgos around Oña. Fernán González (912-970) attempted to win independence from León, preparing the way for the creation of the kingdom of Castile. He founded the monastery of San Pedro de Arlanza (Burgos), where he was also buried. Today only ruins remain of the once great monastery. It was here that the poem was written which tells of Fernán González' fight against Almansur and against the king of Navarra. According to this tale González sold the king a hunting falcon and a horse. They agreed that the price

would double for every day that the king failed to pay. When the king finally remembered his debt, it had risen so high that he was forced to surrender the whole of Castile in payment. Fernán González was captured and temporarily imprisoned, but the daughter of the king promised to let him go if he married her.

Castile was conquered by Navarra in 1029. When Sancho the Great of Navarra died, he divided his kingdom amongst his sons, and Fernando I became King of Castile and León. When Fernando I died his kingdom in turn was divided amongst his children: Castile went to Sancho, his first-born; León was given to his favorite son Alfonso, Galicia went to García. His daughters Urraca and Elvira were given Zamora and Toro respectively, but on condition that they did not get married.

Mío Cid Campeador

But Sancho II of Castile was not satisfied with the situation, and for eight years he waged war against his brothers

and sisters in an attempt to reunite the empire. When he and his vassal El Cid besieged Zamora he was murdered by a traitor. His brother Alfonso VI inherited the entire empire. But before he and his men swore allegiance to the king, El Cid had him swear in the church of Santa Agueda in Burgos that he had had nothing to do with his brother's death. The king agreed to take the oath, but afterwards banished the nobleman. The heroic epic poem *Mío Cid,* which was written down in the 12th century, begins with the banishment of the hero. In order to travel and to seek his fortune far away, Cid borrowed money from a Jew in Burgos, and left behind a trunk full of sand as security, saying it contained gold. In San Pedro de Cardeña he bade his wife Jimena and his daughters Elvira and Sol farewell. With his followers he then went to the lands of the Moors, conquered Zaragoza and Teruel, and took the Count of Barcelona

Above: Roman baptismal font, Redecilla del Camino (Burgos).

prisoner. Then he conquered Valencia and sent Alfonso VI one hundred horses in an attempt to persuade him to allow his family to join him. He defeated the Almoravid Yussef, who had tried to conquer Valencia, and sent part of the booty to Alfonso VI, who then took him back into his entourage. This caused great envy amongst the princes of Carrión. The two infantes of the family asked to marry Cid's daughters and the weddings took place in Valencia. But on the journey home both men beat their new wives and abandoned them tied to trees in an oak wood. Cid killed both men in a duel and had his daughters married to other members of the royal family.

In 1085 Alfonso VI and El Cid conquered Toledo and advanced the Reconquista front southwards in several great military campaigns. The king called himself the ruler of three religions and allowed Jews, Christians and Arabs to practice their faith freely.

The next campaign moved the front further south. The Mosque of Toledo, where later the cathedral was built, continued to function as such, but in his absence the king's wife, Constance of Burgundy, threw the Arabs out of the mosque and had it consecrated in the Christian faith. The Muslims rose up in anger at this sacrilege. When Alfonso VI heard the news he returned immediately to take revenge on the rioters. There would have been a terrible bloodbath, had a Moorish architect, an *alfaquí*, not come forth, and told him what had really happened while he had been away. He can still be seen depicted on the altar of the cathedral of Toledo today. The Castilian kings moved their residence to Toledo and remained kings of all three religions.

Aragón and Catalonia

The kingdom of Aragón emerged from the crown of Navarre at the same time as the kingdom of Castile, following the death of Sancho III. It consisted of the small Pyrenean states of Sobrarbe and Ribagorza, along with various other states of the Spanish March, which had broken with Charlemagne. They joined forces and advanced to the valley of the Ebro, the Arab line of defense. Alfonso I, the Warrior, took Zaragoza in 1118. The daughter of Ramiro II, the Monk, married the Count of Barcelona Ramón Berenguer IV, who thereafter called himself Prince of Catalonia and Aragón. With united strength the two realms fought for supremacy in the Mediterranean.

Languedoc, Provence, the Balearic Islands and Valencia were annexed in their turn by this new great power, which preferred to pursue a policy of trade rather than one of conquest by force. In the 13th century the country was the most important trading power in the Mediterranean. The new emphasis on the Mediterranean is reflected most obviously in the kingdom's architecture. The Romanesque buildings of Catalonia are very similar in style to those of France and to the architecture of Lombardy in northern Italy. There are imitation brick churches made of carefully cut stone, apses with blind arches, shallow friezes joined to beautiful ornamental arches, most effective in the play of light and shadow, and tall bell towers, reminiscent of campaniles. The artistic development of this Romanesque style reached its peak in the 11th century. Many examples have been preserved in the inaccessible mountainous regions of the province of Lérida. The most beautiful are in the Boí valley.

The Pilgrims' Path to Santiago

The kingdom of Navarra became powerful under its ruler Sancho I, the Great, and achieved significance because of its position along the Pilgrims' Path to Santiago. This pilgrimage route was also a major trade route, on which much wealth entered the country, and a cultural impulse which led to the foundation of a number of towns. These towns were different to those on the front. Built without fortifications or castles, they stretched out along the path taken by pilgrims, which was lined with craftsmen and traders, and shops often opened onto a bridge over a river at the end. Many of these towns were founded by Frankish immigrants who were given special privileges in return for settling in the *repoblación* region.

Flourishing trade brought Christians and Jews into the area. Each group had its own quarter in the town and there were often violent confrontations between the parties. In Pamplona, for example, the quarters had to be separated by walls, but the civil war between locals and the privileged immigrants continued for centuries. Chivalric orders also contributed to resettlement; this was particularly true of the Knights Templar, a military- religious order devoted to protecting pilgrims in the Holy Land and on their way to Santiago. Its members were given land and

controlled the roads. The Santiago Order also settled along the road. But it was rather a military order dedicated to furthering the cause of the Reconquista. At the same time the order of the Cluny monks from France arrived in the area, founded monasteries and created a link between the Meseta and Europe. The Pilgrims' Path to Santiago thus became an important medium for art, culture and trade.

Romanesque was the architecture of the pilgrim era. It can be found all over the north of the peninsula, from Navarra to Galicia. The Romanesque churches are built of massive stone walls and their ground plan is shaped like a Latin cross. They have barrel vaulting and an uneven number of aisles. The windows allow only a minimum of light to fall into the church. The semi-circular apses once served as shelter for the pilgrims. The

main chapel behind the altar was usually painted, often with Jesus as Pantocrator. But it was the expressive sculptures in Romanesque art that reached its highest form.

Capitals, portals, altars and bosses were all covered with bas- reliefs and sculptures. Their main function was informative rather than decorative. Perfection, irony, anecdotes and stories from the Bible constituted the depictions that cought the attention of the on-looker. The decorative elements were conceived for a simple public, for pilgrims who were superstitious and who sought comfort and reassurance from the Church. For us the details of these churches are an esthetic delight. They are like historical comic strips in which we can read up about times gone by.

Las Navas de Tolosa

In the middle of the 12th century an army of warriors from the Atlas Mountains began to move towards Al-Andalus.

Above: The Roman church of San Martin in Frómista. Right: Symbolic Roman pillars, San Pedro in Caracena.

They called themselves Almohads, defenders of the unity of God. At that time Christian Spain was divided into five kingdoms: Portugal, León, Castile, Aragón-Catalonia and Navarra. Three armies, those of Alfonso III of Castile, Pedro II of Aragón, and Sancho VII of Navarra, joined forces against the common threat. Together they succeeded in destroying the Almohads in the battle of Navas de Tolosa (Jaén) in 1212. This was the last great battle between Moors and Christians, and it was after this victory that Al-Andalus's demise began. The next Castilian king, Fernando III, the Saint, was able to extend his realm far into Andalusia and to reduce the kingdom of Granada to a small area which remained in existence until 1492. Fernando III was a far-sighted and successful ruler who promoted the founding of universities, supported the establishment of a navy and sponsored the cathedrals of Burgos and Toledo. He was canonized in the 17th century.

Alfonso X, the Wise

The son of Fernando III was Alfonso X (1221-1284), an intellectual. Under his rule the military activities of the Reconquista diminished, and a new period of scholarship began, in which the three cultures which had lived and fought each other for five centuries on the peninsula finally became integrated. He founded a school of translation in Toledo based in the castle of San Servando. Under his personal supervision, 15 scholars worked on two historical scripts and established a codex of penal, military and civil law, the seven law books, which served as both a political handbook and the basis of a constitution. In addition he commissioned the translation of the most important astrological, astronomical mathematical, philosophical and medical works from Arabic and Hebrew into Latin and Castilian. Three were books about games

too, a book on chess, one on dice and treatises on hunting and mineralogy with enchanting illustrations portraying leisure activities of the day, or the magical powers of precious stones. The books of poetry set to music, written in Galician-Portuguese by the king himself, are of an exceptional artistic standard. In the *Cantigas de Santa María,* the legendary miracles of the Virgin Mary are recounted in 193 poems. There is, for example, the story of the *caballero* who prays to the Virgin Mary before a bullfight, whereupon the bull becomes tame. Every miracle is illustrated like a comic strip by a series of eight drawings. It is an invaluable document of everyday life in the 13th century.

Gothic and Mudéjar Architecture

Supported by royal and papal bulls, the Church had become extremely rich in the 12th century. The income from farming on its estates, the wool trade, tithes and other taxes financed the construction of

 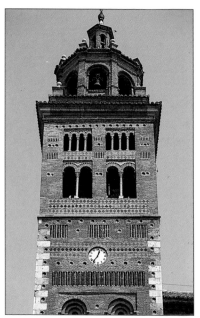

great cathedrals. Countless parishes and dioceses were founded during this period and in Castile in the 13th century, for example, there was one church for every 100 inhabitants. The great Gothic monuments in Castile are to be found on the old wool trade routes. The Cistercians, a reformed Benedictine order, founded in Burgundy as a reaction to the Church's lavish wealth, was the first to introduce Gothic architecture. It was dignified, serious style which has been interpreted as a reaction to the almost playful quality of the Romanesque and an expression of a new spirituality. Light was now let into the church. The windows and the entire construction itself strove upwards to the omnipresent divinity. The large Cistercian monasteries such as Poblet, Oliva, Veruela or las Hueglas and the cathedrals of Avila, Sigüenza and Ciudad Rodrigo

Above left: Burgos Cathedral. Above right: Teruel Cathedral Tower in Mudéjar style. Right: The Catholic Monarchs praying to the Virgin Mother (Anonymous, Prado).

are all pervaded by the unadorned simplicity of the Cistercians. Architects and stonemasons from France, Germany and the Netherlands were brought in to work on the great cathedrals. Masterpieces such as the cathedrals of Burgos or León were built on the model of northern European cathedrals, but they still had characteristic features of their own. One particular aspect of Spanish Gothic architecture was the choir at the center of the cathedral and the ambulatory.

Ever since Fernando III had conquered Andalusia, contact with Arab architects, the *alfaquies,* had not diminished. Impressed by their solid and esthetically refined architecture, Fernando III and Alfonso X also commissioned them to design many religious buildings. This style became known as Mudéjar, and its typical fashion of using brick quickly spread throughout the north in the 13th century and soon towns were filled with Mudéjar churches, towers and *artesonado* wooden ceilings. You will find a number of examples of this architectural style in

Toledo, in the central Duero valley (Cuéllar), in Olmedo or in Castilian towns like Sahagún and the whole area of lower Aragón around Teruel and Zaragoza.

Romance and Intrigue

For reasons of state Don Pedro I of Castile married the fourteen-year-old Blanche of Bourbon, sister-in-law of the French heir to the throne. But without laying a finger on her, he left his young bride at Medina Sedonia castle, while he himself lived in the Alcázar of Seville with his harem and his favorite concubine. Such was the extent to which Arab lifestyles had influenced the lives of Christian kings in the 14th century.

Pedro I is also sometimes known by the title the Cruel. He had five step-brothers and sisters, illegitimate children of his father Alfonso XI. In order to dispose of potential rivals he ordered the heads of all five of his siblings to be brought to him, but his step-brother Enrique of Trastamara escaped and forged

an alliance with the king of Aragón. The French Bourbons, too, were striving to avenge their relative, Blanche, who had been so badly treated in marriage and had died in the meantime, still a virgin. They sent 12.000 men who had been motivated to fight by the promise of "castles in Spain", a phrase which has come to mean the same as "castles in the air". On the other front England and the Arabs joined forces with Pedro I, and this is how Spain came to take part in the Hundred Years' War. After various battles Pedro was finally defeated at Montiel and handed over to his victorious step-brother Enrique de Trastamara, who had him executed in 1369. Enrique II was called the Bastard in folklore. Many romances and folksongs chronicle the events which, recounted in short episodes, form a mosaic of contemporary culture.

Enrique IV of Trastamara was the brother of Isabella the Catholic. He was married to Doña Blanca of Navarre, whom he renounced because she was unable to bear him children. The people nicknamed him the Impotent, for although his second wife, happy Isabella, daughter of the king of Portugal, bore him a daughter, most people agreed that the baby's father was in fact Don Beltrán de la Cueva. Obviously a considerable degree of political interest lay behind this rumor. The daughter, Juana la Beltraneja, became Isabella's rival. In the battle of Toro (1474) aunt and niece fought on opposite sides, Isabella as the ally of her future husband Fernando of Aragón, Juana of her grandfather from Portugal. The victorious Isabella was crowned in Segovia and proclaimed Queen of Castile. Following a vow she had made earlier, she built the monastery of San Juan de los Reyes in Toledo. Two years later she married Fernando. La Beltraneja retired to a convent in Coímbra.

The Catholic Monarchs

After the great campaigns of the Reconquista the peninsula entered a new phase of political stability in the middle of the 13th century. Granada was now only a shadow of its former self, Navarre had finally outlived its imperialistic dream, Portugal and Aragón were devoting all their energies to expansion in the Mediterranean, and Castile had taken over military and political supremacy in the interior. The Trastamara dynasty, which was founded by an illegitimate son of Alfonso XI, married into Castile in 1369 and into Aragón in 1412. The unification of the two kingdoms was completed by the marriage of Isabella and Fernando. They agreed to rule together and to unite their kingdoms as equals. Their motto was *tanto monta, monta tanto, Isabel como Fernando.* They had an itinerant court without any fixed residence. One of their great successes was the capture of Granada, which had until then been excluded from

the Reconquista, partly because of domestic disagreements in the Christian empire, and partly because of its impregnable position. The victory took place in 1492, the year in which Columbus was given funds for an expedition to try and find the western route to India. At the same time the Jews were expelled from Spain.

In 1512 the integration of Navarre was finally achieved, and the whole of Spain was now ruled by one king and had one religion. Both were subsumed under the title of the Catholic Monarchs, given to the Spanish royal house by Pope Alexander VI, a name which still applies to the Spanish royal family today.

Castile's links with Europe were essentially formed by expedient marriages which the Catholic monarchs and their children made. A double link was forged with Austria: Juan married Margarita of Austria and Juana married Philip the Fair. A further well-chosen marriage was that of Catherine (Catalina) of Aragón with Arthur, Prince of Wales, and after his death with the future Henry VIII of England.

Spanish Society at the Time of the Catholic Monarchs

The war for Granada lasted ten years and left the coffers of the Catholic monarchs so empty that they were forced to compensate the nobility which had supported them by awarding feudal rights. This gave rise to the feudal latifundia of Andalusia. Spanish society made a distinction between the nobility and the common people. The nobility paid no taxes, nor did it have to obey most penal laws. Noblemen could not be hanged, they held positions of high office, and had the right to wear certain clothing and to travel in coaches. One group of nobles called the *hidalgos* endued in this system, whose only social advantage was their title, but who were otherwise as poor as

Right: A Gothic tomb in Burgos Cathedral.

church mice. The *cabellero,* the rich nobleman, could pay to have his status elevated. 90 percent of the population was made up of vassals who had to pay heavy taxes and do all the "lowly" work. The main produce was wool, which was exported to Flanders and the towns of the Hanseatic League from the port of Laredo in Santander.

Castile had seven million inhabitants, Catalonia-Aragón barely a million. The church was constantly increasing its wealth, and profited from the custom common among the noble *segundones,* the second-born children not entitled to inherit, of entering monasteries. The Church then assumed responsibility for their educational and other needs. At the tip of the pyramid were the kings, lords of justice who ruled pragmatically.

The Spanish Jews and the Inquisition

The ancestors of the Jews had originally come to the country with the Romans. After a period of discrimination under the Visigoths, they enjoyed greater freedoms again under the Arabs. During the Reconquista they became indispensable to the kings as tax collectors. They took over trade, which was forbidden to Christians, and practiced various crafts because they were not allowed to own land. After Alfonso VI had proclaimed himself king of three religions, his descendants continued to avail themselves of the invaluable services of the Jews. Alfonso VIII had a legendary affair with Raquel, the daughter of his treasurer. Most of Alfonso X's learned translators were Jewish. The Jews were not integrated in the Christian towns, however. They lived in quarters, called the Juderías, which were cut off from the rest of the town. These Jewish quarters have in some cases been preserved – in Ribadavia, for example, or in Allariz, Toro and Zamora, Béjar and Hervás. In almost all the towns near Zaragoza, many Judería streets still exist. The Jewish population, most of which belonged to the urban bourgeoisie, numbered about

35

200.000 in the 13th century. In the 14th century the first violent pogroms took place in many Spanish towns.

During the wars of Granada the Catholic monarchs needed financial help from the Jews, but after the success of the war they passed an edict calling for their expulsion. According to the edict they had to liquidate their assets and leave the country within three months. About 150.000 fled, leaving a financial and intellectual vacuum behind them. These emigrants became known as the Sephardim, a group distinguished by their sophisticated culture. They settled in Portugal, Turkey, North Africa and Romania, where they have maintained their language, the Spanish of the 15th century, and their folkloric traditions until today. About 50.000 preferred to be baptized and stayed in Spain, joining the 20.000 earlier converts, the *conversos.*

Above: Sinister times during the Inquisition, as depicted in Exorcism (Goya).

An Inquisition overseen by Rome had been taking place in Aragón since 1238. In 1478 the Catholic monarchs were granted a papal bull which empowered them to name three inquisitors. These might be bishops, theologians or scholars, who could take action against heretics, false converts and apostates. In 1481 the first auto-da-fé was held, at which several Jews were burned. Some five thousand were to be tried before 1488, and seven hundred of them executed. From 1483 onwards the Dominican Tomás de Torquemada was Inquisitor General. He was introduced by the kings without influence from Rome. Torquemada came from a family of converts himself and remained in office until 1498. The Inquisitors' fanaticism ruled society even into the 19th century. Every town had its own delegation and even today you can still see many of the *picotas or rollos,* the stocks in which the accused were locked and publicly exhibited. This practice is documented in paintings of Berruguete and Goya.

Architecture

The Renaissance in Spain began with the Catholic monarchs and lasted through the whole of the 16th century under Charles V and Philip II. Stylistically, it is impossible to establish clearly-defined bounds of either Gothic or Baroque. The style described by art historians as Isabelline is a continuation of late Gothic, which was retained in Spain until the beginning of the 16th century because it found favor among nobility and clerics. The cathedrals of Segovia and Salamanca both date back to this time. Flemish architects who saw the *horror vacui*, the Arabic tendency to cover everything with ornamentation, began to incorporate Mudéjar elements in the Gothic style.

In 1480 the Breton architect Juan Guas began the construction of San Juan de los Reyes in Toledo and the Palace of Mendoza in Guadalajara. He surrounded the Renaissance façades and portals with scattered decorative elements in the Arabic fashion. The Puerta de la Pellejería and the Capilla del Condestable in the cathedral of Burgos and the Cartuja de Miraflores date from this transition period. With the patronage of families like the Mendozas and Fonsecas, the art of sepulchral sculpture reached a high point in Guadalajara, Sigüenza, Granada, Toledo and Burgos.

The Hispano-Flemish tradition under Isabella the Catholic later became the Plateresque decorative style, named after the engraved works of silversmiths, since the stone was so intricately carved that it resembled silverwork. Stern architectural forms were covered with ornamentation. The first building of this kind was the Colegio de Sta. Cruz in Valladolid (1494), and the Sta. Cruz hospitals of Enrique Egas in Toledo, Santiago and Granada. The stronghold of Plateresque style is Salamanca (university façade, Escuelas Menores, Convento de San Esteban, for example).

When Charles V arrived from Rome he was received as a true Renaissance prince. He brought with him Italian influences and splendid gates were built for him in many towns (Puerta de Bisagra in Toledo). In 1533 he summoned the Italian Titian to be his court artist. The Plateresque style was replaced by a more simple and clear style, perfected in the architecture of Juan Herreras. Under Charles V the Alcázars of Toledo and Segovia were rebuilt in this new style.

The Empire of Charles V

The future Charles I of Spain was born in Ghent in 1500, the son of Philip the Fair of Austria and Juana the Mad. In 1504 Isabel the Catholic died and Juana inherited the throne of Castile. In 1506 Philip died of pneumonia. His death caused Joan to become insane, and she led his corpse in a sad procession through the whole of Castile, until she was locked up under guard in Tordesillas. Her father Fernando the Catholic represented her on the throne until his death in 1516. A year later Charles I arrived from Flanders, where he had been brought up. The interim rule had been carried out by Cardinal Cisneros. But the Spanish did not want to be ruled by a king who had been brought up in a foreign country. His Flemish advisors did not appeal to the nobility, and the king did not even speak Spanish. In 1519 his grandfather Maximillian I of Austria died. Charles inherited his empire, too, and was crowned Charles V, Holy Roman Emperor. This meant departing from Spain again, leaving it in the hands of his mentor Cardinal Adrian of Utrecht. The costs of the coronation celebrations increased dissatisfaction. Many Castilian towns founded *comunidades* and revolted. On a rainy afternoon the *comuneros* in Villalar were defeated and their three leaders executed: Padilla of Toledo, Juan Bravo of Segovia and Maldonado of Salamanca.

SuMa gº ElEmperºᵗ Dº Carlos Quinto ñro.
feñor eneftelugar eftaua afentado Quan=
dole dio elmal alostreintayuno⊚eA=
gofto alas quatro delatarde=Fall=
cio alosveinte yuno de Setiembre
alasdos ymedia delamañana: Año delSºᵗ
de 1558.

Charles V returned to Spain in 1523, having transferred Austria to his brother Ferdinand. After a life-time of battles, the victory over Francis I of France in Pavia, the battle with the Turks at Vienna and the Protestants in the Schmalkaldic War and after conquering Tunis, Mexico and Peru, Charles abdicated and retreated to the Yuste Monastery near Plasencia, where he died. His marriage to Isabel of Portugal had born two daughters and a son, Philip II, heir to the throne. Of his illegitimate descendents, the son of Barbara Blomberg, a beautiful noblewoman from Regensburg, made history as Don Juan de Austria.

Charles V's empire weighed heavily on Castile. The emperor's interests in Central Europe meant that the riches of America were channeled there. Bankers from Germany and Genoa lent him money to finance his many wars. The

Above: Charles V died in the secluded Yuste monastery in 1558. Right: Philip II holding a court council meeting in Segovia.

high interest rates had to to to be met by the Castilian peasants, who became poorer and poorer under this burden. Philip II inherited a state which was forced to declare itself bankrupt in 1557. Some historians interpret the abdication of Charles V as the inability to look ruin in the eye. The normal state budget was about 375 million *maravedis*; the debts which Charles left behind came to 15 billion, not including interest. The annual five billion *maravedis* earned from the colonies went straight into the coffers of the innumerable creditors.

Philip II

Charles V left the Austro-Hungarian part of his inheritance to his brother; Spain, the Colonies, Sardinia, Sicily, Naples, Milan, Burgundy and the Netherlands went to his son. Philip II had the task of defending Spanish politics and the Catholic religion on the Continent. In 1581 he also inherited Portugal and its overseas possessions. Under the leader-

ship of Juan de Austria, the Turks, who had been threatening Europe since the beginning of the century, were finally beaten near Lepanto in 1571. In the Netherlands there were strong moves towards independence, and the Protestant north rose up against Philip II. After even the bloody intervention of the Duke of Alba failed to pacify the area, it finally declared its independence.

Towards the end of his reign Philip armed himself to counter the Protestant fanaticism of Elizabeth I of England and give a somewhat belated response to Francis Drake's attacks on Cádiz, La Coruña and various overseas ports. He built up a huge fleet of ships which was so great that it was called the Unconquerable Armada. On the 20 May 1588 one hundred and thirty ships left the port of Lisbon with 20.000 men. The destruction of the Spanish fleet came about as a direct result of attacks by English galleons, but also as a result of the mistaken strategy of the commander, the Duke of Medina Sidonia, who was no experienced sailor.

Philip II died in the Monastery of El Escorial, which he had built himself. His general confession took three days to be completed.

Mannerism

The Inquisition reached its zenith under Philip II. The king made use of it with gusto. But without contact to the outside world, without the Jews and the Muslims, the generation which followed almost suffocated from lack of culture. Robbed of the opportunity to study the sciences, robbed of its freedom of thought, art remained the only way that it could express itself. The Baroque era was just beginning. In art, in particular, it sought to portray that which was officially denied, the richness of nature, orgies of form and the sensuality of warm colors.

The Counter Reformation also influenced the religious orders. Santa Teresa de Jesús and San Juan de la Cruz reformed the Carmelite Order to put an end to the clergy's loose way of life. Their literary products are masterpieces of mystical-erotic lyrics on the union of the soul with Christ. At this time the picaresque literary genre also emerged. This is a genre in which the world on the fringes of society and the mood of denunciation is dealt with satirically, often by an author hiding behind the mantle of anonymity.

The greatest poet at the time of Philip II was Miguel Cervantes Saavedra (1547-1616), whose life gives us some insight into this era. He was born in Alcalá de Henares, one of several children in a poor family. In 1571 he took part in the Battle of Lepanto, where he lost his arm – hence his nickname, the one-armed man from Lepanto. On his return to Spain his ship was taken by pirates to Algeria, where he remained in captivity for five years until 1580. He then tried to eke out a living as a writer. When he was 58 years old he published *Don Quixote,* which became a best-seller. But Cervantes only received the income from the first of the sixteen editions of his book. The story of Don Quixote tells of an impoverished member of the landed gentry who, inspired by stories of chivalry, believes he is a medieval knight. He embarks on a journey through the Spain of the 16th century, attempting to solve any cases of wrongdoing he encounters. It is a savage picture of society under Philip II. Cervantes died in Madrid in 1616.

Pre-Baroque mannerism was found primarily in the world of art. The genre is perhaps best reflected in Michelangelo's painting *The Academy of Athens.* In Spain the form was represented by the artists Alonso de Berruguete, Luis Morales and El Greco.

Doménico Theotocopulos, called El Greco (1541-1614), was born in Crete. His paintings are clearly influenced by the rigid, solemn art of icons he would

have known there. Later, in Rome and Venice, he studied art under Tintoretto, Titian and Michelangelo. In 1575 he arrived in Spain and settled in Toledo. He attempted to enter the court of Philip II, but his paintings were not liked by the king. The *Martyrdom of San Mauricio* and the *Burial of Conde Orgaz* are two of his most important works. In these two paintings El Greco adopts the position of story-teller, dividing the work into several levels. San Mauricio is a Christian leader of a legion in Thebes. He and his soldiers refuse to make a sacrifice to heathen gods before the battle, and as a result he and every tenth soldier is beheaded. In the foreground one can see Mauricio discussing with military leader; behind this his soldiers are being beheaded in his presence. In the background are the naked soldiers being, from whom the sacrifices are chosen. The picture of the burial recounts the 15th century legend, according to which St. Augustine and St. Stephen appeared in person to bury Conde Orgaz, a local nobleman.

Toledan *caballeros* are shown attending the burial. These are portraits of well-known figures from the period in which the work was painted. One of them is supposed to be Cervantes, another is said to be El Greco himself. At the top of the painting God is seen receiving the soul of the duke from Mary and St. John as an infant. In a narrow gap in the clouds between the heavenly and the earthly spheres, Freudian interpreters have managed to discover a symbolic vagina, through which the soul must pass before it is reborn on the other side.

The architecture of Juan de Herrera (1530-1597) has often been described as an expression of the absolutism of King Philip II. Herrera had been one of Charles V's sentries at Yuste. It was there that he wrote a treatise on geometry. Under Philip II he was given the task of overseeing all the plans of public buildings. He

Right: Scenes from "Burial of Conde Orgaz" (EL Greco).

was responsible for designing El Escorial. The architects from this period were all influenced by Herrera's style: they include Jorge Theotokopulos, Mora, Francisco Bautista and Carbonell.

The Last of the Habsburgs

The 17th century witnessed the end of Habsburg rule in Spain. At the beginning of the century the plague had reached the country, decimating the Castilian population. Strict quarantine had isolated whole areas of land. The army was still engaged in Flanders, this time in the Thirty Years' War, but there were no young people left as reinforcements. The kings delegated their powers to prime ministers, whose activities reflected their vices more than their political foresight.

The Duke of Lerma was a close confidant of Philip III and the very personification of greed. He made himself 40 million *ducados* richer by selling favors. One of his political measures was the final ousting of the Moriscos in 1610. As a result wide areas of the country were simply abandoned and the most fertile areas left untended.

270.000 peasants of Arabic origin left Aragón, Valencia and Granada. Lerma's successor, the Conde Duque of Olivares possessed unparalleled ambition, but was no match for the diplomatic talent of Richelieu. The latter had him sign a series of peace treaties: the Treaty of Monzón, of Rocroi, the Peace of the Pyrenees, the Peace of Westphalia, all of which were retrograde steps from a political point of view.

Philip IV came to the throne at the age of 16. He had two wives and thirteen children. His successor was Charles II, an epileptic who ascended the throne when he was 9 years old and still couldn't read. In 1668 his confessor exorcised him and pronounced him bewitched. This epithet remained with him. After his death the throne went to the Frenchman Philip d'Anjou. He was the beloved grandson of Charles' sister Maria Theresia of Austria and Louis XIV.

41

Baroque and the Churrigueras

With the last of the Habsburgs began the Baroque period. Its main characteristic was the imbalance of its constituent elements – one is usually more strongly emphasized than the others. As *siglo de oro* (Golden Century), it gained acceptance in all areas of art. In literature it is represented by great dramatists, such as Lope de Vega, Calderón de la Barca, Vélez de Guevara and Tirso de Molina, in poetry by Góngora and Quevedo, and in the novella by María de Zayas and Mateo Alemán.

In Madrid, in the first phase of the Baroque, a simple architectural style developed, directly influenced by the Escorial (Plaza Mayor, the Town Hall). The Church was becoming richer and richer and was the only institution which could afford to build great works of architecture. Countless church renovations were

Above: A spinning portrait – The Spinners (Valázquez).

carried out during this period, often at the expense of Gothic architecture. It was at this time, too, that the Jesuit style was developed, the best examples of which are San Juan in Toledo, La Clerecía in Salamanca and Monforte de Lemos. The palatial estates *(pazos)* of Galicia were built at this time, as were the great buildings of Santiago.

Churriguera was the name of three brothers: José Benito (1665– 1725), Joaquín (1674–1724) and Alberto (1676–1750). They created the Churrigueresque style, characterized by ornamental excess and demonstrations of wealth and splendor. The architecture of the period often has twisted columns and intricate sculptures. The style is regarded as an early forerunner of Rococo. José built the town of Nuevo Baztán (Madrid), where Philip V had planned an agricultural experiment. The university colleges of Calatrava, San Bartolomé and Anaya in Salamanca were built by Joaquín; Alberto built the Plaza Mayor, regarded as the most beautiful Baroque square in the country. The masterpiece of the Churrigueresque style is the western façade of the cathedral of Santiago de Compostela, built by Casas y Novoa. The most famous pupil of the Churriguera School was Narciso Tomé, creator of the *Transparente* behind the altar of the cathedral of Toledo and the splendid façade of the University of Valladolid.

Tenebrism dominated painting at this time. Its themes were naturalistic nudity and simplicity, sunken in shade, representing religious absorption and fervor. The Valencians Ribalta and Ribera used dusky candlelight to reflect the same ambience as dominated the churches. Zurbarán was known as a painter of monks and still lifes. Works of sculpture from this period are often polychromatic and concentrate particularly on themes associated with Holy Week. Two schools are especially important: that of Valladolid, with Gregorio Fernandéz, and the Andalusian school.

Diego Rodriguez de Silva y Velázquez, born in Seville in 1599, was also influenced by these developments. He became the court painter of the 17th century. In 1621 Olivares, who was descended from Sevillian nobility, brought Velázquez to Madrid where he was able to complete his artistic education and paint a portrait of the king on horseback. Many pictures of this time were burned in the fire which destroyed the Royal Palace in 1734. In 1628 Velázquez became acquainted with Rubens and began a period of mythological themes, for example the *Drunkards* (Prado), an everyday bacchanalian scene of soldiers in Flanders. At Rubens' request Velázquez made a study trip to Italy. In 1630 he painted *Vulcan's Smithy* (Prado) and *Joseph's Tunic* (El Escorial). When he returned to the court of Madrid in 1641 he began his great portrait of the king on horseback and the wonderful portraits of court jesters and courtesans. His small landscapes of the *Villa of the Medicis* (Prado),

painted on a second visit to Italy, would serve two hundred years later as models for the Impressionists.

Between 1656 and 1658 Velázquez painted his most famous works: these include the *Weavers, Las Meninas* (The Maids of Honor, Prado) and *Venus in the Mirror* (London). These three pictures are captivating, but it is not only their technical perfection which makes them so. Their Baroque playfulness draws the observer into the content of the painting: the weavers seem to have been taken from an everyday scene of carpet weaving, but the Baroque style turns the women overseeing the weaving of the carpet into Olympian goddesses, who might be passing judgment on the works of Arachne and of the goddess Pallas Athene.

Echoing Michelangelo's *Ephebes,* the goddess of weavers can be seen in the foreground in the form of an old woman, together with Arachne at their mythological contest. The old woman is turning the wheel so quickly that you cannot focus on it. Angry at Arachne's perfection, a little later she will hit her with the shuttle and turn her into a spider.

The painting of the *Meninas* seems to show the artist painting the observer. But in fact he is painting the royal couple who are reflected in the mirror, and must logically therefore be standing behind the observer. The family scene around the Infanta Margarita with the ladies-in-waiting or maids of honor (*meninas*) and the court jester form the focal point of the picture. However, this scene is really only of secondary importance to the content of the work. Finally, Venus is not a woman looking at herself, but Aphrodite, who looks out of the mirror at the observer of the painting. Cupid, who is holding the mirror, has removed his blindfold which usually prevents him from seeing.

In 1660 Velázquez died without leaving a school or followers.

Rococo and Enlightenment

After the death of Charles II the question of his successor grew into a European conflict. The opponents were the Bourbon Philip V, who represented the hegemonic interests of Louis XIV and Archduke Charles of Austria, who was supported by Aragón and the Grand Alliance of Britain, Austria, Portugal, Savoy and the German Princes. Louis XIV was defeated elsewhere, but, supported by Castile, he defeated the alliance in Spain (which had been able to advance on Madrid twice). In the Peace of Utrecht (1713) Philip was awarded the Spanish crown, but had to surrender large portions of the empire. Portugal was ever more closely linked with Britain and the borders up to the territory of Olivenza were drawn almost as they are today. The Island of Majorca was occupied by the

Above: A Rococo statue in Aranjuez Park.
Right: Charles IV's family, as immortalized by Francisco de Goya.

French and the British until Spain won it back in 1782. Gibraltar remained in the hands of the British.

The end of the War of Succession heralded a new era of stability which brought with it a significant increase in population. A wave of migration from the countryside to the towns also began. French artists flocked to the courts of the Bourbons, bringing the Rococo style with them. Small palaces, boudoirs, the royal palace in Aranjuez and the Granja date from this period.

The Bourbons also brought French centralism and a new administration to the Spanish state. Under Charles III the country was divided into provinces for the first time, essentially along the lines of the old historical borders. This king was called the mayor of the court, for he had a prestigious capital built by the architects Ventura Rodriguez and Sabatini. His secretary Jovellanos designed new laws concerning agriculture. He believed that the Jesuits had too much power overseas, particularly in Paraguay, and he banned them from Spanish soil. Instead the Freemasons spread throughout Spain.

On the day that Philip V died, Francisco Goya was born near Zaragoza. In 1799, when he was 50 years old, he became Charles IV's court painter, and his paintings can be read as a chronicle of his time. Goya had his own special style which was influenced more by his personal biography than by European artistic genres.

Charles IV did not accede to the throne until he was 40 years old. He was a kind man, but he was dominated by his wife, Maria Luisa, an ambitious woman who loved pomp and splendor. Goya painted both of them on many occasions. In his portraits he tried to represent the personalities of the ruling couple as they really were. Charles IV's first act of government was to change Philip V's Salian law, according to which no woman could ascend the throne. His reign was domi-

nated by debate on the ideas of the French Revolution. His Prime Minister was the 28-year-old Manuel Godoy, who had originally come to the court as a simple guardsman and who made a rapid career, it seems not entirely without the protection of the queen. Godoy attempted to save Louis XVI from the guillotine and allied Spain with the opponents of the Revolution. When the Peace of Basle was signed Spain was forced to surrender Santo Domingo to France and Godoy was given the title of Prince of Peace. One year later he joined with France against Britain and conquered the areas of Olivenza and Gelves from Portugal in the so-called Orange War. In support of its French allies, the Spanish Armada was sacrificed once more in the Battle of Trafalgar, where Nelson was killed. Following this battle Godoy made an agreement with Napoleon that French troops could march through Spain to Portugal. 30.000 French soldiers spread out through Spain and many more waited on the border. Godoy's unpopularity now grew so great that the people rose up in what is known as the Aranjuez Uprising and the king was forced to abdicate in favor of his son Fernando VII, who had to promise to remove Godoy from office.

Napoleon

The French Revolution and the subsequent European wars which Napoleon instigated also influenced Spain of the early 19th century. The march into Spain was important to Napoleon, particularly because he was determined to carry out an effective blockade against Britain (1807), and to do this it was imperative that he have Portugal under his power. The Spanish monarch supported Napoleon's aims and decided to give in to the demands of the Emperor and leave the country. Napoleon then put his brother Joseph on the Spanish throne. But on 2nd May 1808 the people rose up against the French in protest at the deportation of the royal family, and there ensued a violent and bloody battle.

45

The War of Independence lasted for eight long years and had all the characteristics of a Romantic struggle. The grass-roots uprising and the guerrillas who encouraged individuals and small groups to take up arms against the enemy turned the fight for independence from France into a more general idealistic battle against archaic law and order. In Cádiz a government in exile was formed, known as the *Cortes,* which promulgated the first liberal constitution in Europe (1812). The Spanish kept the courageous revolt alive in Zaragoza and Gerona. But it was not until the year 1814 that France finally retreated from the peninsula.

The 19th Century

Once the French had retreated, Fernando VII faced a delicate political situation. He thought he could end the battle between the liberals and the traditionalists through the imposition of an absolutist regime. But this only resulted in the first liberal putsch attempts in the country. These were carried out by the former military heroes of the War of Independence. One after the other they failed.

Riego's coup in Cádiz was supported by La Coruña, Zaragoza and Barcelona. It forced the monarch to recognize the Constitution of 1812 for three years that is, until the French army came to his aid with 100.000 men. But with that a decade of repressive absolutist rule began. Many liberals and intellectuals were forced to flee the country. Most of them went to England. Goya, too, left Spain for France. He died in Bordeaux in 1828. In 1830 the future Queen Isabel II was born and in 1833 Fernando VII died. His wife María Cristina ruled as regent. Her opponents, referring to Philip V's Salian law, called first for the Infante Don Carlos, the king's

brother, to come to the throne, and later his son and his grandson, the three Charles. This brought about the three Carlist Wars which accompanied Isabel II's rule.

Whilst the civil war continued in the north the progressive government of Isabel II's Prime Minister Mendizábal embarked on a policy of secularization. With the support of the people the progressive General Espartero took over the government at the end of the second Carlist War, forcing María Cristina to give up her official government duties. He held onto power for three years, years which were punctuated with many bloody coup attempts. In 1843 Isabel II was declared of age and ruled until she was dethroned in 1868 by General Prim. In the seven years before her son Alfonso XII came to the throne, the political scene was in constant turmoil and chaos. From 1868 to 1871 there was a provisional monarchist government under Serrano, who attempted to introduce a new dynasty of monarchs. For this, Amadeus of Savoy, the son of the Italian king Victor Emmanuel, was chosen. But he only ruled for two years. He was dethroned and the First Republic was proclaimed. But the political situation in the Republic was still unstable. It had four presidents in one year and ended with a further transitional government.

The End of the Empire

Attempts to reform the administration in Cuba collapsed because of the lethargy of the Imperial governments and the intransigence of the ruling classes on the island. The independence movement had been growing steadily since the middle of the 19th century and had led to two wars. The Cuban separatists were supported by the imperialist forces of North America, and finally the United States declared war on Spain. This was fought on two fronts: in Cuba and in the Philippines. Hostilities ended with two major defeats. In 1898

Right: The intellectuals in their regular cafe (La Tertulia del Pombo, J. G. Solana).

the entire Spanish colonial empire simply disappeared into thin air. National pessimism was crystallized in "the generation of '98", a group of writers who wrote on Spanish themes, of the attractions of the landscape and the history of the country. Conscious of the nation's disillusionment following Spain's defeat by the Americans, they attacked the deplorable state of affairs in the country in critical writings. They came from a variety of areas, but presented themselves as a single intellectual force in Madrid. Unamuno, who came originally from Bilbao, was the leader of the movement and the author of *El Sentimiento Trágico de la Vida*. Pío Baroja was from San Sebastian, Valle Inclán from Galicia, Azorín from Monóvar near Alicante, the Machados from Seville, Perez de Ayala from Oviedo, and Blasco Ibáñez from Valencia.

The 20th Century

At the turn of our own century there were, broadly speaking, two social fronts in Spain: the traditional peasantry, a social grouping whose way of life had hardly changed since the Middle Ages, and a very different, modern, industrial nation, which had arisen from the developments in Europe in the 19th century. The former had the greater influence on the Spanish economy because the small farmers' parcels of land and their undeveloped technological skills made economic growth almost impossible.

Latifundia in the south and southeast, mini-farms in the whole of the north, and short leaseholds in the other regions were the pillars of Spain's unstable agricultural sector. The industrial centers were few: the north had mines and metalworks, Catalonia had a textile industry. Secondary industry was made almost impossible, due to the low income of the rural population and protectionist foreign policies. Gradually a working class with revolutionary ideals emerged: the anarchists formed groups primarily in the south, the Levant, in Aragón and its center Barcelona. The socialists spread throughout the Meseta, the mining regions and industrial areas of León, Asturias and the Basque provinces. Passions had not yet cooled after the events of 1898, when the independence movements in the Basque region and in Catalonia originally began. The military presence in Morocco cost many human lives and provoked a general strike in Barcelona, defeated in what came to be known as the Tragic Week.

The First World War finally opened foreign markets to Spain again, when the country declared itself neutral, but it also brought about significant price increases. A temporary boom was experienced in the large cities, which were now following developments in other European cities. The Gran Vía in Madrid and the modernist buildings of Barcelona by the architects Antoni Gaudí, Domènec i Montaner and Puig i Cadafalch all date from this period.

In the years which followed there were many workers' revolts and peasant uprisings. In 1923, after a certain amount of parliamentary indecision, General Primo de Rivera took power in a coup d'état. The military regime, which was supported by Alfonso XII, imposed a number of measures including the closing of the Ateneum in Madrid. It also banned intellectuals and founded industries under state monopoly. The anarchists of the CNT union organized underground. The economic collapse of 1929 added to Spain's foreign debts, and it was economic problems like these which finally brought about Rivera's resignation in 1930. The Republicans won a majority in communal elections, and in 1931 the Second Republic was declared. The king left the country.

It is somewhat surprising that in the midst of all this confusion a group of poets came to the fore who are usually regarded as Spain's best ever generation of literary figures. They met as a group of friends in 1927, in memory of the 300th anniversary of the death of Góngora, the great poet of the Spanish Baroque era. They included García Lorca and Damaso Alonso, Juan Ramón Jiménez, Altolaguirre and Guillén, and were known as the generation of '27. The artists of this period include Miró, Picasso, Dalí, Luis Buñuel and Pablo Casals.

The Republic brought with it the victory of bourgeois principles and ideals. A parliament with one chamber, general franchise, civil marriage ceremonies and the right to divorce were all established. Catalonia was given its own government. A number of agricultural reforms were introduced including measures to give land to the peasants who worked it. In 1932 a decree dispossessed the latifundia owners. But unemployment remained high amongst the proletariat, and a rivalry formed between the two syndicates: the anarchist CNT and the Catholic CEDA. President Azaña called an election which was won by the right. Azaña's decrees then became ineffective. But in Extremadura, union disagreements continued to ferment. In Asturias a soviet was declared and the coalition of the right collapsed. At new elections the Popular Front, a coalition of workers' parties and Republicans won with a massive majority. A general amnesty was issued, agricultural reforms and the Catalan statute reinstated, and for a short time everyone had their heads in the clouds, thinking they could curb the radical forces of the right and the Falange, founded in 1933 by José Antonio Primo de Rivera. But after the murder of the monarchist Calvo Sotelo on 17 July 1936, General Franco launched a coup from Morocco, supported by the traditional forces and the Carlists in Navarre. On the following day a terrible war broke out.

The Civil War

The resistance of the military and of Catholicism found fertile ground in the

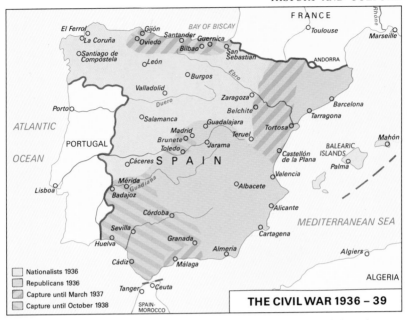

Nationalists 1936
Republicans 1936
Capture until March 1937
Capture until October 1938

THE CIVIL WAR 1936 – 39

Conservatives's fears. The war was a social conflict. It also became an international event: the Axis powers, Germany and Italy, supported the Nationalists, the Soviet Union the Republicans. International Brigades, formed by intellectuals of all countries whose ideals had been smashed in the Nationalist coup, arrived with good intentions but little practical aid, drawn by a love of adventure, humanitarianism, folklore and an ideological sympathy for the working class. Famous writers such as Orwell, Durrell, Hemingway and Malraux have written down their experiences. It seems that the whole world practiced for the Second World War in Spain. The foreign press was enraptured by the war folklore, German pilots practiced air attacks.

On the day after Franco's coup the country divided into two halves, the Republicans and the Nationalists. West Andalusia, the Extremadura and the Alcázar of Toledo (which was besieged by Republicans) fell during the course of the year. In 1937 the Nationalists took Teruel

after a bitter fight, in 1939 they also conquered Catalonia. Only Madrid and the Mediterranean coast remained in the hands of the Republicans. On the 1st April 1939 Franco declared that the war was over and forced an unconditional capitulation. A total of one million lives had been lost during the years of fighting and whole cities had been reduced to rubble. After the war countless Republicans and intellectuals went into exile in France, England or Latin America.

The Franco Era

Franco's power rested on the military, the Church and the Falange. The upper classes and the upper middle classes, helped by laws sympathetic to business and trade, were not opposed to him. The wheel of time was turned back to the time of the Inquisition and to Imperial Spain. Liberals and communists were declared enemies of the state. Freedom of the press and political parties were forbidden. Franco controlled the state himself, like a

49

new Philip II. The Cortes served as a parliament of the estates including representatives of the Church. In 1945 they voted in favor of the monarchy.

As an alliance partner of the defeated powers of the Second World War, Spain was criticized by the UN and boycotted. Starvation forced many people back to the countryside. Agricultural machinery had been damaged and destroyed, and so productivity fell markedly in comparison to the period before the War. The Republic's land reform was reversed.

The post-war era was extremely difficult for Spain. Franco's dictatorial policies led to widespread dissatisfaction and economic problems which came to a head in the '50s. Mounting workers' unrest forced the opening of trade and capital markets and wage discussions. A military agreement with the USA, acceptance into the UN in 1953 and OECD membership diminished Spain's isolation. In the next few years industry was rebuilt, with capital invested in border areas and close to the sources of raw materials. The Basque territories and Catalonia experienced the greatest surge in development during this time.

From 1962 onwards the Catholic lay order Opus Dei took part in government and various development projects were carried out, including the promotion of tourism on the Mediterranean coast.

The '70s, however, brought the oil crisis and economic stagnation, growing inflation and unemployment to Spain, and the renewed emigration of foreign workers. Only after the first treaties with the EC did the economy of the country start to improve again.

In 1975, 39 years to the day after the murder of Primo de Rivero, founder of the Falange, Franco died, following a long period of illness and continuous attempts by his family to keep him alive ar-

Right: Parade of the International Brigade in Barcelona in 1936.

tificially. His last words were: "Everything I leave behind is in order – in very good order indeed." The grandson of Alfonso XIII, the Bourbon Juan Carlos, came to the throne.

Modern Spain

Modern Spain begins with the declaration of the new constitution in 1978. A military coup attempt was nipped in the bud in 1981, and the democracy showed itself to be "ripe for Europe". Since 1983 there has also been a reformed regional administrative structure.

17 regions, Comunidades Autónomas, now form the state. The people of the autonomous regions of Galicia, the Basque region and Catalonia have also been recognized as separate ethnic groups. They have the right to use their own languages in education and administration according to the Statute of Autonomy of 1983, which was accepted throughout the country in a referendum. In most regions since then links with central government have been relaxed. Only in the Basque provinces is the independence movement still strong, terrorism the order of the day. Castile's population is decreasing. The two regions of Castilla La Mancha and Castilla y León have 14 provinces and 35 percent of the land but only 4 million inhabitants. Greater Madrid has a population of 4.8 million.

The traditional industrial areas are the coastal region of Asturias, the Basque region and Catalonia, with their large ports and raw materials industry. Since the crisis in the coal and steel industry the situation along the northern coast has been a particular problem. Heavy industry there was subsidized by Franco, but cannot compete in world markets. Catalonia suffered in the European textile crisis but the automobile and petrochemical industries soaked up a lot of the capital and the workers. However, unemployment in the country is still 20 percent at the time

of writing. More than three quarters of foreign investment now flows into the conurbations of Madrid and Barcelona, while in the rest of the country cost increases are felt without the benefits to the employment market. The most important sectors of the economy are the petrochemical industry, heavy industry and the electrical and automobile industries. Food production is also being promoted in the large centers. The intention is to make those products which are aimed at a domestic market suitable for export too. Soon Spanish bacon, paprika, marzipan and wine will be found on sale in shops and supermarkets all over Europe.

1992

The Spain of the 1980s experienced all the processes well-known in other industrial nations, but more rapidly and more severely than elsewhere. Capital concentration and company closures, unemployment, debt and inflation – all these are the well-known accompani- ments to national economic booms in countries seeking to become part of Europe. Productivity in Spain remains only 60 percent of the European average, and foreign capital is aimed at the financial sector rather than production.

In the face of all its problems, the whole nation seems to be clinging to the magic word 1992 because 1992 is the 500th anniversary of Columbus's discovery of America, when Spain expelled the Jews and began to exploit the colonies; 500 years ago the Moors were finally defeated, and Spain became Spanish. 1992 will be celebrated in style, and world attention is to be focussed on Spain. In 1992 the Olympics are to be held in Barcelona, a world exhibition will be mounted in Seville, and Madrid will become Europe's cultural capital. 1992 will also witness the final chapter in Spain's integration into the EC. When the country finally becomes part of Europe, the Spanish people hope to see an increase in their standard of living, and hope to show a new face to foreigners.

THE CAPITAL OF CATALONIA

BARCELONA

Barcelona lies in the middle of Catalonia in northeastern Spain, a region rich in a variety of resources. In the 1st century B.C. the Romans founded the settlement of Julia Augusta Paterna Faventia Barcino on the **Taber hill**, today the site of the cathedral. After the Franks had destroyed the settlement in the 3rd century the area of the present-day **Barrio Gótico** was fortified. In the 4th century the region was Christianized, and by the 5th century the town had become a fairly important political and religious center under Visigoth rule. At the beginning of the 8th century it was captured by the Moors, but by 801 it had already been liberated again by Luis I, the Pious. The Carolingians ruled Catalonia in the 9th and 10th centuries. During this period trade in the town developed; the population grew to 15.000 and began to spread beyond the fortified area.

In 1217 Jaime I, the Conqueror, came to the throne, introducing a new period of expansion during which Barcelona became one of the most important trading powers in the Mediterranean, governed by the Consolat de Mar, an institution whose laws applied all over Europe for

centuries. In 1260 the erection of the town walls began, a project which lasted for a hundred years. Initially the walls were built along the **Ramblas**, at that time the natural course of a stream; the section running from the **Pl. de Catalunya** to the **Ciudadela** was built. By 1374 it was already necessary to build a further section of wall, running from the Pl. de Catalunya along the **Ronda de Sant Antoni**, the **Ronda de Sant Paul**, to the **Drassanes**, to defend the new town quarter of **Raval**.

The town had already experienced its Golden Age and had entered a phase of social crisis, which continued with its ups and downs until the 16th century. The construction of the harbor mole can be interpreted as a symbol of a new economic upswing. In the 17th century the growth and wealth of Catalonia stood in marked contrast to Castile's demise and the crown's attempts to maintain its hegemony in Europe. Philip IV tried to suppress the separatist tendencies in the various regions and to build an absolutist monarchy on the French model. Catalonia was to be integrated into the Castilian ruling system. On 7 June 1640 revolution broke out in Barcelona. With the bloody Corpus de Sangre, the War of Independence began, sometimes called the reapers' uprising *(Segadores)*. In 1659 a

Preceding pages: Castilian vineyards. Evening relaxation after a hard day's work. Left: Barcelona cathedral.

peace treaty was finally signed. Catalonia lost Roussillon to France, which had emerged as Castile's ally. The town made a remarkably rapid economic recovery, and by the 17th century already had a population of 50.000.

Ferdinand I, the Catholic (1479-1516), was the last sovereign to have his residence in Barcelona. It was here that he received Columbus after he had docked in **Puerta de la Paz** on his return from discovering America. Today you will see the city's emblems in the port: a tall monument showing the famous navigator with his caravel at his feet. During the rule of Charles V Barcelona was the port of embarkation for expeditions leaving for Africa. The emperor loved the city, and it was here that he held a gathering of the Order of the Golden Fleece.

The Habsburg kings established their capital in Madrid and lived far from Barcelona. In the battle for the succession to Charles II, Barcelona was on the side of the Habsburg Archduke Charles and against the Bourbon claimant to the throne, Philip V, who besieged the town for 13 months in 1714. After Barcelona had been taken by force, he destroyed all the state machinery in Catalonia and subjected the country to the laws of Castile. In order to maintain control over the conquered town he built a citadel on the site of the present-day Parc de la Ciudadela. Life in Barcelona sank to the level of life in a provincial town. Between 1808 and 1815 during the time of Napoleon it was ruled by France.

Barcelona's attempts to free itself from its various fortifications lasted until the first half of the 19th century. When all the walls had finally been demolished in 1860, the city began to expand. The World Exhibition of 1888 heralded a new cosmopolitan phase. Barcelona, reduced in the 19th century to the role of a simple provincial capital, regained its position of capital of the old principality with the foundation of the so-called Mancomuni-

tat by Prat de la Riba from 1914 to 1924. With the creation of an autonomous Catalan government (1931–1939) during the Republic, Barcelona became a capital again under President Macía (1931–33). After the Civil War General Franco's dictatorial regime took its anger out on the inhabitants and held court martials, following which thousands of civilians were executed for betraying the fatherland. These purges not only dissolved Catalan institutions, but public and private Catalan customs were also forbidden. The measures were intended to emasculate a society from which an independent industrial revolution had grown, with an eye on developments in neighboring European countries, and which repre-

sented a threat to the stability of the dictatorship. Whilst a majority of the upper middle classes worked with the new ruling class in order to retain its economic position, the rest of the population supported an underground movement which kept the democratic spirit alive.

In the 1950s Spain began to open up. The first treaties with the USA were signed, but the regime held on to the bitter end until the death of General Franco in 1975. With the transition to democracy the autonomous status of Catalonia was reinstated and bilingualism was officially introduced. In 1979 Joseph Taradellas, the Catalan president in exile, returned to Barcelona following long negotiations in Madrid. His greeting to the Catalan people was *Ja sóc aqui* (I am here). It was answered by the cheers of the crowds who still celebrate the *Diada de Catalunya,* the festival of the new Catalonia, every year on 11th September. The new Catalonia seeks to be a part of Iberian society and hopes to simultaneously contribute its special talents to the building of a nation which sees before it a Europe without frontiers.

The City of two Millennia

In order to view the buildings of the city chronologically we should start from the **Plaza de Sant Jaume**, the administrative and historical center of the city, on the Taber hill, where locals dance the traditional *sardana* every Sunday afternoon. Protected by the old Roman walls are the remains of the heathen **Temple of Augustus**, which can be viewed at the **Centre Excursionista de Catalunya**. If you walk from the **Plaza Berenguer III** over the **C/Tapinería** you can still see some of the sections of the 4th century wall which served to protect the town until the 13th century. Part of this complex was preserved, even after Jaime I's new walls, because it served as support for the newer buildings.

On the **Plaza del Rei** on the other side of the wall you will find the **Museum of Municipal History**, housing exhibitions of other interesting excavations dating back to Roman times. At one time there were thermal baths here, with pools, amphorae and water canals.

During the lively period of development when Barcelona was the capital of the Catalan-Aragonese crown, a large proportion of the Romanesque buildings were rebuilt and extended. But some of the monuments survived intact: these include the **Chapel of Santa Lucia** (13th century) in the cathedral, elements of the **Sant Iu portal** and the cloister, the **Monastery of Sant Pere de les Puelles** (12th century) and the old Benedictine Monastery of **Sant Pau del Camp** not far from the Rambla. The church ground plan is shaped like a Greek cross; its cloister has beautiful capitals. Visits are also recommended to the Romanesque **Chapel of San Lazaro** (12th century) in the old **Hospital dels Meselles** and to the gallery of the bishop's palace (13th century).

Gothic Buildings

Barcelona has many Gothic monuments dating back to its Golden Age.

Right: A view of the city from Tibidabo.

Many, though by no means all, are to be found in the Barrio Gótico. Only the most important are listed here: the **Casa de la Ciutat** on the Pl. Sant Jaume is the historical and present seat of the municipal administration. Important parts of the building from 1370 have also been preserved; it was extended in the 19th and 20th centuries. The original façade on the **Calle de la Ciutat** has a splendid portal and beautiful windows. On the belle étage you will find the **Saló de Cent**, the meeting room of the Council of Hundred, with Gothic arches supporting a wooden ceiling. The cathedral mansions *(canónigos)* date from the same period. The passage which joins them to the **Palau de la Generalitat** is a neo-Gothic reconstruction. Today the president of the Generalitat of Cataluña has his official headquarters here.

The **cathedral** was built on the site of a Roman building which in its turn had replaced a pre-Christian temple. The general interior design features a nave and two aisles, and a chancel and chapels between the buttresses. The towers are eight-sided, in the Catalan Gothic style. The tower on the gable end of the nave, called the *aguja* or needle, and the main façade were not built until 1885, based, however, on plans drawn up in 1408 by the architect Carlí. The portals of Sant Iu, the **Piedad** and the Santa Lucía Chapel on the cloister are the most beautiful details of this building. The cloister was built in various stages from the 15th century onwards. Muted light falls through the inset windows. The choir has unusual carvings in its upper part which date from the end of the 14th century. The lower part was decorated with the coats-of-arms of the various orders in honor of the gathering of the Order of the Golden Fleece in 1519. In the **Crypt of Santa Eulalia** under the main altar you can see a fine alabaster sarcophagus. The altar retables on which San Gabriel, San Ambrosius and San Martín are portrayed and

the depiction of the Transfiguration are among the church's most important and valuable treasures. In the sacristy, goldsmith's works, including the monstrance and the silver chair of King Martí (circa 1400) are exhibited.

In the **Palau Reial Major** of the Catalan-Aragonese crown the most important sights are the **Chapel of Santa Agueda** and the **Saló de Tinell**. The former was built in 1302. The altar retable of the *Condestable* is one of Juame Huguet's best works (1464/65). The throne room dates back to 1359 and is spanned by six supporting arches. This is where the Catholic Monarchs received Columbus after he returned from his first voyage in 1493. The **Palau del Lloctinet**, the Viceroy's Palace from the 16th century, is also on the Plaza del Rei, and houses the archive of the Crown of Aragón.

The medieval shipyards near the harbor, **Les Drassanes**, are the largest and best preserved shipyards of this period. They were built in the 14th century on the site of a smaller shipyard and today house

the **Sea Museum**, which includes amongst its exhibits a model of the ship of Juan de Austria from the battle of Lepanto (1571). Next to the Drassanes is the only section of the 14th century medieval wall to have been preserved. The **Hospital de la Sta. Cruz**, built by the Council of a Hundred to unite the various hospitals of the city, is arranged around a central inner courtyard. Over the years extensions have been added, including the Baroque house of convalescence and the classical College of Surgery. Today you will also find the Library of Catalonia here. The **Llotja** is the 14th century trading exchange. It has a neo-Classical façade. Curiously it still functions as Barcelona's official stock exchange. In the Baroque church **La Mercé**, once part of the convent of the Brothers of Mercy, the patron saint of Barcelona, the Divine Mother of Mercy, is worshipped.

The **C/Montcada** runs through the quarter of **Ribera**, with its surprising grid network of streets. It was built in the 12th century, and was the area where the most

61

powerful noble families of the 14th and 15th centuries had their palaces built. In the **Palau Aguilar** and the **Palau del Baró de Castellet** (15th century) you will find the **Picasso Museum**, which exhibits the estate of Sabartés, comprising all of Picasso's graphical works, his works from Barcelona and 58 works from his *Meninas* series. Amongst others, the *Harlequin* (1917) and the *Portrait of Señora Cabal* from the artist's rose period are particularly noteworthy. Next to this museum in the **Palau del Marqués de Llió** (13th/14th century) you will find the **Textile and Costume Museum**. Another Gothic Chapel has been preserved and incorporated in the splendid Baroque **Palace of the Dalmases** (17th century). **El Pi** is one of the oldest parish churches in the city (14th century). Its tower stands out as one of the most memorable monuments of the Barrio-Gótico. The large rosette in the façade is

Above: An eternal building site – Sagrada Familia, Gaudi's life-time master piece.

particularly eye-catching. The **Church of Sta. Anna** has managed to retain some of its seclusion, despite its proximity to the busy Pl. de Catalunya. It was built between the 13th and the 15th centuries, and illustrates well the transitional style between Romanesque and Gothic. **Santa María del Mar** is regarded by many as the best example of Catalan Gothic. It was built in the 14th century. Its harmony and its clear lines are its most impressive features. The light and the clarity of its elements are emphasized by its stylized octagonal pillars.

The final gem of Gothic Baroque is to be found on the edge of the city. The **Pedralbes Convent** was founded by Queen Elisenda de Montcada in 1326. The rapid construction of the complex made for harmonious architectural unity of church, cloister with three galleries and convent buildings. In the presbytery next to the main altar you will find the grave of the founder with a statue showing her dressed in the habit she wore during the last years she spent in the convent.

Building Boom after a 400 Year Gap

With the Renaixença, the revival of Catalan culture at the turn of the century, a new art movement began: that of modernism. Its architecture has become the emblem of Barcelona. The most important representatives were Antoní Gaudí and Lluís Domènech i Montaner. Their most important buildings are listed here in brief:

Gaudí: **Casa Vicens** (22, C/Carolines); **Güell Palace** (3, C/Nou de la Rambla), today the Museum of Theater; the **Theresian Convent** (85, C/ Ganduxer); **Güell Park**, Casa Batlló (43, P. de Grácia); **Casa Milá**, also called La Pedrera (92, P. de Grácia); and the **Sagrada Familia**, an unfinished, intensely personal temple of atonement and hallmark of the city.

Domènech i Montaner: **Castell dels Tres Dragons** on the Paseo Picasso, today a zoological museum; the publishing house **Montaner i Simón** (255, C/ Aragon), today the Tápies Foundation; the **Palau Montaner** (8293, C/Mallorca); **Fonda Espanya** (9, C/St. Pau); the **Hospital de Sant Pau** (Av. Gaudí; and his masterpiece, the **Palau de la Música Catalana**.

Barcelona for Relaxation

Barcelona has a variety of open spaces where to while away some idle hours. To the north on the **Tibidabo** there is a pleasure park next to the **Sagrado Corazón Church**. From here you can go on a number of pleasant walks through the wood, which has many wonderful views of the city.

Bordering on the harbor is the **Montjuic Hill** with a variety of places to see. The **Catalan Art Museum** in the National Palace of the International Exhibition of 1929 includes a wonderful collection of Romanesque and Gothic frescoes and treasures from all over Catalonia. In front of this is the **Fuente** **Mágica** fountain, a symphony of light and sound. There is also the reconstruction of the **German Exhibition Pavilion** from 1929 designed by no lesser figure than Mies van der Rohe.

The **Puebla Español** is a model Spanish village displaying a cross-section of regional architecture from the whole country, and its restaurants and bars guarantee pleasent refreshment. You can also visit the **Miró Foundation**, with its permanent exhibition of the artist's work and other rooms for contemporary exhibitions. There is another pleasure park, the old castle, and the **Olympic Ring** (Anilla Olímpica) currently being prepared for the Olympics in 1992. This includes the Olympic Stadium and the Olympic Hall of Sant Jordí, recently completed by the Japanese architect Arata Isozaki. And last but not least there is a cable car which will take you from the Miramar observation terrace, across the harbor, and over to the beach at Barceloneta.

Barceloneta was once a fishing quarter. Today it is filled with countless restaurants and dock-side bars, which set tables outside and on the sand in summer, and which serve every fish speciality imaginable. The most famous bar is probably the **El Salmonete**. Hanging on its walls are photos of all the personalities who have enjoyed the fruits of its kitchen. As aperitif one must taste the specialties approximately called *bombas*. These are breaded potato balls filled with meat and covered with a spicy sauce, usually accompanied by a beer. And talking of beer, we must not omit to mention the ever popular bar of the **Vaso de Oro**, even if it is only to witness the serving of *flautas* and *filarmónicas*, which the regulars order "at 50 %", or dark and light beer mixed.

The beach at Barceloneta is very busy and well-maintained. If you prefer a quieter swim, try the beaches of the **Maresme** (Premiá de Mar, Vilassar de Mar) or go to

Castelldefels. All these places can be reached by train in half an hour from the center.

Bordering Barceloneta you will find the **Park of Ciudadela** in the grounds of Philip V's citadel, with the Catalan parliament and the city's **Zoo**. But if you want to stretch your legs, your best bet is the **Ramblas**. This avenue joins the harbor with the Plaza de Catalunya. Watching the people of all kinds and all nationalities going to and fro is a spectacle in and of itself. Outdoor cafés, kiosks, flower stands and bird-sellers all contribute to the general hubbub. Along the Ramblas you will find the **Gran Teatro del Liceo**, where the Opera performs in the winter, and the **Palace of Virreina**, wife of the Viceroy of Peru, which now houses the Museum of Decorative Art. You will also see the Baroque **Church of Belén**, and roam around **La Borquería**, probably the best and most picturesque

Above: Bargaining on the Ramblas flower market.

market in the city. Off to one side is the **Plaza Real**, a closed neo-Classical square with arbors, where the stamp market is held every Sunday in front of the sidewalk cafés.

The **Plaza del Pi** is another picturesque square where you can sit awhile in peace. Its only bar has a Bohemian atmosphere, underlined by the art market on the square, where works of art of varying quality are sold under colorful parasols. The most typical bars and cafés around the Ramblas are the **Café de la Opera** opposite the Liceo, the **Bar Pastís** (C/ Sta. Monica), with the ambience of Montmartre, and the **London Bar** (C/ Nou de la Rambla).

The streets near the harbor, especially in the **Barrio Chino**, west of the Ramblas, for example, are regarded as disreputable because of their large and transient population. But they become increasingly commercial and middle-class, the further up the Ramblas you go. From the Plaza Catalunya onwards the street is called **Rambla de Catalunya**, and with

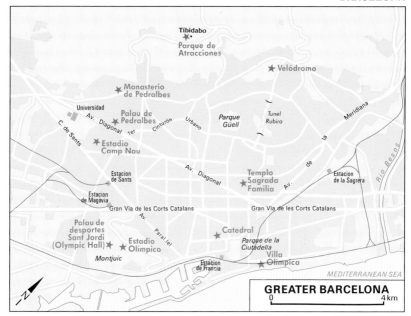

Tibidabo
Parque de
Atracciones

Velódromo

Monasterio
de Pedralbes

Universidad
Palau de
Pedralbes
Av. Diagonal
1er
Cinturón
Urbano
Parque
Güell
Tunel
Rubira
Meridiana

C. de Sants

Estadio
Camp Nou

Av. Diagonal

Templo
Sagrada
Familia

de

la

Rio Besos

Estacion
de Sants

Estacion
de la Sagrera

Estacion
de Magovia

Gran Via de les Corts Catalans

Gran Via de les Corts Catalans

Palau de
desportes
Sant Jordi
(Olympic Hall)

Av.

Parallel

Estadio
Olimpico

Montjuic

Catedral

Parque de la
Ciutadella

Villa
Olimpica

Estacion
de Francia

MEDITERRANEAN SEA

GREATER BARCELONA

0   4 km

the **Paseig de Grácia** it forms the core of Barcelona's **Ensanche** (*Eixample* in Catalonian), the expansion of the city which took place in the late 18th century, today the center of the urban middle class. Banks, luxury shops, shopping centers, restaurants, bars in the modern *diseño,* cinemas and art galleries are all concentrated in this area.

Further up, the **Paseo de Grácia** leads to the quarter of the same name, the most popular night spot for young people. The **Café del Sol**, on the eponymous square, or the **Bar Candanchú** on the Pl. del Reloj are popular meeting places for students and artists. Two other areas should also be mentioned while we are speaking of rest and relaxation: Beyond the intersection with the **Paseo de Grácia** there are various bars on the **Av. Diagonal**. Their number and diversity increases along the **Pl. Francesc Macià**. Why not try the Mecca of the nocturnal in-crowd, starting with the most fashionable place to go, the **Universal**? Further south along the **Av. Parallel** you will find most of the city's theaters. The spirit of the revue and music hall has been retained in places like **El Molino** or **Theater Arnau**.

Summer weather will probably drive you outdoors. The season begins with the *Grec*, the summer festival which takes place in July. Musical and theatrical events are staged outdoors, in the Greek theater or in the Pueblo Español on Montjuic. In the middle of August the quarter of Grácia celebrates its fiesta, turning all its streets and squares into a large, open-air ball room. 24th September is the day of the *Merced*, the city biggest festival. Immediately after this the autumn festival begins *(Festival de Tardor),* followed by a jazz festival and the International Film Days.

If you enjoy the morning sun and love browsing amongst unusual objects, there is the antique book market of **San Antonio** every Sunday morning. Or why not have a look around the flea market at **Les Encants**, where you might have the good fortune to discover an inexpensive antique amidst the usual heaps of junk.

65

BARCELONA

(Telephone area code: 93-)

Accommodation

LUXURY: **Hesperia**, C/ Los Vergos 20, Tel: 2045551. **Ramada Renaissance Barcelona**, Ramblas 111, Tel: 3186200. **Colón**, Av. Catedral, 7, Tel: 3011404. **Meliá Barcelona Sarriá**, Av. Sarriá 50, Tel: 4106060. *MODERATE:* **Rey Don Jaime I.**, C/ Jaime I. 11, Tel: 3154161. **Mayoral**, Pl. Real 2, Tel: 3179534. **Montserrat**, Paseo de Gracia 115, Tel: 2172700. **Paseo de Gracia**, Paseo de Gracia 102, Tel: 2155824. **Montecarlo**, Ramblas dels Estudis 124, Tel: 3175800. **Gaudí**, C/ Nou de la Rambla 12, Tel: 3179032. **Astoria**, C/ Paris 203, Tel: 2098311. *BUDGET:* **Rembrandt**, Portaferrisa 23, Tel: 3181011. **Internacional**, Ramblas 78, Tel: 3022566. **La Lonja**, Paseo de Isabel II. 14, Tel: 3193032.

Information / Telecommunication

Oficina de Turismo: Aeropuerto del Prat: 8 a.m. –8 p.m., Sundays and public holidays 8 a.m.–3 p.m. Ayuntamiento, Pl. de St. Jaume I, Mon–Fri 9 a.m.–9 p.m., Sat 9 a.m.–2 p.m., Tel: 3182525. Estación de Francia, Mon–Sat, 8 a.m – 8 p.m., Tel: 3192791. Generalitat de Catalunya, Gran Vía de les Corts Catalanes 658, Mon–Fri 9 a.m.– 1.30 p.m. and 4.30 – 8.30 p.m., Tel: 3017443. **Post offices:** 9 a.m.–1 p.m. and 5–7 p.m.; Main post office Pl. Antonio López, C/ Aragón 282. **Telefonica:** Pl. de Catalunya.

Transportation

Metro = Underground: Although underground-tickets are valid for travel throughout the underground-network, they don't cover travel on the suburban *Generalitat*-trains. Multiple-ride tickets (10 rides on one ticket) are a good bargain. The **Tranvía Azul** (blue tram) departs every half hour from Av. Tibidabo, Balmes to Pl. Dr. Andreu. **Cable Cars:** Funicular Tibidabo, from Pl. Dr. Andreu, 7.30 a.m.–9.20 p.m. Funicular Montjuic, from Av. Parallel to Av. Miramar, 11 a.m.– 8.15 p.m., Sundays from 12 noon to 2.45 p.m. and 4.30–9 p.m. Funicular de Vallvidrera, from Av. Vallvidrera to Pl. P. Ventura. Transbordador Aeri del Port (cable car across the harbor), leaves the harbor Torre Sant Sebastiá, glides over to Torre Jaume I. and to Jardins de Miramar, Montjuic, 11 a.m–6.45 p.m., June–September 11 a.m.–10 p.m. Teleferico de Montjuic, from Av. Miramar on Montjuic to the Castell de Montjuic; runs during summer weekends only, 11 a.m.– 2.45 p.m. and 4–9 p.m. **Golondrinas**: the swallowtail boats flitting across the harbor depart daily from the Columbus Monument, March–October 10 a.m.–8.30 p.m., and cross over to the jetty in 15 minutes only.

Rail Terminals: Estación Central, Barcelona Sants, Pl. Paisos Catalans. Estación de Francia, Paseig Nacional. Estación Cercanías (short-distance trains): Paseig Nacional. Suburban trains (Ferrocarriles de la Generalitat): see section on Pl. Catalunya. **Bus Terminals:** Julia (to Germany, France, Great Britain, Switzerland, Scandinavia, Italy and Portugal): Pl. Universitat, 12, Tel: 3183895. Iberbus (France, Belgium, Netherlands, Italy): Av. Paral.lel 116, Tel: 3296406. Alsina i Graell (to Andorra): Rda. Universitat 4, Tel: 3026545. Les Courriers Catalans (Paris): C/ Pau Clarís 117, Tel: 3025875. **Airport**: 14 km outside of town in Prat de Llobregat. Flight information Tel: 3013993. Train connection from Barcelona Sants Station to the airport every 20 minutes from 6 a.m. to 10 p.m. **Passenger Ships:** Estación Baleares, Moll de les Drassanes; Estación Internacional: end of Moll de Barcelona.

Museums

ON MONTJUIC: **Fundació de Joan Miró**, 11 a.m.–7 p.m., Sundays and public holidays 10.30 a.m.–2.30 p.m., closed Mon. **Museu d'Art de Catalunya** and **Museu de la Ceramica**, 9.30 a.m.–2 p.m., closed Mon. **Museu Arqueológico** and **Museu Etnológico**, 9.30 a.m.–1 p.m., 4–7 p.m., Sundays and public holidays 10 a.m.–2 p.m., closed Mon. **Museu Militar,** Castell de Montjuic, 9 a.m.–2 p.m., 4–7 p.m., sundays and public holidays 10 a.m.–7 p.m., closed Mon.

MORE MUSEUMS: **Museo Picasso,** C/ Montcada 15- 17, 9 a.m.–2 p.m. and 4–7 p.m., Sundays and public holidays 9 a.m.–2 p.m., Mon 4– 8.30 p.m. **Museu Textil de L'Indumentaria** (national costumes), C/ Montcada 12, 9 a.m.–2 p.m. and 4.30–7 p.m., Sundays and public holidays 9 a.m.–2 p.m., closed Mon. **Museu d'Art Modern**, Parc de la Ciutadella, 9 a.m.– 7.30 p.m., Sundays and public holidays 9 a.m.–2 p.m., closed Mon. **Museu de la Ciéncia** C/ Teodor Riviralta 55, 10 a.m –8 p.m., closed Mon. **Casa Museu Gaudí**, C/ Olot (inside Parque Güell), 10 a.m.–2 p.m. and 4–7 p.m.; closed Dec–Feb. **Museu del Teatre**, Nou de la Rambla 3 (in the Gaudí-designed Palau Güell), 10 a.m.–1 p.m. and 5–7 p.m., closed Sun and public holidays. **Museu de la Historia de la Ciutat**, Pl. del Rei, 9 a.m.–2 p.m. and 3.30–8.30, Sundays and public holidays 9 a.m.–2 p.m., Mon 3.30– 8.30 p.m.(in the 15th century Casa Padellas). **Museu Maritim**, Pl. Portal de la Pau 1, 10 a.m.– 1.30 p.m. and 4–7 p.m., closed Sun and Mon. **Museu de Artes Decorativas**, La Ramblas 99, 10 a.m.–1 p.m. and 4–6 p.m., Sat, Sun and public holidays 10 a.m.–2 p.m. **Museu de la Musica**,

Av. Diagonal 373, 9 a.m.–2 p.m., closed Mon (in the modernistic building designed by Puig i Gadafalch). **Museu Clara**, C/ Calatrava 27-29, 9 a.m.–2 p.m., closed Mon. **Museu Frederic Marés**, C/ Comtes de Barcelona 10, 9 a.m.–2 p.m. and 4–7 p.m., closed Sun and Mon. **Museu del Perfum**, Paseig de Grácia 39, 10 a.m.–1.30 p.m. and 4–7 p.m., closed Sat and Sun. **Museu de Zoología** (in the "Expo 1888" exposition complex designed by Domènech i Montaner), Paseig del Tillers, 9 a.m.–2 p.m., closed Mon.

Sightseeing

Pavillon Mies van der Rohe (World Exposition 1929) in the exposition park in front of the Montjuic. **Acuario de la Barceloneta**, Paseig Nacional. **Casa de los Canónigos**, C/ del Bisbe. **Centro Excursionista de Catalunya**, C/ Paradís 10. **El Gran Teatre del Liceu**, Rambla de Caputxins, 61. **La Font Mágica** (fountain) Pl. Carles Buigas. Performance of waterworks Thur, Sat, Sun 9 p.m.–midnight, in winter Sat and Sun 8–11 p.m. **Llotja** (Lonja), Paseig de Isabel II. **Museu-Monestir de Pedralbes** (Monastery-Museum), Baixada del Monestir, 9: 9.30 a.m.–2 p.m., closed Mon; Metro: Palau Reial. **Museu Futbol Club Barcelona**, Arístides Maillol, Estadio C.F. Barcelona, 10 a.m.–1 p.m. and 4–6 p.m., Sundays and public holidays 10 a.m.–1 p.m., closed Mon. **Palau (Palacio) de la Música Catalana**, C/ Amadeu Vives 1, modernistic building by Domènech i Montaner. **Palacio Real Mayor** and Salon de Tinell, 14th century. **Parque Güell**, by Antoní Gaudí, C/ Olot. **Planetarium de Barcelona**, C/ Escoles Pies 103, Demonstration 9.30, 10.30, 11 a.m., 3 and 5 p.m., Sun 12 noon, 1 and 6.30 p.m., closed Sat. **Poble Español**, Av. Marques de Comillas, Parc de Montjuic, 9 a.m.–8 p.m., in winter until 7 p.m. (Restaurants may close later). **Sagrada Familia**, Pl. de la Sagrada Familia. **Museum of Waxworks**, La Rambla 4–6. **Zoo**, Parc de la Ciutadella, 9.30 a.m.–7.30 p.m.
CHURCHES: **Cathedral**, Sta. María del Mar, 14th century. **Sta. María del Pino**, 14th century, Pl. del Pi. **San Pablo** (Pau) del Campo, 12th–14th century, C/ Huerto de San Pablo. **La Mercé**, 18th century, Pl. de la Merdé.

Restaurants

CATALAN: **Can Massana**, Pl. del Camp 6; **Agut**, C/ Gignás 16; **Agut d'Avignon**, C/ Trinitat, 3; **El Petit Dorado**, C/ Dolors Moncerdá 51; **Florian**, C/ Beltrand i Serra 20.
FISH: **Casa Chus**, Av. Diagonal 339; **Senyor Parellada**, C/ Argentería 37; **Can Majó**, C/ Almirante Aixada 23. For good restaurants also try the La Barceloneta quarter.

SPANISH: **Azulete**, Via Augusta 281; **La Balsa**, C/ Infanta Isabel 4; **Cas Isidro**, C/ Flors 12; **Tirton**, C/ Alfambra 16; **Botafumeiro** (Galician), C/ Gran de Grácia 81.
VEGETARIAN: **Illa de Gracia**, Domenec 15; **Macrobiotico Zen**, Muntaner, 12; **Govinda**, Pl. Villa de Madrid 4-5;
DISCOTHEQUES: **Distrito Distinto**, Av. Meridiana, 104; **Studio 54**, Av. Paral.lel 54; **Up and Down**, C/ Numancia 179. *MUSIC BARS:* **Els Quatre Gats**, C/ Montsió 5 (Jazz); **Sisisi** (Jazz), Av. Diagonal 442; **Este Bar**, C/ Consell de Cent 257; **Frank Dube**, C/ Buscarons 24; **Humedad Relativa**, Pl. Mañe i Flaquer 9; **King Bar**, Av. Diagonal 618; **Mas i Mas**, C/ María Cubí 199 (St. Gervasi); **Metropol**, Passage Domingo 3; **Mirablau**, Pl. del Funicular, Mirasol, Pl. del Sol 3; **Nick Havanna**, C/ Roselló 208 (Eixample); **Particular**, Av. Tibidabo 61 (Sarriá-St. Gervasi); **Universal**, C/ María Cubí 182-184 (St. Gervasi); **Velvet**, C/ Balmes, 161 (Eixample); **Zig-Zag**, C/ Platón, 13 (Sarriá, St. Gervasi); **Boliche**, Av. Diagonal 508.
FLAMENCO BARS: **Bandolero**, C/ Muntaner 244; **El Patio Andaluz**, C/ Anibal 242; **El Cordobés**, Rambla Caputxins 35; **Blanca Paloma**, C/ Napols, 222.

Festivals / Public Holidays

April 23 *Sant Jordi* (St. George), patron saint of Catalonia; May 11 *Fiesta Sant Ponç*, market for herbs and health food in the C/ del Hospital; June 24 *San Juan*, street festival during the night from June 23 – 24; September 11 is the *Diada*, the Catalan national holiday; September 9 *Virgen de la Merced*, patron saint of Barcelona. Fiesta in the town quarter Grácia around August 15. **Bullfights** are not as common in Catalonia as in other parts of Spain. In Barcelona they take place on Sundays from April to October: Plaza de Toros Monumental, Gran Vía Corts Catalans 747.

Shopping

Boutiques: Luxury fashion and jewellery shops offer their goods on the Paseig de Grácia between Pl. Cataluña and Av. Diagonal; trendy fashion boutiques entice the customer in the sidestreets to the left, C/ Aragón and C/ Valencia; Rambla de Cataluña, Av. Diagonal between Paseo de Grácia and Pl. Francesc Macia with northern sidestreets; upper C/ Muntaner; garments of all kinds: El Mercadillo, C/ Portafgerrisa 17. **Antiques**: Centro de Anticuarios, Paseo de Grácia 55. **Craft Shops:** Artespaña, Rambla de Cataluña 75. **Rare Books:** Mercado del Libro, Mercant de Sant Antoni: Sundays 10 a.m.–2 p.m. **Markets:** La Bocquería: Rambla des San José; Mercado de Sant Antoni: C/ Urgell; Medir, C/ Cáceres.

THE PYRENEES

LÉRIDA
ANDORRA
HUESCA PROVINCE

One of the most beautiful sceneries in Spain extends in the remote Pyrenean heights of Catalonia and Aragón, a region loved by mountain climbers, walkers, skiers, nature enthusiasts and ornithologists alike. Long walks often separate its valleys from the more populated, industrial regions. Its inaccessibility also spared it the Moors and the many wars, leaving a number of genuine Romanesque churches to posterity in the mountain valleys.

Almost all of them had almost intact frescoes inside. Most were in the apse of the church, and showed Christ the Pantocrator, surrounded by the four evangelists. Next to them were representations of the saints or of Mary. Often the entire interior was painted. In 1931, following the appearance in the Boston Museum of frescoes from the **castle of Mur** near **Tremp**, the museum administration of Barcelona decided that all other frescoes should be removed and taken to the National Museum of Art of Catalonia. In some cases reproductions replaced the originals. The churches themselves remain unchanged, just as they have been for 800 or 900 years. Seeking them out provides an excellent leitmotif for a round trip of the region.

Left: Fresh water springs in the Pyrenees.

LÉRIDA (LLEIDA)

In **Lérida** you are greeted by the cathedral, with its cloister hanging like a balcony over the mountain of the Arab fortress **La Zuda**. The old **Cathedral of La Seu Viella** (1203), a Romanesque building with Gothic and Mudéjar elements, was used as a barracks in the 18th century because of its strategic position. The view from the tower includes the town and the hill with the Templar castle of **Gardeny**. In the main street, which follows the Roman Vía Augusta, stands the **Pahería**, the 13th century mayor's building, now the town hall. The Baroque **New Cathedral** was built in the time of Carlos III of Sabatini.

The former **Hospital Santa María** is the site of the archeological museum. The medieval quarter, **Canyeret**, still has remains of walls dating back to the 13th century. Today Lérida is one of the most important trading centers for agricultural products. The produce from the fertile **Segre Valley** is marketed here at the Eurofruit fair.

The road from Lérida to the northeast forks at the village of **Balaguer**, which lies in the shadows of a ruined castle. The valley of the Segre runs to Andorra and that of the Noguera- Pallaresa far into the Pyrenean heights.

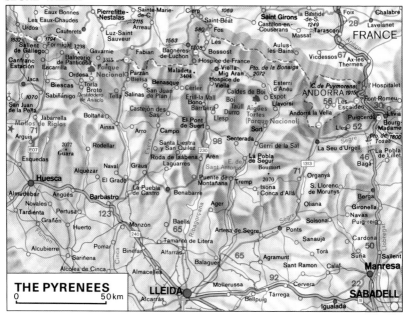

The Valley of the Segre

If you choose the road through the Segre Valley it is worth stopping at **Agramunt**. It has two pretty squares and a Romanesque church with a funnel portal with 15 archivolts. Chocolate is the local speciality here, to be found in many shops. Another worthwhile stop is **Solsona**, the center of the Catalan textile industry since the 15th century. It has an interesting **Salt Museum**, displaying crystal formations from the mines of Carmona.

Seo de Urgell lies on the fertile river plain at the confluence of the Segre and the Valira. The little town has picturesque streets with arbors, old façades and beautiful balconies everywhere. The oldest cathedral in Catalonia, **La Seu**, stands here. The bishop of La Seu has been the Co-Prince of Andorra since the 12th century. The cloister dates from the 11th century, and has beautifully decorated capitals. A further Romanesque church is that of **San Miguel**. The town hall from the 15th century and the Diocesan Museum are also worth a visit. Nearby you will find the monastery of **San Sadurní de Tabernoles**, an interesting example of early Catalan Romanesque architecture.

The border with France runs to the east the Segre Valley, along the mountains of the **Sierra del Cadí** to La Molina and **Puigcerdá**. This area is a favorite holiday spot for the people of Barcelona. **Llívia**, a Spanish enclave on French territory, surrounded by the 28 villages of the Cerdanya, was granted to France in the Peace of the Pyrenees in 1659. The area was awarded a town charter and remained Spanish. **Berga**, reached through the tunnel of Cadí, is always worth visiting during the Feast of Corpus Christi.

ANDORRA

The principality of **Andorra** is only 10 km from Seo de Urgell. When Charlemagne crossed the Pyrenees, the Andorrans served him as guides through the mountain valleys. In gratitude, his son

Louis the Pious gave them their independence in 819. There are also other legends about the origin of this curious state, which is ruled by the Bishop of Seo de Urgell and a representative of the French president who lives in Perpignan. At the moment around 40.000 people live here, most of whom are French and Spanish. Only 8.000 are native to Andorra. The state derives most of its income from people who come to buy tax-free electrical equipment, alcohol and stereos. Andorra is a colorful French, Spanish and Catalan mix.

The capital **Andorra la Vella** lies at a height of 1.079 m, and is one giant supermarket. The roads leading to it are completely choked with traffic in summer. The little town has an old center. Since the 15th century it has had a *Consell General*, a sort of parliament, once elected by the heads of the most important families. But since 1839 all adult men have had the right to vote. Women have been able to vote since 1970. The council meets in the **Casa de lo Val** (1586), a typical Catalan mountain palace. On the left next to the entrance is the 18th century coat-of-arms. In the building itself the records of the entire country are kept in a cupboard with six locks. Each member of the council keeps one key. You can tour the kitchen and the dining room, the council chamber and the **San Armengol Chapel**, in which the bishop and Co-Prince celebrates the mass before every council meeting.

Andorra is a 468 km mountain valley embraced by peaks reaching almost 3.000 m, a mountainous landscape with glacial lakes, two clean rivers, the **Valira d'Orient** and the **Valira del Nord**, which join in **Les Escaldes** to become the **Gran Valira**. The valleys are removed from the crowds of consumers and offer wonderful panoramas and beautiful hikes. The **Vall d'Inclés** forks beyond Soldeu; the **Vall de Ranso** is narrower and has rare plants which will interest botany enthusi-

asts; the **Vall d'Arinsal** leads to the highest mountain in Andorra, the **Pic de la Coma Pedrosa** (2.946 m). Of all the valleys this is the most open to tourists. To the south, the major road leads towards Spain, but the **Vall d'Aós** will take you to a pass and a town of the same name, already on Spanish territory. Finally, to the south-east, far from the tourist track, are the **Vall d'Madriu** and the **Vall d'Perafita**, carved like ravines between steep cliffs. They meet at **Les Escaldes**, a spa town in which iron-enriched water bubbles up from 85 m. In all these valleys there are many hotels, restaurants and camp sites.

HUESCA PROVINCE

The second road from Balaguer runs to **Tremp**, a 12th-century market town on the southern end of the Antoni reservoir. It is a favorite starting point for trips to **Pobla de Segur** at the beginning of the reservoir, at the confluence of the **Flamicell** and **Noguera-Pallaresa**, or into the Flamicell Valley, called Vall Fosca higher up. Another popular excursion is to the isolated **Mañanet valley** and the town of **Benés**. In the Noguera-Pallaresa Valley, beyond the **Desfiladero de Collegats** gorge, you will find **Gerri de la Sal**, named after its salt-works, which were established as far back as Roman times. A Roman bridge takes you to the 12th-century church on the other side of the river. This is where the festival of the Morisca is celebrated with a dance said to have been made up by a young girl to save the town from the Moors. Above **Sort** you will find the ski valley of **Llesui** and north of **Llavorsi** the **Vall de Cardós**, with its little villages whose slate roofs disappear among the highest peaks of Catalonia (Pica d'Estats 3.143 m).

From the C-147 a path leads to the ski resort of **Espot** and further on to the eastern entrance of the national park of **Aigües Tortes** and the **San Mauricio** Lake.

The road continues beyond **Esterri d'Aneu** over the **Bonaigua Pass** at a height of 2.072 m. From there you can look into the **Valle de Arán**, formed from the upper reaches of the Garonne, the only Spanish Pyrenean river which flows into the Atlantic. The valley is easier to reach from France than from Spain. Its 6.000 inhabitants speak Aranés, a mixture of Gascón and Catalan. They live in scattered villages with forgotten Romanesque churches. The valley originally belonged to Aquitaine, but became Catalan in the 13th century. Its most important town is **Viella**. A visit to the church to see the 12th century figure of **Cristo del Mig Arán** is a must. This valley has the best ski resorts in the Spanish Pyrenees. Good resorts are **Baqueira-Beret**, **Salardú** and **La Tuca-Betrén**.

The tunnel of Viella will take you south to the valley of the **Noguera Ribagorza** and the large town of **Pont de Suert**. The town has an avant-garde

Above: Hiking in the Ordesa National Park.

church (1955), built when the old monastery of Lavaix disappeared under the waters of the Escales reservoir. The whole course of the river is dammed and is lined with hydroelectric power stations.

To the northeast of Pont de Suert, in the little **Valley of Boí**, amateurs of architecture will find some of the finest Romanesque churches. They date from the time when the valley was ruled by the powerful Erill family. The Lombard influence is obvious in the blind arches of the apses and in the towers with square ground plans. You will find one of these Romanesque churches in every village: San Martí in **Llesp**, Sant Feliu in **Barruera**, La Nativitat in **Durro**, Santa Eulalia in **Erill-la Vall**, Sant Joan in **Boí**; but none can compete with the two churches of **Taull**. **San Clemente** is on the edge of the town, probably intended as a monastery which was never built, and **Santa María** is the parish church in the center of the town. Both were consecrated on consecutive days in 1123. The last of these churches, Sant Quirce, lies high in the valley between ski slopes near **Caldes de Boí**, a spa with 37 thermal springs once used by the Romans.

The Aragonese Pyrenees

A little to the north of Port de Suert, a road runs west to the **Valley of Benasque**. A little road immediately to the left takes you to the peaceful **Valley of Isábena** in the direction of **Graus**. **Roda de Isábena** had 13 bishops and a cathedral in which all of them are buried. A Renaissance portal has replaced the Romanesque portal.

You can get to the Valle de Benasque via **Castejón des Sos**, the commercial center of the area whose streets and squares are lined with arcades. Higher up, at the foot of the highest Pyrenean peak, **Monte Aneto** (3.408 m), is the town of **Benasque**, a base for ski and mountain tours. Even further up is the ski resort of **Cerler**. Down the valley on the Rió Esera is **Campo**. A side road runs to the thermal pool of **Vilas de Turbón** and **Graus**, with its old Plaza Mayor, watched over by the *Virgen de la Peña* (15th century). From Graus it is not far to **Barbastro**. On the way you will pass a turning to **Torreciudad**, a modern place of pilgrimage right next to the **Grado** reservoir, where followers of the Opus Dei commemorate its founder, who was born in Barbastro. To the north of Barbastro on the Río Vero is the medieval town of **Alquézar**, clustered around its fortified church. Many houses have been built from adobe, and the square is one of the most picturesque in the region. The town is dominated by the castle, which dates back to Moorish times and is surrounded by a double wall.

Valleys around Ordesa

You can get to the **Ara Valley** and **Aínsa** on the winding roads north of Alquézar or on the larger road from Bar-

bastro along the banks of the **Cinca** and via the **Alto de Pino**. The **Peña Montañesa** towers behind, at its feet sprawl the ruins of the **San Victorián monastery**. To get there you have to leave the road coming from Campo in the Esera Valley over the **Foradada Pass**, and turn off to the north at the town of **Arro**. Keep going until you reach the hamlet of **Los Molinos**. What is left of the monastery is a romantic skeleton of arches and broken cupolas, overgrown with blackberry bushes. In the 11th century it was the most important monastery in the whole region, the burial place of the kings of Sobrarbe, the medieval mountain kingdom, whose capital was at Aínsa.

Aínsa is today a lively Pyrenean village, daintily spread between the Cinca and the Ara, both of which flow into the Mediano reservoir. It is the region's market town and a favorite base for mountain climbers, hikers and anglers. The lower part of the town is full of hotels, bars, cafés and shops; the old town, a Romanesque ensemble of a square and the collegiate church from the 12th century, is under preservation order.

Aínsa's castle has Arabic origins. Long after the Reconquista, many Moriscos lived in the town. This is commemorated by the biennial **La Morisma** production, in which all the 500 inhabitants take part, dressed as *Moros y Cristianos*, Arabs and Christians. Further up in the Cinca Valley there are other picturesque valleys, but it is not always obvious how to get to them. From **Escalona** a road leads to **Puértolas** to the isolated town of **Escuaín**, from which you can hike to the valley of the Río Yaga or to the 300 m gorge of **Garganta de Escuaín**. Another road will take you along the **Río Vellos** to the **Valley of Vió**, the most isolated of all the Pyrenean valleys.

The villages of the valleys of Fanlo, Sarvisé and Vió are joined by paths which are most suited to hiking. The Río Vellos runs from the **Añisclo Gorge** in

the north, cut so deep that sunshine rarely reaches the bottom. The path through the gorge takes you to the foot of the "Three Sisters", **Monte Tres Sorores** (2.383 m), in the middle of the **Ordesa National Park**. The scenery here is wild and breath- takingly beautiful.

Further up in the Cinca Valley, there is a small turning to the left which leads to **Tella**. Beyond Lafortunada the road slips into the **Desfiladero de las Devotas** and winds back and forth until you reach **Salinas** and **Bielsa**. In **Salinas** the Gistaín Valley, also called **Valle de Plan**, will take you to the town of **San Juan de Plan**. These valleys have only recently been discovered by mountain tourists. The villages are inhabited by shepherds and small mountain farmers and have retained their traditional architecture.

In the Gistaín valley an episode took place a few years ago which might have

Above: Unspoiled countryside in Maladeta National Park. Right: A village in Tena Valley in winter.

come from a movie. Most of the young women of the region had moved to the towns to find work, rather than spend their lives in the hard conditions of the villages. The priest put a notice in the national newspapers advertizing for young women for the bachelors of the valley. Two or three bus-loads of girls arrived. A dance was arranged and some stayed. Every year this festival is repeated in San Juan de Plan, apparently with good results.

The little town of **Bielsa** is the last town in the valley. In summer all the traffic passing through the **Aragnouet Tunnel** from France arrives here. It is also the gateway to the **Valle de Pineta** and the valley basin before **Monte Perdido** (2.784 m), which makes up the second half of the Ordesa National Park. You will find a *parador* here which makes an ideal base for mountain tours.

The third entrance to the Park near **Torla** is reached by following the Ara Valley from Aínsa. The villages here are foothill villages rather than mountain vil-

lages. Many of them are half deserted. The valley stretches for 700 m, has a mild climate and Mediterranean vegetation. To return to the mountains you have to climb to **Broto** and the waterfall of **Sorrosal**, then follow the winding road to Torla. The medieval roads are lined with guest houses, hotels and restaurants, but people often get lost in the wide valleys which run into the national park from the west and then fork into the surrounding mountains. Away from the roads you will always be able to find a quiet path through almost untouched natural landscape.

Río Gállego

You can get to the last of the mountain valleys from Torla by crossing the **Cotefablo Pass**, just before **Jaca** and the old mountain crossing of the pilgrims. The **Tena Valley** is formed by the **Río Gállego**, one of the region's best rivers for swimming. To the north of Biesca it has carved itself one of the prettiest Pyrenean valleys in Aragon.

Small villages, chapels of Mozarabian origin and green meadows line the road up to the ski resort of **Formigal** and the 1.800 m high **Pourtalet Pass**, the crossing to France. If you cross the **Garganta de Escalar** from Escarilla you will come to the **Balneario de Panticosa**, and an inviting reservoir, which even in summer is only just above freezing. The half-deserted spa at a height of 1.636 m provides a good base for winter sports and hikes. There are also some wonderful paths to various mountain lakes.

A series of foothills separate you from Huesca. In **Sabiñánigo** the industrial harbingers of the Ebro Valley begin to pollute the river. The town has an interesting ethnological museum. Further south you can see a wide panorama from the **Monrepós Pass**. To the west lies the **Sierra de Loarre** with the castle of the same name – an impressive complex from the 11th century, formerly a fortress, royal palace and a monastery. Beyond, moving downstream along the Gallego you will see the two cylindrical and 200-m high

cliffs, the **Mallos de Riglos**, also called the Gateway to Upper Aragón. East of the pass is the **Sierra de Guara**, a dolomitic mountain range which has spawned unique ecosystems. The rivers **Flumen**, **Guatizalema**, **Alcanadre** and **Vero** form the largest gorges of the system, the most spectacular of which is the gorge of **Mascún** near **Rodellar**.

The untouched landscape is home to wild boar, deer, mountain cats, otters, bearded eagles and a great number of birds of prey. South of Huesca the rivers flow to the plain, through the desert of **Los Monegros** and to the Ebro.

Huesca

Huesca was once the capital of Aragón, and between the 14th and the 19th centuries it had a university, the setting of the gruesome legend of the bell of Huesca.

Above: The Alquézar (Huesca) is nestling snugly at the foot of the fortress.

In the 12th century, the nobility under Ramiro II refused to become subjects of the king. He invited them to the inauguration of a bell which was to be heard tolling throughout the land. The noblemen were beheaded as they entered and their heads hung in a circle in the tower with one in the middle as a clapper.

The building now houses the **Provincial Museum**, with prehistoric and Roman finds and Gothic paintings, including some by Maestro de Sigena. The Gothic **cathedral** is a fortified building with a beautiful portal, in the tympanum of which there is a representation of Mary and the infant Jesus and the Adoration of the Kings. Inside in an alabaster altar and Renaissance choir stalls. Opposite the cathedral is the Renaissance town hall. The cloister of **San Pedro el Viejo** is a further gem of Romanesque architecture.

The old town of Huesca seems deserted today and has lost much of its former splendor. But on the 10th August it magically comes alive again when celebrating the festival of Saint Lorenzo.

PROVINCE LÉRIDA (Lleída)
(Telephone area code: 973-)
Accommodation
LÉRIDA: *LUXURY:* **Condes de Urgel II.**, Avda. de Barcelona 17, Tel: 202300. *MODERATE:* **Pirineos**, Pº de Ronda 63, Tel: 273199. *BUDGET:* **El Centro**, Anselmo Clave 29, Tel: 237653. **Principal**, Pl. Pahería 8, Tel: 230800.
BALAGUER: *LUXURY:* **Conde Jaime de Urgel**, C/ Urgell 2, Tel: 445604. *MODERATE:* **Hostal Solanes**, General La Llave, Tel: 445002.
SOLSONA: *MODERATE:* **Pensión Sant Roc**, Pl. San Roque 2, Tel: 480827. **Gran Sol**, Crta. de Manresa, Tel: 8110975.
SEO D'URGELL: *LUXURY:* **El Castell**, Ctra. de Lleida, Tel: 350704. *MODERATE:* **Nice**, Avda. Pau Claris 4-6, Tel: 352100. *BUDGET:* **Hostal Ignasi**, C/ Capdevila 17, Tel: 351036.
TREMP: *MODERATE:* **Siglo XX**. Pl. La Creu 8, Tel: 650000. *BUDGET:* **Alegret**. Pl. Cruz 15, Tel: 650100.
POBLA DE SEGUR: *MODERATE:* **La Manduca**, San Miguel del Puy 35, Tel: 680100.
SORT: *MODERATE:* **Pey**, Avda. Montserrat 8, Tel: 620254.
ESPOT: *MODERATE:* **Saurat**, C/ San Martín, Tel: 635063. *BUDGET:* **Sant Maurici**, Ctra. Sant Maurici, Tel: 635009.
ESTERRI D'ANEU: *MODERATE:* **Hostal Costa**, Majo 14, Tel: 626061. *BUDGET:* **Sant Maurici**, Ctra. Sant Maurici, Tel: 635009.
VIELLA (Vielha): *LUXURY:* **Tuca**, Crta. Salardú s/n, Tel: 640700. *MODERATE:* **Bonaigua**, Sta. María del Villar 5, Tel: 640144. *BUDGET*: **Pensión Casa Vicenta**, Camí de Reiau 7, Tel: 640819.
SALARDU: *LUXURY:* **Montarto,** Baqueira-Beret, Tel: 645075. *MODERATE:* **Lacreu**, Ctra. Viella Esterri, Tel: 645006. *BUDGET:* **Garona**, C/ Cardenal Casañas, Tel: 645010.
VALL DE BOÍ: *MODERATE:* **Pensión Benería**, in Boí, Pl. Trayo, Tel: 696030.
PONT DE SUERT: *MODERATE:* **Pensión Can Mestre**, Plaza Mayor 8, Tel: 690306.
Excursions / Sport
The **National Park Aigües Tortes y Lago San Mauricio** is an ideal place for excursions; hike to the lakes (Estany) Ratera, Amitges and Negre, take a break in the alpine huts on the Estany Negre (J. M. Blanc), or on Lake San Mauricio, Lake Amitges, in Certascan or in Vallferrera.
The Noguera Pallaresa river offers excellent canoeing-conditions downstream from Sort, and a canoeing-school gives instructions to would-be canoeists. Don't miss the „International Rallye" in July and the downstream-race on August 15.

Tourist Information / Post
LÉRIDA: Oficina de Turismo: Arc del Pont; Tel. 248120. **Post:** Rambla de Ferrán, 16.
Fishing Permits and information: Generalitat, C/ Camp de Mart 35, Tel. 246650.

PROVINCE HUESCA
(Telephone area code: 974-)
Accommodation
HUESCA: *MODERATE:* **Sancho Abarca**, Pl. Lizana 15, Tel: 220650. *BUDGET:* **El Centro**, C/ Sancho Ramírez 3, Tel: 226823.
AÍNSA: *MODERATE:* **Apolo**, Pineta 4, Tel: 500888. *BUDGET:* **Hostal Sánchez**. Avda. Sobrarbe 10, Tel: 500014.
PANTICOSA: *MODERATE:* **Hotel Escalar,** C/ La Cruz, Tel: 487008. *BUDGET:* **Continental**, in Baños de Panticosa, Tel:487161.
BENASQUE: *MODERATE:* **Hostal El Puente**, Cl. San Pedro, Tel: 551279. *BUDGET:* **Hostal Avenida**, Av. de los Tilos, Tel: 551126.
BIELSA: *LUXURY:* **Parador Monte Perdido**, Valle de Pineta, Tel: 501011. *BUDGET:* **Hotel Bielsa**, C/ Medio, Tel: 501008.
BIESCAS: *BUDGET:* **Hotel Giral**, Crta. de Francia, Tel: 485005.
SALLENT DE GALLEGO (Skiing-Station Formigal): *LUXURY:* **Formigal**, Urbanización el Formigal, Tel: 488000. *MODERATE:* **Nievesol**, Estación de Formigal, Tel: 488034. *BUDGET:* **Balaitus**, Francia 16, Tel: 488059.
TORLA: *MODERATE:* **Edelweiss**, Ctra. Ordesa, Tel: 486173. *BUDGET:* **Viñamala**, C/ Fatás 5, Tel: 486156.
Tourist Information / Post
HUESCA: Oficina de Turismo, Coso Alto 23, Tel: 225778. **Post:** Coso Alto 16.
Museums / Sightseeing
HUESCA: Cathedral, 8 a.m.–1 p.m., 4–6.30 p.m. **Museo Arqueologico Provincial**, Pl. Universidad, 10 a.m.–2 p.m., closed Mon. **City Hall** (with the painting of the „Bell of Huesca"), weekdays 10 a.m.–2 p.m., 4–6 p.m. **San Miguel**, 10 a.m.–12 noon, 4–6 p.m. **San Pedro el Viejo**, 10 a.m.–1 p.m, 4–6 p.m., in winter 4–6 p.m. only.

ANDORRA
(Telephone area code: Spain 9738-)
Accommodation
ANDORRA LA VELLA: *LUXURY:* **Andorra Park**, Av. Roureda, Guillemó, Tel: 20979. *MODERATE:* **Calones**, Barrio Antiguo, Tel: 21312.
Tourist Information
Sindicato de Iniciativas, C/ Doctor Vilanova, Tel: 20214.

COSTA VERDE
The Green Coast

THE BASQUE PROVINCES
CANTABRIA
ASTURIAS
GALICIAN COAST

THE BASQUE PROVINCES

The Basque region (*Euskadi*) consists of the three provinces of **Guipuzcoa**, **Vizcaya** and **Alava**, with their capitals San Sebastian, Bilbao and Vitoria (Donostia, Bilbo and Gastiez). The language is ancient and of unknown origin. It was banned under Franco, but is now experiencing a renaissance as an expression of national pride. Modern Basque is constantly forced to create new words, as the old vocabulary is insufficient for the modern world. Officials, teachers and politicians are often heard getting their tongues in a knot trying to speak a language they have to learn in order to practice their profession.

Peculiar to the Basque provinces are a number of sports played only in this area. In **Markina**, a town a little inland from **Ondarroa**, there is an **Academy for Pelota Vasca**, a game similar to hardball that is played throughout northern Spain. In the Basque region, however, it is played using baskets with which the ball is projected at two walls standing at right angles to each other. This game is regarded as the origin of modern squash.

Preceding pages: The Basque coast. Left: The docks are a threatened source of employment today.

Other Basque sports include a game with stones called *arrijasotzale* and competitive wood cutting, *aizkolaris*. And finally, Basque cuisine must be mentioned, for it is the best in Spain. Seafood takes pride of place. Even if you were on an extended holiday you could never hope to taste all the different dishes. But it is worth at least making a start!

San Sebastian and the Coast

From the French border onwards everything seems to be one large suburb of San Sebastian. Behind the border town of **Irún** is **Fuenterrabía** (Hondarribia), where the old town wall still survives. Two main streets lead from the harbor area to Charles V's castle, now a parador. The **Calle Mayor** boasts wrought iron balconies, coats-of-arms and the **Church of Santa María**, and the **Calle Pampinot** with its jutting, decorated roofs. **Pasajes** (Pasaia) is just behind **Monte Jaizkibel**. It is divided into three districts. Victor Hugo lived in exile at no. 63 on the only street in **Pasajes de San Juan**, which is full of brightly painted fishermen's houses. At the end of the street you come to a splendid panorama, crowned by the **Faro de la Plata**, the lighthouse. At the end of the bay lies **Pasajes Ancho**, San Sebastian's fishing and commercial har-

bor. You can cross to **Pasajes San Pedro** by boat.

San Sebastian was the fanciest resort on the Atlantic coast between 1845, when Isabel II made it popular, and 1923, when Primo de Rivera banned casinos. Today it is a border industrial town and the site of an increasingly important film festival. It offers pretty walks and well-maintained town areas which blend well into their natural surroundings, and many impressive views. The wide **Alameda del Boulevard**, which begins at the town hall, a former casino, divides the old town from the 19th century town extension and the middle class residential areas dating back to the second half of the last century. They are full of wide avenues and richly ornamented façades with glassed-in balconies. The **Avenida de la Libertad** joins **La Concha** with the bank of the river **Urumena**. On both sides there are squares and parks surrounded

by arbors. In the north you will find the **Plaza de Guipuzcoa**, with the monumental palace of the provincial administration, and in the south the **Plaza del Buen Pastor** with its neo-Gothic cathedral. Beautiful promenades line the river. On the left bank you will discover what has made San Sebastian famous: the three splendid bridges, the luxurious **Maria Christina Hotel** and the **Victoria Eugenia Theater**, surrounded by gardens. A walk through the de Gros quarter on the other side of the river takes you to **Monte Ulía**, where you will have a fine view of the town.

The **old town** at the foot of **Monte Urgull** was built up around the **Constitución Square**. Few buildings survived the plundering of the town during the War of Independence: they include the **Santa María Basilica** (18th century), the **Church of San Vincente** and the **Convent of San Telmo** (16th century), now the city's museum. It has a rich collection including paintings by El Greco, Goya and Zuloaga. In the cloister there are an-

Above: La Concha, the shell-shaped beach of San Sebastian.

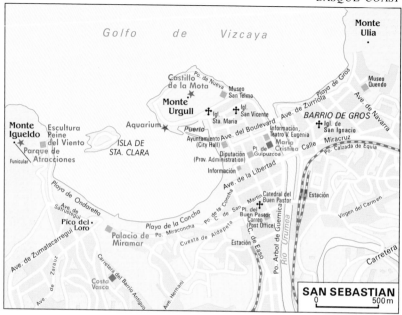

SAN SEBASTIAN

0   500 m

cient graves and archaeological finds. On the side of town facing the bay is the fishing port and a very interesting aquarium. This old quarter is a center of seafood restaurants, bars and cafés, where everyone meets from early evening onwards to drink a glass of *chacolí*, a light Basque wine, or a *zurito*, a beer, accompanied by various tasty *tapas*. There are several roads from the old town to the **Urgull Mountain**, site of the **Castillo de la Mota**, and a huge figure of Christ and a cemetery of the English soldiers who fell in the Carlist wars. A pleasant walk skirts the mountain along the shore.

The mussel-shaped bay and its two beaches lie between Monte Urgull and **Monte Igueldo**. The beaches of **La Concha**, the more popular, and **Ondarreta**, the more elegant of the two, are separated by a small mountain called **Pico del Loro**. This is where the **Miramar Palace** was built, the former royal holiday residence. **Monte Igueldo** gazes across the bay to **Santa Clara Island.** You can get to the pleasure park at the top along

marked paths or by cable car. The modern sculpture by controversial Basque sculptor Chillida stands at the foot of the mountain. It has a rather beautiful name: *Peine del Viento*, which translates as "wind comb".

Basque Coast

The Basque coast is wild, with steep cliffs, wave-swept shores and usually small sandy beaches. Isabel II made the entire stretch as far as Bilbao fashionable amongst holiday makers. The small coastal settlements enjoy great popularity as bathing resorts and summer residences. Today members of the Basque middle classe have their second homes along this coast, which is full of attractive fishing villages and fine walks. In summer it is almost impossible to get a room in the few hotels in this area. Each resort has a more or less well-preserved castle in its 15th century town center, as well as a fishing harbor around which a fishermen's quarter is usually clustered. Gaily painted fishing boats are reflected in the glassed-in balconies. In most cases a new town center developed alongside the old section.

The prettiest towns in this area are the aristocratic **Zarautz** and **Getaria**, with its natural port and memorial by Vitorio Macho of Sebastian Elcano, the first man to sail around the world, and **Zumaia**, with a museum devoted to the artist Zuloaga (1870-1945), famous for his portraits of Basque sailors.

The best view of **Lementza Mountain** is from **Lekeitio**, which has the usual picturesque port and the Gothic **Church of Sta. María**. The town has acquired dubious notoriety for a festival, in which young men in boats tear off the heads of geese hanging from ropes across the harbor basin.

Elanchove, a small isolated village with an almost vertical street running down to the harbor, is good training for your lungs. Basque is practically the only language spoken here.

Bermeo, which has a large fishing port, is not far from **Cabo Machichaco**, where you can enjoy a wonderful view of the coast, and to the **Chapel of Gaztelugache**, which stands defiantly on a rocky promontory to the west. Beware of the beaches between the Cape and the **Ría of Bilbao**, for many are not suitable for swimming. The villas of the present-day Basque moneyed class are to be found in the towns in this region.

Guernica has been the center of Basque nationalism since it was razed in 1937 by the German *Legion Condor*. This act of devastation was immortalized in Picasso's famous painting bearing the town's name. Only a part of the old oak tree still stands under which the Basques once used to meet. It is estimated to be about two thousand years old and is a steady reminder of the kind of grass roots democracy that existed here for so many years alongside the *fueros*, a set of special privileges.

Bilbao

With its population of 430.000 **Bilbao** is one of Spain's largest cities and an important center of heavy industry. Its harbor was modernized after the floods of 1983.

Many small communities had sprung up along the Ría, the bay-like estuary which stretches far inland. But the small town of Bilbao was able to gain significance in 1300, despite the fact that the larger ships could not reach it. Goods had to be unloaded onto smaller ships and brought into Bilbao to be sold. The former old town around the Gothic **Cathedral of Santiago** consisted of seven streets, which are now free of traf-

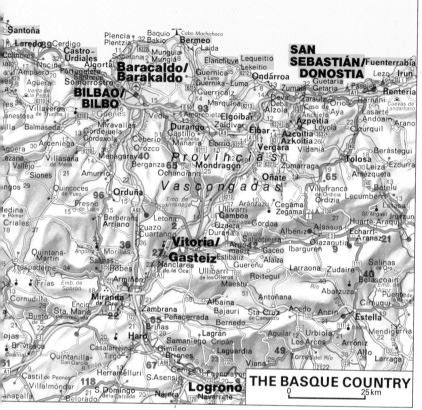

THE BASQUE COUNTRY

0   25km

fic and full of cafés and small shops. Nearby is the **Plaza Nueva**, a square surrounded by an arcade where traditional events are staged. Between the old town and the river is the **Paseo del Arenal**, a shaded avenue on which you will find the **Arriaga Theater** and the octagonal **Church of San Nicolás de Bari** (14th century). Behind the church a lift climbs up to the **Church of Begoña**. Not far away is the **Historical Museum of Vizcaya**, in the former **Monastery of San Juan**. The museum has traditional objects and archaeological finds on display.

On the other side of the river, Nervión is the sailors' traditional recreational quarter. The large buildings and wide streets of the new town lie in the bend of

the river around the **Square of F. Moyúa**. It is intersected by the **Gran Via de Lopez de Haro**, on which the most important buildings can be found, such as the provincial administration and the bank of Vizcaya. It leads to the **del Arenal Bridge**, that join the old and new towns. The **Museum of Fine Arts** on the edge of the large city park has one of the best portrait collections in Spain, with paintings not only from the Spanish schools, but the Italian, Dutch and Flemish schools as well.

Opposite the new town you can cross a bridge to the huge town hall, which is graced with splendid marble steps. The **Jesuit University** is on the same side. The **State University of Bilbao** is further

85

downstream. The Ría is, unfortunately, the backyard of Bilbao, lined by industrial compounds and the poorest residential areas. But at the end, where the river flows into the sea, you will find the towns of **Portugalete**, with its curious hanging bridge, and **Santurce**, to which the people of Bilbao flock to eat sardines down by the harbor.

Trips into the Basque Mountains

South of San Sebastian the countryside is beautiful, although the valleys are narrow and beset with industry. Nevertheless there are always towns worth visiting, and the Basque restaurants certainly deserve their excellent reputations. In **Azpeitia** you can see the **Casa de Anchieta**, the only example of Mudejar architecture in this region. **Loyola** is the home town of the founder of the Jesuit Order, whose birthplace and the enormous Baroque

Above: From up there, she doesn't miss a thing (Pasajes de San Juan).

Church have become popular destinations for pilgrims. **Oñate** was a university town between the 16th century and the beginning of this century, and in the 19th century it was also a Carlist stronghold. Today the university building is a school. The town has many old palaces, but its most famous building is the chocolate factory. In **Elorrio**, too, there are palaces and mansions. Further west in the valley of the same name is an industrial town named **Durango**, which also has an old center and beautiful town gates. Above the town is the village of **Garay**, at the foot of **Mount Oiz**. Here, from the **Balcón del Duranguesado**, you can look across the entire valley.

The **Valle de Mena**, behind the coastal mountains, is really part of the province of Burgos, but it is so close to the Basque region, that weekend tourists come here from Bilbao. You can get to it from **Balmaseda**, which lies southwest of Bilbao. A walk through the mountain valley of Río Cadagua will take you past clean streams, but the reservoir of **Ordunte** holds Bilbao's drinking water, so you are not allowed to swim in it. The area between the mountains of Ordunte and **Peña**, where the river grows from small waterfalls, is ideal for hikes, and the weather is often good here, even when it is pouring rain along the coast. Important sights include **Villasana de Mena** with its Romanesque old town, **Lezana,** with the **Torre de los Velasco** (15th century), **Vallejo** and the temple church of **Siones**. At the other end of the Mena Valley is **Espinosa de los Monteros**, which has a series of medieval churches, palaces and castles. The town is best visited on a Tuesday, or market day, when the streets and plazas fill with people. The caves of **Sotoscueva** are not far away. In the **Ermita** the walls are painted with scenes from the life of San Tirso (17th century). From here it is only a stone's throw to the **Ebro reservoir**, where you can swim when the water level is suitable.

Vitoria

In the 12th century Sancho the Wise of Navarre transformed the Basque-Visigoth **Gasteiz** into a fortress against the Castilians. He accorded the town *fueros* and called it *Nueva Victoria*. The old town center dates back to this time. It has since expanded because of the grain, wool and iron trade between the coastal area and the interior. A wealthy bourgeoisie built mansions in **Correría** and **Cuchillería**. They include one which now houses the **archaeological museum** (16th century) and the palaces of **Alava-Esquibel** and **Escoriaza-Esquibel**.

In 1813 the English defeated Napoleon's troops here. The French Emperor had camped in the **Casa Etxetxanda** on the **Paseo del Prado**. The battle inspired Beethoven to compose a "symphonic poem on the Battle of Vitoria", and a memorial on the Square of the Virgen Blanca commemorates the event. The old town on the hill and the old cathedral seem a little deserted during the day, but the area fills with people in the evening, who sit in the countless cafés drinking wine from the *Rioja Alavesa* and eating *tapas*. The new town spreads out on the other side of the **Plaza de España**, a typical neo-Classical square with an arcade and town hall. The **Plaza de los Fueros** close by is a modern project dedicated to Basque independence. From here a 3-km long, shaded walk ambles past the most important buildings in the town and to the **Basilika of Armentia**. You then cross the **Parque de Florida**, site of the Basque parliament and the neo-Gothic **cathedral**, and across the **Paseo de la Senda** and **Paseo de Fray Francisco de Vitoria**. Here you will find the **Art and Playing Card Museum** and the **Ajuria - Enea**, seat of the *Lehendakari*, the President of Basque autonomy. The **Museum of Armaments** is situated in the neighboring building. The walk continues through the **Parque del Prado**, across the **Paseo de Cervantes** and the **Avenida San Prudencio**, until the Romanesque **Basilica San Prudencio** suddenly towers before you on the outskirts of the town.

The province of Alava is small and has few surprises. But the town of **Salinas de Añana** with its three salt water springs is interesting. The water evaporates on the 5000 flat terraces originally laid by the Romans. Villagers have still work on over half of the saline ponds during the dry period of the year. To the west of Vitoria is **Estíbaliz** with a Romanesque church, and just outside **Argómaniz** is the **Palace of Larrea**, the *parador* of the area. Further into the plain is **Salvatierra**, a village with unaltered medieval streets. Near **Gaceo** and **Alaiza** you can see some naive early-Gothic paintings.

CANTABRIA

To get from the Basque region to Santander you follow the protracted coastline of Cantabria, with its fishing villages and beaches. From the 16th to the 18th century the ports in this area were regarded as the "Sea of Castile". The four most important towns were the *Cuatro Villas del Mar:* Castro- Urdiales, Laredo, Santoña and Santander.

Later the *Indianos* exerted their influence on the coast: at the end of the 19th century, when the last colonies in Cuba and the Philippines were lost, emigrants and traders returned with great wealth. They built extravagant villas and invested capital in the building of harbors and fleets. The harbors of Castro-Urdiales and Laredo were extended at this time to relieve the pressure on Bilbao.

Castro-Urdiales is now the Bilbao bourgeoisie's favorite summer residence. Its silhouette is marked by the ruins of the medieval Templar castle, its lighthouse and the fortified **Church of Santa María**. The church was planned in the 13th century, but later built in Gothic style. The interior has supporting arches which must have been added in the Renaissance to forestall the building's collapse. The upper part of the town is the medieval center, in the lower part you will find the harbor promenade and a grandiose residential area dating to the turn of the century.

On the **Ría de Oriñón** there are some wonderful beaches. The shellfish farms in the area leave you in no doubt as to what you should order in the restaurant in the evening. The Ría is the starting point of a wonderful tour to one of the most beautiful Cantabrian valleys, the **Valley of Guriezo**, which has a well- preserved old smithy in **La Yseca**.

Despite continuous building and land speculation, the charm of the 5-km long beach (**Playa de Salvé**) of Laredo has been retained. In **Laredo** the steep main street, **Rúa Mayor**, leads to a square with

Right: The town hall of Castro Urdiales (Cantabria) well- lit at night.

a Gothic church and a Renaissance town hall. You can still make out the eight blocks that formed the original town, which was extended in the 14th century around the quarter near the **Convent of San Francisco** and the **Chapel of the Holy Spirit**. The town is the site of a festival in August at which a flower battle takes place. The port of Laredo was the most important bridgehead in the direction of Flanders and northern Europe. It has also been linked with several romantic doings. This is where the daughters of the Catholic Monarchs boarded their ships to enter strategically conceived matrimony – Catalina (Catherine) to Henry VIII of England and Juana with Philip the Fair of Habsburg. And 60 years later the son of Charles V landed here, old and suffering from gout, on his painful final journey to the Monastery of Yuste in the Extremadura. With him came Barbara Blomberg, his lover from Regensburg and the mother of his illegitimate son. She lived in the La Madama district of **Colindres**, and her grave is in the **Monastery of San Sebastian de Ano** in Santoña. **Colindres** is now nearly joined to Laredo, and today has one of the largest fishing ports in Cantabria.

On the other side of the bay, at the foot of a steep cliff, lies **Santoña** with its Gothic **Church of Santa María del Puerto** and the large fortified complex dating back to the time when Napoleon landed here. Juan de la Cosa also came from Santoña. He was the cartographer who made the map of the world which Columbus used on his journey to America. The bay is a waterfowl reservation.

You can get to the **Valley of the Río Asón** from Colindres, and to the picturesque villages of **Limpias, Ampuero, Rasines** and **Ramales de la Victoria**, with their elegant houses with glassed-in galleries and palatial villas. The Río Asón is famous for its eels, trout and salmon. Near **Ampuero** in **Udalla** you will find the **Church of Bien Aparecida** (18th

century), the patron saint of Cantabria. **Ramales** has one of the most interesting palaeolithic settlements in Spain: the Caves of la Haza, Cullalvera and Covalanas. Further up in the **Valley of Soba** you will find small villages nestling in untouched large woods.

Cabo de Ajo, the coastal formation before Santander, has sandy beaches with many little cliffs and is an area which is becoming more and more popular amongst tourists. Pretty little towns line the coast: **Noja**, with the Playa de Ris beach; **Isla**, with palaces, towers and noblemen's *casonas* (mansions); **Bareyo**, with its Romanesque Church of Sta. María; and **Ajo**, with its small beaches and many hotels.

Santander

Santander was an important harbor in the Middle Ages. Today many inhabitants of Madrid spend the hot summer weeks here. The town center is relatively new and modern, rebuilt after a fire in 1941. It is a commercial center as well as an industrial and university town. In the royal **Palacio de la Magdalena** on the tip of the peninsula, where Alfonso XIII spent the summer for 27 years, is the summer university of **Menéndez Pelayo**, where many foreigners come to learn the language. The former stables now serve as classrooms. You can cross the bay by boat to the golf course of Pedreña and the beaches of **Somo** and **El Puntal**.

The **cathedral** was rebuilt after the fire, but the Romanesque crypt and the tomb of the scholar Menéndez Pelayo survived the blaze. The town also has an excellent small **museum of prehistory** and an **art museum** which includes works by Mengs and Goya. There are countless small pubs and bars around the **port**, which serve everything from the smallest seafood snacks to gourmet fish delicacies. Behind the extensive parks are several fine, sandy beaches, the most famous of which is **El Sardinero**.

In summer Santander has a comprehensive cultural program with concerts and productions of all kinds. Many of them are staged on the **Plaza Porticada**.

Around the town are many beautiful walks and excursions. One might visit the **lighthouse of Cabo Mayor**, for example, or the **caves of El Pendon** in **Camargo**. One can also take a trip to **Maliaño**, to see the church in which the famous Renaissance architect of the Habsburgs, Herrera, is buried. Nearby, in **Muriedas**, the ethnographical museum is housed in the **Casa Verlarde**, a 17th century palace. Typical furnishings and tools from the region are exhibited here. To the south of the Bay of Santander, in **Carbarceno** near Obregón, lies a bizarre stretch of abandoned iron mines which has been transformed into a zoo, accessible by car only.

The mountains south of Santander can be reached via the valleys of the **Río Miera** and **Río Pas**. These valleys are more gentle than those of the high mountains to the west. Beyond the spa of **Solares** you come to **Liérganes**, also a spa, which grew up around the royal arms factory in the 17th century. The whole town seems to consist of Baroque palaces. Liérganes is the origin of a curious 17th century legend, known throughout the country. The carpenter Francisco de la Vega disappeared on a swim in the Río Miera. Years later he was discovered in Cádiz. He had lost his memory and only knew the most important words: Liérganes, bread, wine and tobacco. Webs had grown between his fingers and toes, and his skin had become scaly. He was nicknamed the fish-man.

In **Puente-Viesgo** there are various caves with prehistoric wall paintings, some of which are open to visitors. This is where the **Valle del Pas** begins, formerly an isolated mountain valley, whose inhabitants traveled about trading. The most popular sweet dishes of the re-

gion come from here: cheese cake, or *quesada*, and *sobaos pasiegos*, a kind of butter cake. Typical villages are **Vega de Pas**, **San Roque de Riomiera** and **San Pedro de Romeral**. The mountain villages are dotted with holiday homes.

To the west of Santander is a particularly popular stretch of coast. The little village of **Santillana del Mar** has not changed since the 17th century. All its buildings are typical examples of the architecture of the landed nobility of Santander: tall roofs, aristocratic coats-of-arms on the façades and glassed-in balconies, covered with geraniums. The **Casa de Tagle**, the **del Merino Tower**, the **Casa de los Hombrones** and the **Casa Barreta** are just a few cases in point. In one of the palaces is a *parador nacional*. The collegiate **Church of Sta. Juliana** is the most important example of Romanesque architecture on the northern coast. Traffic is banned from this pretty town, but on weekends in high season there is rarely room to move. Santillana is known, among other things, for the nearby caves of **Altamira**. Not far away is **Comillas**, a holiday town in a beautiful setting, made famous by the Count of the same name who returned a rich man from Cuba in the last century. Along with a palace and a playful modernist summer castle – the **Capricho**, built by Antoni Gaudí – much of the wealth went to the Jesuits, who had a theological high school built by Domenec i Montaner.

From the long bridge spanning the Ría you can look out over **San Vicente de la Barquera**, a particularly beautiful town, dominated by the ruins of a castle, a fortified Gothic church with a Romanesque portal, the remains of the town wall and the picturesque Plaza Mayor.

Cabezón de la Sal, the gateway to the mountain valleys of **Cabuérniga** and the **Valley of Nansa**, was formerly a natural starting point for immigrants who resettled the Castilian areas freshly won back from the Moors. These immigrants

Right: Beach life along the Cantabrian coast has something to offer for everyone.

came from the mountains and were called *foramontanos*. On their trail, following the **Valley of Saja**, you come to **Ruente**, which prides itself in its clear spring. Nearby you can take a nice walk to **Aá Mountain** with its ancient oak stock.

The towns of **La Bárcena Mayor**, **Carmona** and **Tudanca** are model settlements, preserved in their historical form for tourists. But while Bárcena seems like a museum, you will still find genuine cow patties in the alleys of the other two towns. Tudanca is the setting for the novel *Peñas arriba* by Pereda, the Cantabrian regional poet. The house in the novel is the **Casona Tablanca**, today a museum. Above Tudanca a narrow, winding mountain road runs to a dam wall, built between steep cliffs. The road meets the Valle de Liébana at a height of almost 1.400 m. At the head of the **Valle de Cabuérniga** and the **Valle des Nansa** is the **Pico de Tres Mares** attaining the proud height of 2.222 m. Its waters flow into the Cantabrian Sea, the Mediterranean and the western Atlantic.

In the **Valle de Liébana** you will find the famous Mozarabian church of Lebeña, standing before an impressive mountain panorama. A side street takes you to the **Monastery of Santo Toribio de Liébana**, famous for its 8th century *Commentary on the Apocalypse*, a splendid example of Mozarabian culture.

From **Potes** you can get to the steepest and highest valleys of the Cantabrian mountains. When you have finally fought your way through the narrow **Desfiladero de la Hermida**, the valley basin of **Fuente Dé** suddenly opens up before you. In summer this is the largest car park in the northern Cordilleras, surrounded only by the *parador nacional* and a few cafés and pubs. In the background you will see the **Picos de Europa**, the highest peaks of this range, which tower to heights of up to 2.648 m. The owners of the cars are usually nowhere to be seen. They have been taken to a station 1.847 m up the mountain. Once there, the people disperse: some admire the view, others go on one of the wonderful mountain tours. There is also a jeep which carries guests to a modern mountain hotel.

This area has enjoyed an enormous tourist boom over the last few years. Tourists are now offered everything their hearts might desire, from mountain hikes to horseback riding, or from hang gliding to mountain bike tours.

South of the Cantabrian Mountains

The gorge of **Hoces de Bárcena** steers you from Torrelavega to a high valley and the small industrial town of **Reinosa**, at the beginning of the Ebro reservoir. Near the town, in **Retortillo**, are the remains of the Roman settlement of **Julióbriga**. Stones from the Romans building were used in the construction of a 12th-century Romanesque church. Another church with a splendid portal is to be found in **Cervatos** farther south.

In **Aguilar de Campóo** one arrives at the north rim of the Castilian **Meseta**. Despite the large reservoir, grain growing dominates the local economy. Entering the town you will immediately smell what is made from the grain. A huge biscuit factory blocks the view and the entrance to the busy town center with its beautiful main square, colonnades and fountains. A surprise is in store for you at the **Monastery of Sta. María la Real**, whose history can be traced back to the 9th century. It was turned into a restoration school, and one is allowed to look around the rooms where the pupils themselves are doing restoration work. In one room there are photos and replicas of some of the most beautiful of the 125 Romanesque churches which have been preserved in the district of Palencia.

Further west you come to the nature reserve on the source rivers of the Carrión, the **Fuentes Carrionas**. From **Cervera de Pisuerga** you can get to a beautiful,

Right: The Riaño Reservoir – there was a farm here a few years ago.

clear mountain lake with a campsite, the **Pantano de Ruesga**. The only building, the huge *parador nacional,* stands on its shore. A number of paths lead to several crystalline mountain reservoirs and rivers, up to the watershed of the **Pico de Tres Mares**. To the west is another nature reserve, the **Reserva Nacional de Riaño**. Riaño lies on the shore of the huge reservoir of the same name, spanned by futuristic bridges. It made headlines in the 1980's when the village with a population of more than 5.000 was flooded to make way for a dam. Present-day Riaño is a daring urban construction, home to only about five families from the original village. The rest was bought up by townspeople who come here in summer for watersports, fresh summer air and the mountain scenery.

ASTURIAS

The Christian armies in Asturias rebelled against the Moors only 11 years after the latter's occupation of Spain. In this, the oldest Spanish kingdom, hidden behind the great Northern Cordilleras, an individual breed of people has survived along with its traditions. They are rather like their Celtic ancestors and do not fit the clichée of the fiery southerners. Asturian villages and minifundia still exist in the mountainous elevations. Towns and industrialization have only been able to develop in the seaports and in the plains of Oviedo, behind the first coastal mountain range.

The scenery of Asturias is probably the most beautiful in Spain. The deep mountain valleys with countless, clear rivers, green meadows, wild hedges, chestnut woods, red tiled roofs on wooden houses, tall store houses *(horreos)*, fields reaching right up to the rocky Atlantic coast, the palatial villas of the *Indianos* – all this makes Asturias a unique area. You need time to drink a glass of bubbling *sidra* or eat a heavy Asturian *fabada* with big

beans. These *fabes* are a staple food eaten in every possible combination – with mussels, for example. On the coast *caldereta de pescado*, a type of fish stew, is also tasty. A favorite snack is bream or sea pike in *sidra – besugo, merluza a la sidra*. Among the cheeses the *queso de cabrales* is particularly recommendable.

On the coastal road, the **Río Deva** marks the border to Asturias. On the road to **Llanes** is the **cave of Pindal** with unique prehistoric wall paintings, and in **Vidiago** you will find the neolithic rocks of **Peña-Tu**. Llanes is an important fishing port with Renaissance houses and Baroque palaces. From the **Paseo de San Pedro**, a promenade on the steep coast above the town, you can see right across the harbor, the old and the new town centers and the beach **Playa de Sablón**. The beaches between Llanes and Ribadesella are regarded as the finest in Asturias.

Ribadesella has an old town center and a town hall in a Renaissance palace. A 300-m long bridge over the river Sella

takes you to the wide sandy beaches. On the first Saturday in August the Fiesta de las Piraguas takes place, an international canoe competition, which runs from **Arriondas** down the Río Sella. In this area there are also many caves with stalactites and stalagmites. The most interesting is the **cave of Tito Bustillo**, with animal paintings more than 20.000 years old.

From Arriondas you pass the **Monastery of San Pedro de Villaneuva** (16th century) on your way to **Cangas de Onís**, the first capital of the Asturian kingdom, with its famous Roman bridge, *el puentón*, and the Asturian cross underneath. Carriages and carts have to be pulled across this steep bridge by oxen. In the **Ermita de la Santa Cruz** you will find a carved dolmen. From here you can get to the Picos de Europa and **Covadonga**, site of the legendary battle in which Don Pelayo conquered the Moors. Steps lead to the cave where the soldiers hid. Here the figure of the Virgin of Covadonga, the Santina, and the graves of Don Pelayo and his family are worshipped. A water-

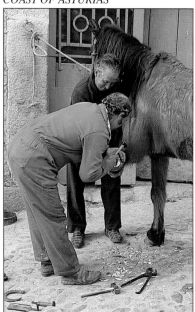

fall plunges from the cave into a basin. Its waters are said to have miraculous powers and are drunk by young girls wishing for a *novio,* a fiancé. Next to it is the collegiate Church of **San Fernado** (16th century) with a cloister and Romanesque graves. A tunnel has been dug to the **Basilica of the Virgen de las Batallas** from the last century. Make sure you take a trip up to the queen's look-out and the lakes of **Enol** and **Ercina** at the foot of the Picos de Europa, in the middle of beautiful landscape that has been declared a national park.

Some fine tours into the mountains begin in **Cangas**. The road to **Panes** follows the gorge of **Río Cares**. Near **Alles** in **Besnes** you will find the Hotel La Tahona, in an old bakery. From this hotel you can go on walks, riding trips and mountain bike excursions. In **Arenas de Cabrales** a side street takes you to **Poncebos** and **Bulnes**, running directly

Above: Rural craftsmanship is still a part of daily life in Asturias.

beneath the sheer walls of the **Naranjo** (2.519 m). From Poncebos you can walk through the gorge to **Caín** (15 km), also known by the name of *garganta divina* (divine gorge). The **de los Beyos gorge** on the mountain road from Cangas to Riaño in León is impressive, as is the **gorge of Pontón** near San Juan de Beleño through which you can walk to the cheesery at **Neyos**.

From **Arriondas** a road runs to the coast and the beautiful beach of **La Isla**. Along the road there are many good views of the coastlines, the mountains and the **Sueve Nature Reserve**, where the last remaining Asturian wild horses, the *asturcones*, roam. In **Gobiendes** you come across the first early-Romanesque Asturian church, the **Church of San Salvador**. Another church of the same name is in **Priesca**. But the majority of these unique little churches are in the parish of **Villaviciosa**. The Romanesque **Church of San Juan de Amandi** stands on the edge of the town. Before reaching Villaviciosa you come to the picturesque sea-side town of **Lastres**, where you can get the freshest seafood dishes. In **Villaviciosa**, with its typical squares and alleys (and the **Church of Santa María** in transitional Romanesque-Gothic style), you should also pay a visit to the *sidra* bottling plant. In **Valdediós**, a little further along the road to Oviedo, is the **Monastery of Santa María** (13th century) and another gem of Asturian pre-Romanesque style, **San Salvador**, also called El Conventín (893). On the tip of the bay is the pretty harbor of **Tazones**, where Charles V first set foot on Spanish land in 1517. The beaches to the east of Gijón are not the cleanest in Asturias, although some of the countless small rocky bays could turn out to be small paradises.

Gijón is the largest town in the region, with a population of 260.000. An industrial town, with a huge loading and container port, it also has a 5-km long beach in the **Bay of San Lorenzo**. Be-

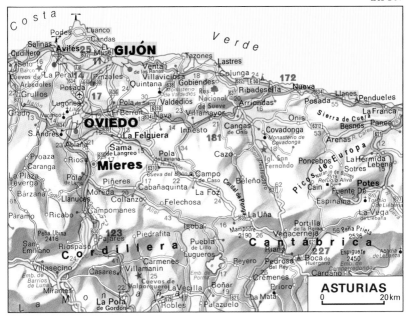

tween the beach and the harbor is the
fishing quarter of **Cimadevilla**, the old
town center with steep streets full of
sidra bars *(chigres)*, where you can drink
fresh apple cider and eat sea urchins *(ori-
cios)*. Below this quarter is the **Renaissance Palace of Revillagigedo**, the Casona, birthplace of the great politician
and writer of the Spanish Enlightenment
Gaspar de Jovellanos, and the Roman
baths of **Campo Valdés**. At the other end
of the bay, in the **Isabel la Católica
Park**, is the town's *parador* in an old
mill. The buildings of the **Universidad
Laboral** on the edge of the town are also
interesting – a strange neo-Baroque technical college from the time of Franco,
with a 150-m tower.

From Gijón you can continue your
journey directly along the coast. Against
the backdrop of the steep faces of the
Cabo de Peñas, where the wind blows
constantly, are the quaint towns of **Candás** and **Luanco**, the latter with a sailing
museum. **Avilés** is dominated by the steel
industry, but also has an old town worth

visiting. Its beach in **Salinas** used to be
an elegant holiday resort in the 19th century. The old buildings still reflect this
past glory. A little way off the main road
are the stalactitic and stalagmitic caves of
Arbedales. The industrial areas, the airport and the Río Nalón, which carries the
waste waters of the coal industry from
Pravia into the sea, should bypassed as
quickly as possible. **Cudillero** lies off the
main road. It has a deep harbor basin with
houses arranged around it like an atrium.
This is one of the finest fishing villages in
Asturias, and has a whole series of seafood bars. From here to the west, the
steep coast opens up repeatedly onto
clean sand (**Cadavedo**) and pebble
(**Cabo Busto**) beaches. If you walk a
little way, you are bound to find a very
private rocky bay (e.g. at **Las Escaladina**
in Barcia, before Luarca). **Luarca**, the
old "white fishing village", is a sprawling
town, hemmed into the narrow space
around the **Ría** of the **Río Negro**. It has a
pretty fishing port and narrow streets in
which tourists and locals throng in an ap-

95

parently perpetual holiday mood. From the center of **Navia** a promenade lined with eucalyptus ends at the beach and the open sea. A little way above the town is the **Castro Coaña**, a Celtic settlement of which only the foundation walls have survived.

As you approach the town of **Ribadeo**, the beaches become busier and more touristy. The sea rolls in massive swells, suitable for surfing. **Tapia de Casariego** is another amiable fishing town with countless seafood bars. The Ría del Eo gives its name to the towns of **Ribadeo** and **Vegadeo** (bank and meadow of the Eo). Both are lively coastal and holiday resorts. The townscape of **Castropol** is known for its palaces.

Oviedo

The main road of the region runs parallel to the coast, through a fertile plain, and on to **Oviedo**. One fun stop on the

Above: It's a long way to Cambridge.

way is **Nava**, famous for its *sidra* festival, and **Pola de Siero**, a place known for its pilgrimages and for the Easter feast of the painted eggs, on April 17, a custom otherwise unknown in Spain.

Oviedo, the petty bourgeois "Vetusta" of Clarín's novel *The President's Wife*, is now a thriving town. The tower of the late-Gothic **cathedral** rises over the roofs of the town between green hills and mountains, "a poem in stone", as Clarín describes it. Near the cathedral you can still find traces of past centuries. Dusty shops with devotional objects, old-fashioned pastry shops, quiet squares in the shade of old churches, the streets of **Sto. Domingo**, **San Vincente**, **Cimadevilla** or **Salsipuedes** ("leave me if you can").

Perez de Ayala describes this old center as being traditional and authentic. Everywhere there are *chigres* with wooden floors where *sidra* is served with great ceremony. The **Plaza Mayor** and **El Fontán** (the market place) are typical squares with arcades.

The **cathedral** of Oviedo, essentially a Gothic building with a simple interior, has an overwhelming late-Gothic altar retable. In the southern transept you will find the **Camara Santa** (9th century), a chapel extension built for the imperial treasury and brought here after the fall of Toledo to the Moors. It includes treasures such as an agate chest and the legendary **Cross of Los Angeles** and the **Cross of Victory**, with the coat-of-arms of Oviedo and Asturias. Finely worked ivory altars and religious relics can also be admired, including one of St. Peter's sandals, a few of Mary Magdalene's hairs, a singed bone of St. Eulalia and one of Judas' 30 pieces of silver. Apart from the Camara Santa Oviedo has other unique buildings from pre-Romanesque times: in the center the apse of the **Church of San Tirso** and the fountain of **Foncalada**. A little further out, in the suburb of **Santullano**, is **San Julian de los Prados**. But the two churches at the foot of the **Mt. Naranco**, about 3 km northwest of the town, are especially beautiful: **Sta. María del Naranco**, originally the residence of Ramiro I, and **San Miguel de Lillo**, a royal chapel with fine interior decorations and the typical cord motifs. It is worth taking a walk there just for the pretty surroundings and the *sidra* bars along the way. The **Church of Sta. María de Bendones** is on the road to **La Felguera**.

In the town center the **Convent of San Vincente** houses an archaeological museum. Next to this is the **Convent of San Pelayo** (17th/18th century). The beautiful 16th century Renaissance university building is also worth seeing, as are the town hall (16th century), the **San Feliz Palace** (18th century) with an apostle series by El Greco, and the 17th century hospital, now the **Hotel Reconquista**. The main street in modern Oviedo is called **Uría**, and runs past the **San Francisco Park**.

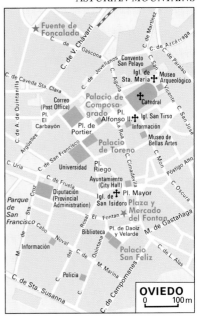

OVIEDO
0   100 m

The Asturian Mountains

Along the coast of Asturias, the mountains also offer a fascinating panorama. Facilities are often lacking, but some tourist centers are now in the process of being built.

From **Castropol** a road runs through the angler's paradise of **San Tirso de Abres** to **Taramundi**. From a lovely, not exactly cheap mountain hotel in a former nobleman's house from the 18th century, you can embark on excursions into the surrounding area. Marked hiking paths through river valleys and woods take you to the neighboring towns with their typical artisans: cutlers, potters, weavers, and a water-driven smithy, for example. To the south, in the border area near Galicia, lies the **Oscos**, an isolated mountain region which has retained its rural lifestyle, its typical architecture *(caseríos)* and traditions. The landscape is green and exceptionally beautiful.

South of Oviedo, toward León, you come to the coal mining area of **Mieres**, where the small villages sport winding towers that rise against the green landscape. In **Pola de Lena**, above the motorway, you will find a true gem: **Sta. Cristina de Lena**, a church (9th century) overlooking the whole valley from a hill. In **Lluances** the **Palacio de los Miranda** with its holiday flats makes an ideal base for hikers.

If you cross the **Pajares Pass** instead of driving through the tunnel you can enjoy the wide panorama of the mountain valleys of Asturias and León. These mountains are the ideal location for various hikes from the **Valleys of Pigueña**, **Trubia**, **Aller** and **Río Negro**.

The **Río Luna Dam** with its reservoir, the **Barrios de la Luna** (moon quarters), is on the south side of the Pajares Pass next to the motorway. Not far from the country road, south of the pass, are the **Caves of Valpoquero**, which have three entrances and three and a half kilometers of labyrinthian, subterranean passageways.

THE GALICIAN COAST

The Ría Eo separates Asturias and Galicia. Galicia is the third region of Spain with its own language, Gallego, from which Portuguese developed. It is the northern region furthest from Castile, but not only in kilometers. Culturally heavily influenced by the Celts, it is often more reminiscent of Ireland than the south of the country, with its architecture and its bagpipe music. Galicia is full of legends and superstitions: witches and fairies, imaginary castles and ghostly visions which come and go in the Galician mists like the *saudade*, Galician melancholy, much written and sung about. The many wonderful beaches can only be used during the two summer months, and are abandoned for the rest of the year, leaving a paradise for solitary beach walkers. In October they fill again with locals who collect tons of mussels and shellfish from the sand. The Galician villages scattered through the fields have unique, traditional architecture: the stone crosses with a figure on each side, called *cruceiros;* the long stone *horreos,* maize granaries which are clearly distinguishable from the wooden Asturian ones; and *pazos,* small noblemen's castles with a little more than the usual tiny parcels of fields. The best of Galicia's many festivals are those associated with the catching of wild horses in the mountains, at which bagpipes are played and fresh *pulpo,* cooked octopus, is eaten. Once a year, usually in spring, the horses' manes and tails are clipped *(rapa),* the vet examines them and individual animals are selected for taming. In Viveiro, Cedeira, Valadouro and Sabucedo local holidays have developed from this tradition. Most of them have maintained authentic flavor because they occur outside the tourist season.

The coast of Galicia has four main regions. The north coast up to **Cabo Ciprián** with its large breakers and small

Above: The Asturian maize storage huts on stilts are safe from mice.

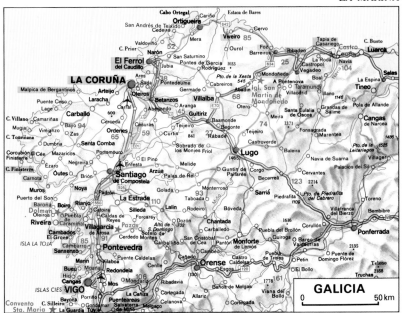

river valleys is called **Mariñas**. The **Rías Altas** consists of the raw atlantic firths of the northern coast to **La Coruña**. The northwestern rocky coast around **Cabo Finisterre** is called the Coast of Death, *Costa de la Muerte*. The southwestern coast from **Padrón** has river estuary valleys reaching further inland. **Rías Bajas** has a milder climate and a settlement with white villages and colorful shutters, and is similar to Portuguese settlements.

La Mariña and the Rías Altas

The coastal strip between **Ribadeo** and **Viveiro**, towards Asturias, is full of small parcels of maize and vegetable fields, meadows and eucalyptus woods reaching right down to the shoreline. The beaches are larger and more open than in Asturias, all clean with fine sand, populated by visitors from the immediate area. From **Foz** you can visit **Mondoñedo**, a small surprise in the middle of misty mountains. For a long time the town was the bishop's seat, and it has an almost forgotten **cathe-**

dral from the transition period between Romanesque and Gothic, with a Baroque façade. Inside you will find very fine frescoes from the 15th century. The spirit of the old convents floats through the little town, in the **Calle de las Monjas** you can hear the nuns' hourly prayers. It is the town's inhabitants who give it its particular charm: the "cake king" who marches proudly through the town and who has a shop where only one kind of cake is sold, or "Merlin the magician" who loves to show you his junk shop full of dusty nostalgia. In the old mill quarter, **Os Muiños**, there are pleasant bars and cafés serving cheap meals. If you go on from here to **Lugo** you will come to the **Terra Chá**, the "flat land", with the small *parador* of **Villalba** in the medieval tower of the **Andrade**. It is exclusive, with only 6 rooms. On the way to Foz is the early Romanesque Church of **San Mart de Mondoñedo**.

The busiest town in the area is **Viveiro**, a popular summer resort with steep streets, a Plateresque town gate from the

99

time of Charles V, and two Romanesque churches. The **Ría**, with its large fishing port, has charming sandy beaches surrounded by cliffs. The favorite section of the coast for the local townspeople is between Viveiro and Ferrol. The port towns of **Porto de Bares**, **Ortigueira**, **Cariño** and **Cedeira** beyond **Cabo Estaca de Bares**, the northernmost point of the peninsula, are small and attractive. Their beaches are covered in wonderful white sand. Those who don't get as far as **San Andrés de Teixido** when they are alive, a local saying goes, come back as lizards or frogs, and there are indeed many of these animals here. It is a small place of pilgrimage, situated directly by the sea at **Cedeira**, made famous because of superstition. People come here to pray for healing from terminal illnesses, to pick the grasses which are supposed to bring love, or to gather the reeds which are said to guarantee an easy birth. You can buy

Above: The Cape Finisterre – until the 15th century the world came to an end here.

colorful figures made of bread dough as souvenirs, said to bring good luck.

Around the large bay formed by the three Rías of **La Coruña**, **Betanzos** and **Ferrol** is the largest industrial zone in Galicia, with over 400.000 inhabitants. Fish canneries, wharfs, tin works and other heavy industry brought jobs for the locals who could no longer live off the land – at least until the European coal, steel and wharf crises hit this area too.

Ferrol, nicknamed "del Caudillo" because Franco was born here, has a small old town center, next to a beautifully preserved neo-Classical part of town built up during the Industrial Revolution. To the west, on the tip of the bay, is the fortified compound of **San Felipe**, which once defended the harbor area.

Pontedeume has a long history. It was named for the medieval bridge supported by 58 arches crossing the **Río Eume**. It belonged to the Andrade family, who fought with the Order of the Knights Templar for supremacy in the area in the 13th century. A tower in town commemorates this powerful dynasty. **Betanzos** is a little further away from the industrial hubbub. It has some well-preserved medieval churches and an old town wall.

The city of **La Coruña** has Celtic and Roman origins. It is guarded by the **Lighthouse of Hercules** on the most extreme tip of the peninsula, built under Trajan in the 2nd century. The name La Coruña (crown) was first mentioned in a document from the 12th century. The arcaded **Plaza de María Pita** on the edge of the old town is also the ciy center. The square is named after a heroic damsel who helped the town to victory against the English under Francis Drake in 1589. The English burned down the entire old town including the harbor quarter. The most attractive part of this largest city in Galicia is the **Avenida de la Marina**, with its white glassed-in balconies and the old town on a promontory on the peninsula which leads to the island of the **Castillo de San Antón** (16th century) and an archaeological museum. In the old town are the Romanesque collegiate **Church of Sta. María del Campo**, the Romanesque **Santiago Church**, and **Sto. Domingo**, a good example of Galician Baroque (17th century). Here one also finds **Azcarraga Square**, **San Carlos Park** and the remains of the old town walls which surrounded this part of the city. La Coruña has an impressive art museum, the **Museo Provincial de Bellas Artes**, with works from Italian, Dutch, and Spanish schools.

To the west of La Coruña are the wonderful, big beaches cherished by the local townspeople. Beyond the village of **Malpica de Bergantiños** begins the Coast of Death. Its name derives from the many accidents at sea which have taken place near the rocky promontories, and reflects the deep-rooted superstition of the local population. The area up to **Cabo Finisterre**, regarded as the "end of the earth" until the 15th century, has many cliffs, is inaccessible and has ravishing beaches, many of which can only be reached by long paths cut through fields. Thousands of tourists flock to this area every summer to enjoy the wonderful views, the beaches and to taste the best and freshest fish and shellfish in Galicia.

The Rías Bajas

South of Finisterre, before the famous beaches of Muros, is **Carnota**, with the longest *horreo* in Galicia. **Muros** and Noia are the main towns on the first of the **Rías Bajas**. **Noia** was the traditional port of Santiago. Today it is silted up, but it still has traces from the time when pilgrims arrived here in their ships from northern lands. In the **cemetery of Sta. María** (14th century) a number of old gravestones have been found with puzzling stone carvings which some experts believe may be guild symbols. A path runs from **Porto do Son** 500 m up to the **Sierra de Barbanza** and the **Ermita Magdalena**, from which you have a grand view over the sea.

Everywhere in this region there are traces of the Celts and the Suebis, and of their old, uneven stone streets. From the beach near **Baroña** you can take a tour around a Celtic settlement, the **Castro**. Near Oleiros sign-posted roads will take you to the prehistoric **Dolmen of Axeitos**. On the beach at **Ladeira**, at the tip of the peninsula, there are large sand dunes.

Don Rámon de Valle Inclán, one of the writers of the '98 generation, was born in **Puebla de Caramiñal**. The mysterious atmosphere of his homeland is a recurring theme in his writings. From the town you can reach the observation point at **Mirador de la Curota**, which is situated high above the firth.

The little town of **Padrón** lies at the beginning of the **Ría Arousa** on the **Río Ulla**. The boat containing the body of the apostle Santiago is supposed to have been tied to a *padrón* here, a stone post

which can still be seen today. Rosalia Castro lived and died in Padrón. She was a Galician lyricist and the author of sad and melancholic poetry. Her house on the outskirts of town, is open to the public.

The towers of **Oeste** in **Catoira** are all that remains of a Roman fortress, built in the 11th century to defend Santiago from the Normans. This event is commemorated today in a "Viking pilgrimage" to the early Romanesque chapel, ending in a festival with red wine and mussels. In the town some of the old windmills and tide-driven watermills still stand. In **Villagarcía de Arousa**, after which this Ría is named, there is a Celtic castro, **San Cristobal de Alobre**, a convent next to the *pazo* of **Vista Alegre** (16th century) and **Lobeira Castle**. There are a number of other pretty *pazos* near by, including the **Pazo de Golpelleira**, the **Pazo Rubianes** (14th century)

with its beautiful garden and the **Pazo O Rial**, which has now been converted into a luxury hotel. The town has an important harbor where the large ships filled with emigrants set off for distant shores in the 19th century. It is full of stately houses, reflecting its long tradition as an estival holiday resort. Today, too, the town is busy in summer and has a number of good and interesting restaurants and cafés serving tasty food.

Cambados is the center for **Albariño** winegrowing. Its vines were originally brought in from the Rhine and the Moselle by Cistercian monks in the 12th century. These excellent white wines become drier the further inland they are grown. The wines from **Ribadumia** and **Fefi** are particularly recommended with *pulpo* (octopus) or oyster dishes. In the **Pazo de Bazán** you will find the *parador* and the park in which the Albariño wine competition is held every year.

The Ría de Arousa sports three islands. The beaches of **Isla de Arousa** can be reached by crossing a long bridge from

Above: The freshly cought sword fish are being unloaded. Right: Tobacco fields in full bloom in Sta. Comba de Bande (Orense).

Vilanova. You have to take a boat to get to the island of **Sálvora**. But the most famous of the islands is undoubtedly that of **La Toja**, connected to the mainland by a bridge in El Grove. La Toja is a spa, and its waters are said to be particularly beneficial for skin ailments. It has been the most luxurious spa in Galicia since the 19th century. The healing powers of the waters are said to have been discovered by a farmer who abandoned his old and very sick donkey on the island to die. But after the donkey had swum for a time in the spring he recovered completely and turned up at his master's house the following day, much to the amazement of the farmer! Today the spa is full of very expensive holiday apartments. The peninsula of **El Grove** and its beaches are far quieter and less busy, except for the huge and famous **Playa de Lanzada**.

The Ría de Pontevedra is guarded by the islands of **Ons** and **Oceta** at its entrance. They are maintained by the Office for Environmental Protection, and can be reached by boat in summer from **Bueu** and from **Sanxenxo**. The mouth of the river, like that of the other Rías, is full of mussels which hang from *mejilloneras* on long strings for six to eight months until they are exactly the right size to be served up and eaten.

If you have time, pay a visit to **Pontevedra**, which has a charming old town. It is named after the old bridge, *pontis veteris*, which spanned the **Río Lérez**. It lies at the beginning of the Ría of the same name. Formerly an important harbor, it has now silted up and only the fishing quarter with the Plateresque **Sailors' Church of Sta. María la Mayor** still remains. The old town sits between the two bridges spanning the Lérenz. The Baroque pilgrim's church, **La Peregrina**, was built in the shape of a mussel. The small streets are filled with beautiful shops, excellent cafés and have many pleasant little corners and squares where you can sit and relax for a while. The streets are for pedestrians only so that you can escape the traffic chaos which

rumbles on the edge of the old town. The **Provincial Museum** is housed in several buildings around the **Plaza de la Leña**. It has a variety of exhibitions and displays, and is certainly worth a visit. In the former **Dominican Convent** at **La Alameda Park** is the **Archaeological Museum**. In the center you will find the **Casa del Barón**, the old **Pazo de Maceda** (16th century), now a *parador nacional*. On the edge of the town is the **Monastery of San Juan de Poyo**, which dates from the 12th century but has been restored in Baroque style. The 18th century grave of St. Trahamunda is still intact. He was patron saint of vagabonds. It is said that his body floated up to the adjacent island of **Tambo** in a ship made of stone, while bells were heard chiming in the heavens.

Combarro is a good example of a local 18th century fishing village. The inhabitants live in the more than fifty *hor-*

Above: Cruceiro in Hío (Pontevedra). Right: A fisherman repairing his fishing baskets.

reos that stand next to each other along the shore, each facing the sea wind for ventilation. The whole **Ría de Pontevendra** is dominated by visitors, but has hardly any hotels to offer. The only accomodation it does have is holiday flats. The beaches here are lovely and, being far removed from the larger towns, are also very clean.

Between Ría de Pontevedra and Ría de Vigo is the quiet bay of **Ensenada de Aldán**, in which you will find the most beautiful *cruceiro* in Galicia. It stands beside the Romanesque **Church of San Andrés** in **Hío**, and shows Christ being taken from the cross (19th century). **Ría de Vigo** is densely populated, but its beaches get larger the closer they lie to the open sea, and are rarely too crowded to find a spot to sunbathe.

At the mouth of the Ría de Vigo are the **Cíes Islands**, which form one of Galicia's three nature parks as well as a sea bird reserve. There are no hotels on the islands, but there are a few cafés and restaurants, fresh water sources and camp sites. Both islands are a paradise of peace and have wide beaches, walks, and a small lake and wooded hills. The larger is about 4 km long. Boats cross regularly from Vigo in the summer months.

Vigo, the Roman *Vicus Espacorum*, a former fishing village, experienced enormous growth during the 19th century. Today it is the most important Atlantic port for the large Spanish fleet of sardine fishermen and the fish industry connected with it. Since Spain joined the European Community, other factories and businesses have opened here as well, and Vigo is now the industrial center of Galicia. Artists, fashion designers and the like have all taken part in this boom. In the harbor area of **Barrio de Berbés**, the only relic which remains of the old town, you will find the restaurants and cafés of the self-confident local *movida*. Of the booming 19th-century expansion, the most elegant buildings in the C/del Principe have been preserved. The **City Museum** in the **Pazo de Castrelos** (17th century) is in the **Quiñones de León Park** and has a collection of paintings, archaeological finds and artefacts of Galician folk culture. Everywhere there are beautiful sights: in the town center you can see the park with the ruins of **Castillo de Castro**, and on the edge of town you can climb up to the **Mirador de la Guia**.

On the northern side of the Ría is the port of **Moaña** and a lovely Romanesque church. A short trip inland will take you to **Mondariz**, formerly a fashionable spa, where the two springs housed in Art Nouveau buildings are still in operation. The spa's palaces, however, burned down and were abandoned. Hardly any of its former splendor has been retained, but the town has a clean swimming pool on the river and many people come here during the summer months.

On the southern end of the Ría de Vigo is the town of **Baiona**, with a well-preserved old town and a Gothic collegiate church with a Romanesque portal. The castle, the **Castillo Monterreal** (14th century) with its three medieval towers, beckons visitors. In the *pazo* next to it, the **Palace of Gondomar**, you will find a *parador.* The **Playa de America** is world-famous. It is a large beach on the **Ría of Baiona**. Its name commemorates the fact that Columbus's ship docked here on his return from his voyage of discovery to what was then (1493) considered the western coast of India.

The coastal strip to the south of Baiona, stretching up to the mouth of the **Rió Miño**, is exposed to the sea and the breakers, and is therefore never very busy. There is a picturesque, originally Romanesque Cistercian monastery here, **Sta. María de Oia**, with a Baroque façade and a beautiful cloister which dates from the 15th century. It is said that Christian ships pursued by Turkish pirates fled to the harbor at Oia and that

the monks then chased off the pirates with fireworks.

La Guardia guards the mouth of the river. Above it, on the hill of **Sta. Tecla**, there is a well-restored Celtic *castrum* with an interesting museum. The river Miño (Minho in Portuguese) forms the border here between the two countries.

Inland on the Miño is the Portuguese **Valencia do Minho**, and opposite it, joined by a 19th century bridge, **Tui**, a Greek settlement, which has often been the object of territorial disputes in the past. It has frequently changed hands between Spain and Portugal. The narrow streets of the town run steeply up to the hill where you will find a Gothic **cathedral**, a sturdy fortified construction with an interesting cloister and three transepts. The portal shows the three kings worshipping Jesus. The most impressive church treasures are displayed in a museum. The church of **Sto. Domingo**, originally Gothic, but rebuilt in the Baroque style, is located in the park of Sto. Domingo at the foot of the hill.

PROVINCE GUIPUZCOA
(Telephone area code: 943-)
Accommodation
FUENTERRABÍA: *MODERATE:* **Parador de Hondarribia**, Pl. Armas, Tel: 642140. OÑATE: *BUDGET:* Hosp. del Monasterio de Aranzazu; Tel. 943-781313. GETARIA: *MODERATE:* **Azcue**, Alto de Meagas, Tel: 841008. SAN SEBASTIAN: *LUXURY:* **Londres y de Inglaterra**, C/ Zubieta 2, Tel: 426989. *MODERATE:* **Alameda**, Alameda del Bulevard 23, Tel: 421687.
Museums / Sightseeing
SAN SEBASTIAN: **Museo de San Telmo**: 9 a.m.–9 p.m., Sundays and public holidays 9 a.m.–2 p.m., Mon 5–9 p.m.. in winter 10 a.m.–1.30 p.m., 3.30–7 p.m. **Monte Igueldo** with amusement park 10 a.m.–10 p.m.
Tourist Information
SAN SEBASTIAN: Oficina de Turismo: C/ Reina Regente, Tel. 421002.

PROVINCE VISZCAYA
(Telephone area code: 94-)
Accommodation
LEKEITIO: *MODERATE:* **Beitia**, Av. Pascual Abaroa 25, Tel: 6840111. GUERNIKA: *MODERATE:* **Gernika, Tel: 6854948.** DURANGO: *MODERATE:* **Hostal Juego de Bolos**, San Augustinalde 2, Tel: 94-6811099. BILBAO: *LUXURY:* **Aranzazu**, C/ Rodriguez Arías 66, Tel: 4413200. *MODERATE:* **Hostal Gurea**, C/ Bidebarrieta 14, Tel: 4163299.
Tourist Information
BILBAO: **Oficina de Turismo**, Alameda Mazarredo.
Museums / Sightseeing
Museo de Bellas Artes and **Mus. Historico de Vizcaya**: 10.30 a.m.–1 p.m., 3.30–7 p.m., Sun. a. public holidays 10.30 a.m.–1.30 p.m., cl. Mon.

PROVINCE ALAVA
(Telephone area code: 945-)
Accommodation
SALVATIERRA: *MODERATE:* **Parador de Argomaniz**, 20 km east of Vitoria, Ctra. N-240, km 361,7; Tel: 282200. VITORIA: *MODERATE:* **Dato 28**, C/ Dato 28, Tel. 232320.
Tourist Information / Post
VITORIA: Oficina de Turismo, C/ Ramón y Cajal. Post: Plaza Correos
Museums / Sightseeing
VITORIA: **Museo Provincial, Museo de Armería, Museo Arqueologico, Museo de Ciencias Naturales**: 11 a.m.–2 p.m. and 5–7 p.m., Sat and Sun 11 a.m.–2 p.m., closed Mon.

PROVINCE CANTABRIA
(Telephone area code: 942-)
Accommodation
CASTRO URDIALES: *MODERATE:* **Miramar**, Av. de la Playa 1, Tel: 860200. LIÉRGANES: *MODERATE:* **del Balneario**, Barrio de Calgar, Tel: 528011. SANTILLANA DEL MAR: *MODERATE:* **Parador Gil Blas**, Pl. Ramón Pelayo 11, Tel: 818000. COMILLAS: *MODERATE:* **Josein**, C/ Santa Lucia 27, Tel: 720225. CABEZÓN DE LA SAL: *MODERATE:* **Conde de Lara**, Vista Alegre 4, Tel: 700312. CARMONA: *MODERATE:* **Venta de Carmona**, Tel: 728057. VALLE DE LIÉBANA: *MODERATE:* **El Caserío**, Camaleño, Ctra. Potes-Espinama, Tel: 730928.
ESPINAMA, FUENTE DÉ: *LUXURY:* **Parador Río Deva**; Tel: 730001. POTES: *MODERATE:* **Rubio**, C/ San Roque 17, Tel: 730015.
REINOSA: *MODERATE:* **La Corza Blanca**, Ctra. Reinosa-Tres Mares, km 24, Tel: 751099.
SANTANDER: *LUXURY:* **Real**, Paseo de Pérez Galdós 28, Tel. 272550. *MODERATE:* **Alisas**, C/ Nicolás Salmerón 3, Tel: 222750.
Tourist Information
SANTANDER: **Oficina de Turismo:** Pl. Velarde 1, Tel: 310708.
Museums / Sightseeing
SANTANDER: **Museo Marítimo del Cantábrico**, C/ San Martín de Baja Mar, 11 a.m.–1 p.m., 4–7 p.m., Sundays and public holidays 11 a.m.–2 p.m. **Museo de Prehistoria y Arqueología**, C/ Casimiro Sainz 4, 8 a.m.–2 p.m., closed Sun. **Museo Municipal de Bellas Artes**, C/ Rubio 6, 10 a.m.–1 p.m. and 5–8 p.m.
CAVES OF ALTAMIRA: You will need a special permit to visit these famous caves; applications must be made in writing at least half a year before the prospective visiting date to: Centro de Investigación de Altamira, Santillana, Cantabria 39330; stalactite-room and didactic rooms 10 a.m.–1 p.m. and 4–6 p.m.
PUENTE VIESGO: Caves 10 a.m.–12.15 p.m. and 3–6.15 p.m., in winter 10 a.m.–2.15 p.m.

PROVINCE PALENCIA
(Telephone area code: 988-)
Accommodation
CERVERA DE PISUERGA: *LUXURY:* **Parador Fuentes Carrionas**, Tel: 988-870075.
AGUILAR DE CAMPOO: *MODERATE:* **Pórtico de Castilla**, C/ Féréz, Tel: 122225.
Sightseeing
AGUILAR: **Monasterio Sta. María la Real**, weekdays 10 a.m.–2 p.m.; 5–8 p.m., Sundays and public holidays 11 a.m.–2 p.m., 5–8 p.m.

PROVINCE ASTURIA
(Telephone area code: 985-)
Accommodation
CANGAS DE ONÍS: *MODERATE:* **Hospedería del Pelegrino**, Covadonga, Tel: 846047. **GIJÓN**: *LUXURY:* **Casona de Jovellanos**, Pl. Jovellanos 1, Tel: 342024. *MODERATE:* **Pathos**, Contracay 5, Tel: 352546. **LUARCA**: *MODERATE:* **Baltico** (local dishes), Paseo del Muelle, Tel: 640991. **POLA DE LENA**: *MODERATE:* **Puerto de Pajares**, Lena, Tel: 496023. **TARAMUNDI**: *LUXURY:* **La Rectoral**, Tel: 634060. **OVIEDO**: *LUXURY:* **Reconquista**, C/ Jil de Jaz 16, Tel. 241100. *MODERATE:* **Asturias**, C/ Uría 16, Tel: 214695.

Museums / Sightseeing
GIJON: Museum Jovellanos, Cimadevilla 10 a.m.–1 p.m., 4–8 p.m., Sun. and public holidays 12 noon–2 p.m., closed Mon, (keys for Roman Baths). **Museo Etnográfico**: Asturian village on the right bank of the Río Piles, open from 10 a.m. until dusk. **VILLAVICIOSA: San Salvador** and **Santa María de Valdediós**, 11 a.m.–1.30 p.m., 4–6.30 p.m., closed Mon. **RIBADEDEVA: Cave of Pindal** 10 a.m.–12.30 p.m., 4.30–6.30 p.m., closed Mon. **RIBADESELLA: Cave of Tito Bustillo**, 10 a.m.–1 p.m., 3.30–5.15 p.m., closed Sun in summer, Mon in winter. **LUANCO: Museo Marítimo**, 11 a.m.–1 p.m., 5–7 p.m., closed Mon. **CANGAS DE ONÍS: Cave of Buxu**, 10 a.m.–1 p.m., 3.30–6.30 p.m. **COAÑA: Celtic Castro**, 10 a.m.–2 p.m. and 4–5.15 p.m., Sat and Sun 10 a.m.–2 p.m. and 3.30–7.30 p.m., closed Mon. **POLA DE LENA: Sta. Cristina**: 11 a.m.–1 p.m. and 4.30–6 p.m., closed Mon. **OVIEDO: Museo Arqueológico**, C/ San Vivente, 3: 10 a.m.–1.30 p. m., 4–6 p.m., Sundays and public holidays 11 a.m.–1 p.m., closed Mon. **Museo de Bellas Artes**: 11 a.m.–1.30 p.m., 4–7 p.m., Sundays and public holidays 12 noon–2 p.m., closed Mon. **Cathedral** and **Camara Santa** 10 a.m.–1 p.m., 4–7.30 p.m. **Diocesan Museum** 10 a.m.–1 p.m., 4–7 p.m., closed Mon. **San Julián de los Prados**, 11 a.m.–1 p.m., 4.30–6 p.m., in winter 12 noon–1 p.m., closed Mon. **Santullano** and **Sta. María de Bendones**, 11 a.m.–1 p.m., 4.30–6 p.m., closed Mon. **Santa María del Naranco**, 10 a.m.–1 p.m., 3–7 p.m., in winter until 5 p.m., Sun 10 a.m.–1 p.m.

Tourist Information
GIJÓN: Oficina de Turismo, C/ Marqués de San Esteban, Tel: 346046. **OVIEDO: Oficina de Turismo**, Pl. Alfonso II el Casto 6, 9 a.m.–2 p.m., 4.30–6 p.m., Tel: 213385. **Fishing-Information**: Consejería de Agricultura, C/ Uría 10, Tel: 222748.

PROVINCE LUGO
(Telephone area code: 982-)
Accommodation
RIBADEO: *MODERATE:* **Voar**, C/ Os Garitos, Tel: 110685. **VIVEIRO**: *MODERATE:* **Aguadoce**, Playa de Areas, Tel: 560944. **VILLALBA**: *LUXURY:* **Parador de Villalba**, C/ Valeriano Valdesuso, Tel: 510090. **MONDOÑEDO**: *BUDGET:* **A Taberna do Valeco**, Os Muiños, Tel: 521861.

PROVINCE LA CORUÑA
(Telephone area code: 981-)
Accommodation
LA CORUÑA: *LUXURY:* **Finisterre**, Paseo de Parrote, Tel: 205400. *MODERATE:* **España**, C/ Juana de Vega 7, Tel: 224506. *BUDGET:* **Hostal Centro Gallego**, C/ Estella 2, Tel: 222236.

Tourist Information
LA CORUÑA: Oficina de Turismo, Dársena de la Marina, Tel: 221822, 9 a.m.–1 p.m., 4–7 p.m., Sat 9 a.m.–1 p.m., closed Sun.

Museums / Sightseeing
LA CORUÑA: Museo de Bellas Artes, 10 a.m.–2 p.m., 4–6 p.m., Sun 10 a.m.–2 p.m. **Museo Histórico-Arqueologico**, 10 a.m.–2 p.m., 4–8 p.m., closed Mon. **Tower of Hercules**, 10 a.m.–1.30 p.m., 4–7 p.m., closed Sun. **PADRÓN: Casa Museo de Rosalia Castro**, 9.30 a.m.–2 p.m. and 4–10 p.m., closed Mon.

PROVINCE PONTEVEDRA
(Telephone area code: 986-)
Accommodation
CATOIRA: *LUXURY:* **Pazo O Rial**, El Rial 1, Tel: 505622. *MODERATE:* **Hostal Hipólito**, C/ Puente, Tel: 546107. **VILLAGARCÍA DE AROSA**: *BUDGET:* **El Chocolate**, San Cibrán 1, Tel: 501199. **LA TOJA, EL GROVE**: *LUXURY:* **Louxo-La Toja**, Tel: 730200. *BUDGET:* **Balneario**, La Toja, Tel: 730150. **SANGENJO**: *MODERATE:* **Pazo el Revel**, El Revel, Villalonga, Tel: 743000. **PONTEVEDRA**: *LUXURY:* **Parador Casa del Barón**, C/ Maceda, Tel: 855800. *BUDGET:* **Mexico**, Andrés Murvais 10, Tel: 859006. **CANGAS**: *MODERATE:* **Airiños Do Mar**, Av. Eugenio Sequeiros 30, Tel: 304000. **VIGO**: *MODERATE:* **Junquera**, C/ Urugay 19, Tel: 434888. **BAIONA**: *LUXURY:* **Parador Conde de Gondomar**, Monterreal, Tel: 355000. *MODERATE:* **Hostal Carabela la Pinta**, Tel: 355107. **TUI**: *MODERATE:* **Parador San Telmo**, Av. de Portugal, Tel: 600309.

Tourist Information
VIGO: Oficina de Turismo: C/ Las Avenidas, Tel. 430577, Estación Maritima, Tel: 221217.

PILGRIMS' PATH TO SANTIAGO

ARAGÓN
NAVARRA
LA RIOJA
BURGOS
LEÓN
LA CORUÑA

The pilgrims' path to Santiago de Compostela (the field of the stars from the Latin *campus stellae*) was one of the few reasons to travel in the Middle Ages. A pilgrimage involved ridding oneself of one's earthly goods as Christ did, and symbolically following the path of humility. Some medieval pilgrims went on the long and uncertain journey as penance, to safeguard the salvation of their souls or to fulfill a vow, while others were sent on the pilgrimage in chains as punishment. There were also paid pilgrims, who went on the time-consuming and often dangerous pilgrimage in place of those who were too busy to go themselves. Up to 200.000 people were said to come to Santiago every year, many ill and exhausted. Many of the stations along the way, the stone witnesses to this period, have been preserved, for when the fashion of pilgrimages stopped, the area was forgotten. All the cathedrals, churches, hermitages, hospitals and monasteries from the 9th to the 15th century found between the north coast and the large Castilian towns act as markers through a part of Spain which is often disregarded by the general public.

Preceding pages: Galician mountains. Left: The Condestables' chapel in the Burgos cathedral.

Today the pilgrims' path is once again well-marked. The "friends of the path" make sure signs are put up, and maintain pilgrims' guest houses in some parts. In other areas communities and monasteries provide accommodation for pilgrims.

The 25 of July is St. James's day. Whenever this date falls on a Sunday, the year is a holy one, and the stream of pilgrims increases (e.g. 1993). Each year on this day the town of **Santiago** (St. James in English) celebrates a festival. The fireworks set off over the towers of the cathedral on the night of July 24 signal the climax of a summer trip in the footsteps of the pilgrims.

ARAGÓN

Four pilgrims' routes can be traced from France, which flowed into two paths in the Pyrenees. They came from Paris, Vezelay, Le Puy and Arles. Pilgrims also came from Italy, visiting the Monasteries of St. Cugat de Vallés, Sta. Maria de Ripoll or Seo de Urgel in Catalonia on their way. From northern Europe ships sailed directly to Santiago, and from southern Spain and Portugal pilgrims' routes can be traced from the west of the peninsula.

The routes from Germany and France crossed the Pyrenees at Pto. de Somport,

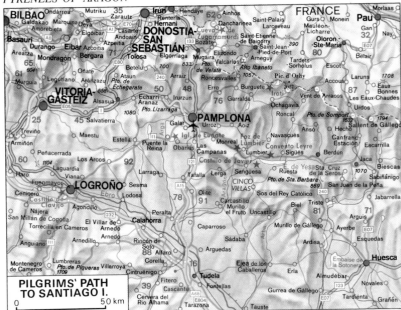

or further west at Pto. de Ibañeta, about 750 km from Santiago. Somport is now a ski resort, the center of which is **Candanchú**. **Jaca**, surrounded by the Río Aragón, was always a military border station on crossing the Pyrenees. The **citadel**, a perfect five-pointed star, was built under Philip II. Jaca was Aragón's first capital in the 11th century. The **cathedral** is the oldest on the pilgrimage route and influenced other church buildings along the way. In many of the Romanesque churches you will find the checkered braid frieze and the monogram of Jesus Christ on the tympanum above the entrance.

Jaca has a lively old town and is the base for excursions into the Pyrenean heights of **Valle del Hecho** and **Valle de Ansó**, the former haunts of smugglers, wood cutters and shepherds. The architecture is typically dominated by slate covered stone buildings. The finest ex-

amples of this village architecture are found in the town of **Ansó**, which earns a living from modest mountain tourism and Spanish summer guests. In summer the valleys are unusually green for Spain, their meadows bloom with camomile and meadow flowers, and are crisscrossed by clean brooks. Further up the valleys become narrower and more picturesque. You can even find gentian here. Mountain paths are marked, and there are many camp sites.

The **Garganta del Infierno** gorge and the **Selva de Oza** forest in the Hecho Valley are particularly charming. The high mountain woods in this area, with oaks, beech trees and hornbeams, stretch all the way to France, and are the last remaining large and unified wooded areas in Spain. In the Ansó Valley, before **Zuriza**, you can go for swim in the **Río Veral**. From Zuriza a wide, high valley leads to the **Roncal Valley**, already part of Navarre and heavily pervaded by tourism.

From Jaca the Río Aragón takes you westwards. A small road runs to the little

Right: A rainy day in the Pyrenees – San Juan de la Peña (Huesca).

town of **St. Cruz de la Seros**, where there is a castle-like church in a monastery from the 11th century. Further up the mountain you come to **San Juan de la Peña**, with its old monastery nestled in a hollow of **Mt. Pano**. A newer monastery was built further up in the 17th century, but has been a ruin since 1809. In the 8th century a hunter called Voto is said to have pursued a deer here in blind enthusiasm, and was only saved from falling into the abyss by a miracle. He discovered the cave of a dead hermit at the same spot and in gratitude founded the monastery.

The building consists of an early-Romanesque lower church (10th century) and an upper church about 150 years older, both of which are built with their backs to the cliff face. Some parts of the cloister were worked on by a French stonemason around 1140 and have survived. Their capitals show truly perfect scenes from the Bible. The old Aragon burial area has since been rebuilt in the Baroque style and some chapels were added later. Hidden high in the mountains, the town still retains some of the feel of the time when the pilgrims sought accommodation in the monastery.

Further along the road to Pamplona you pass **Berdún**, lying like a fortress atop a *mesa* at the bottom of the Ansó Valley. Rather than crossing from the Ansó Valley to the **Valle de Roncal**, you can take the road 17 km north of Berdún.

The Valle del Roncal used to be an isolated valley and many of the old Basque traditions have been kept alive. On June 13 the French village of Barétous had to bring three cows to the village in exchange for guaranteed pasture rights, according to ancient tradition. The valley center is the town of the Roncal with the tomb of the famous tenor Gayarre, sculptured by M. Benlliure.

Westwards along the main road, the valley opens up into the **Yesa Reservoir**, the "Pyrenean Sea", which almost dried out over the last few years. Several abandoned villages show how much cultivated land was flooded for the reservoir. Today water sports flourish in place of farmland. Above the lake, behind steep cliffs, lies **Leyre Monastery** with rest areas and walks to the spring of the monk San Virila. It is told that he spent a full 300 years there, enchanted by the song of a bird, before returning to the monastery. Like the one in San Juan de la Peña, the church consists of an upper and lower church from the 11th century. The lower church, falsely described as a crypt, lies in the dusky light of a small alabaster window and is, with its deep girders and short pillars, a curious early-Romanesque monument.

The road between **Leyre** and **Lumbier** also takes you to the **Foz de Lumbier** gorge, formed by the **Río Irati**. From Lumbier you can get to the **Valley of Salazar** (Foz de Arbayún), originally a gorge. Here lies the town of **Ochagavía**, which still consists entirely of old stone houses. Further up the valley are the **Sierra de Abodi** and the fabled **Irati Wood**, where a few pleasant days could be spent on the camp sites and paths around the Irabia reservoir.

Not far from Yesa is the fairytale castle of **Javier**, commemorating the Jesuit Francisco Javier. On warm summer evenings it is enveloped in a romantic light show. An old-fashioned hotel next to it offers better accommodation than that in the town of **Sanguesa**, which always smells of its paper factory. Along with the noblemen's palaces on the main street, the most important sight there is the **Church of Sta. María la Real**, on the river Aragón (12th century), which has a portal decorated over and over with figures.

To the south the area joins the **Cinco Villas**, the bread basket of this western region of Aragón, whose five medieval villages attest to solid agricultural wealth. In every single one of these little villages there is a surprise in store for the visitor. One might pay a visit to **Uncastillo**,

Right: The Palace of Olite, now a parador.

whose ground plan forms a circle around a mountain surmounted by a castle, or to **Sos del Rey Católico**, where the Catholic Monarch Fernando was born. The village of **Sádaba** has a splendid castle, and **Egea de los Caballeros** was named after the landed gentry. Last but by no means least, there is still **Tauste,** which has one of the oldest Mudejar churches.

NAVARRA

Navarra is one of the oldest kingdoms of the Iberian peninsula, independent up to the 16th century. Its special rights, or *fueros*, were retained until the 19th century. The Navarrans are Basques and today the whole region is bilingual. In contrast to the Basque region, Navarra was on Franco's side during the civil war, which must have influenced the fact that, after the constitutional reforms of 1978, it became a *comunidad autónoma*. It is famous for its excellent cuisine, a mixture of French, Basque and Aragon traditions. Try the *trucha a la navarra* (trout), *cochifrito navarro* (lamb) and *estofado de toro de Pamplona* (beef).

Here in Navarra, in the environs of Cinco Villas, there are further traditional villages. **Olite** was a royal town in the 15th century. It has an impressive palace which has been turned into a *parador*. In medieval **Ujué** is the Church of Sta. Maria la Real, surrounded by a fortified wall. The Cistercian **Monastery of la Oliva** (12th century), near **Carcastillo**, has a Gothic cloister (14th century) and is open to visitors without any formalities. Hardly anyone ever disturbs the peace and solitary calm of this town.

Back on the pilgrims' route, just before **Puente la Reina**, standing all alone on the edge of the path, is the octagonal Romanesque Templar **church of Eunate**, a burial ground for pilgrims. A little further on you will see the **Ermita of Arnotegui** perched on a hill. A mystery play is performed in **Obanos** every year on the

August 20 in memory of its origin. On this occasion the town's 600 inhabitants perform the story of Feliciana, who went on a pilgrimage to Santiago and then decided to remain there in inner contemplation. Her brother Guillén followed her to bring her home again, and when she refused he killed her. As penance he withdrew into the solitariness of the Ermita.

On the crossroads where the routes from Jaca and Roncesvalles meet you will find a modern memorial to the pilgrims. The Frankish settlement of **Puenta la Reina** is nearby. This town grew around the bridge built by Sancha, the wife of the King of Navarra, in the 10th century. The village road leads straight to the bridge spanning the river **Arga**, which has been dammed to form an artificial lake with goldfish in it.

On the Trail of Charlemagne

From **St. Jean Pie du Port** the road climbs steeply through green valleys, via **Valcarlos**, to the second Pyrenean pass,

that of **Ibañeta** (1.057 m), at which pilgrims' crosses, a chapel and a memorial to Roland commemorate the legends surrounding it. This is where Charlemagne is said to have crossed to pray to in Santiago 40 years before the saint's grave was discovered, as reported in the *Codex Calixtinus*, written in the 12th century by the French monk Aymeri Picaud. There are a good dozen of such historical pilgrim's reports describing the journey to Santiago. The *Codex Calixtinus* is the most detailed. It describes the regional characteristics of the country and people, the story of the saint and the journey in 13 stages from Roncesvalles to Santiago. It has been regarded as the most authoritative guide for the pilgrimage since the Middle Ages. In one of its five volumes, the work describes the life of Charles magne and the Roland legends, quoting the *Song of Roland*, written in the 12th century – religious enthusiasm, somewhat falsified history. For example, it tells how the Moors and not the Basques, ambushed Charlemagne's rearguard, and

praises the chivalry of Christian soldiers.

Below the pass is the Augustine monastery of **Roncesvalles,** with a collegiate church from 1130. The chapter room contains the grave of Sancho VII, the Strong (13th century). The marble figure on the coffin corresponds to his actual height of 2.25 m, and depicts his deformed leg. The modern window shows the Battle of Las Navas de Tolosa (1212), where the king was wounded, but ultimately triumphed over the Moors.

Traversing the **Valle de Irati** leads to the **Irati forest** and to the reservoir of Irabia on the other side. Nearby are the ruins of a large cannon factory from the time of the War of Spanish Succession at the beginning of the 18th century. A stream rushes through the factory building and the area only acquires its true ambience under a luke warm summer rain.

The **Valle de Baztán,** with the town of **Elizondo**, an old administrative district

Above: The Pilgrims' Bridge in Puente la Reina over the Rio Arga.

with 15 villages, is somewhat rainy and sleepy. There are a few Basque holiday homes, but little tourism. Nevertheless, it has a variety of things to offer the holiday-maker, including excursions to Biarritz, San Sebastian and Pamplona. At the time of Charles III, in the 18th century, the descendants of lepers *(agotes)* were sent from Arizcun, in Bozate, to resettle the village of Nuevo Baztán, in the vicinity of Madrid. Many of the inhabitants emigrated to the Americas to seek their fortunes. Many of the extravagant houses belonged to the rich returning emigrées, the *Indianos*, the same as in the whole of the north coast. One of them was Pedro de Ursua, who led the famous expedition to El Dorado in the 16th century, and who was killed by mad Lope de Aguirre, referred to as the God's Wrath.

In the north of Baztán, on the French border, is the **Cave of Zugarramurdi**, made famous by the Basque witches' sabbath. In 1610 the Inquisition in Logroño tried 40 women from this town for being witches. 12 of them were burned.

Pamplona is a thriving town today. A Roman *castella* was built here on the site of an old Basque settlement. Later it became the capital of the kingdom of Navarra. Franks, Jews and Navarrans settled here after the Reconquista. They built their own walled quarters, and had some privileges, such as trade with the pilgrims, which repeatedly led to unrest. The fortified churches of **San Nicolás** and **San Saturino** were the centers of such Frankish quarters. In the 15th century Charles the Noble had the borders torn down and put an end to the civil war. Fernando the Catholic annexed Navarra in 1512. The French tried to liberate it. In the battle one Basque nobleman was wounded: Ignatius of Loyola, founder and first general of the Jesuit Order. You can still walk along the town walls, built under Charles V. The citadel was built under Philip II (16th century), and it is said the French conquered it in 1808 with snowballs.

Near the walls in the oldest part of the town stands the **cathedral**. Don't be fooled by its Classical façade. It was built on top of a Romanesque building in the 14th and 15th centuries. The cloister with its tracery and a wonderful **Portal of Mary** is a beautiful work of art.

The patron saint of the town, San Fermin, is celebrated in a fiesta in July, which is heralded by a thunderbolt. The feast days, made famous throughout the world by Hemingway, have a rigid program, associated with ancient bull fighting rites. The feast begins at 8 o'clock on the dot with the *encierro,* when the bulls are driven from the corral to the arena. Young men, who have usually been celebrating all night, test their courage by running in front of the bulls and then jumping to safety over the security fences. Every year there are injuries, usually amongst inexperienced foreigners. After the bulls have been brought in, anyone can practice in the arena with the young bulls, whose horns are covered.

After this the town takes a rest for a few hours. At 12 o'clock the giants come, surrounded by children, and wake up those sleeping in the squares. Following lunch everyone goes out onto the streets again. At 6 o'clock there is a bull fight, and the ensuing nights are spent dancing, singing, letting off fireworks and carousing. During the fiesta the population and the prices in Pamplona treble. If you don't want to end up sleeping in the park, you had better plan your visit well ahead of time.

Modern Pamplona has developed into a lively trading center. The Catholic university with 12.000 students is run by the Opus Dei. Many restaurants and cafés and a lively cultural life mean that a visit to the town is always worthwhile, whatever the time of year.

The medieval pilgrims went on from Pamplona to the bridge called **Puente la Reina**, where the paths from France to Santiago join to form the **Camino Francés**. In **Estella** (Lizarra), on the right bank of the Ega, there was a large Frankish quarter around the **Calle de la Rua**, settled by traders and artisans who earned their living from the pilgrim trade. On this side are the Romanesque church of **San Pedro de la Rua**, a Romanesque royal palace and a town hall in a former Renaissance palace. The quarter was joined to San Martín on the other bank by some steep steps which have been preserved. In San Martín you will find the center of the little town. The **Monastery of Irache**, just beyond Estella, was a pilgrims' hospice and a university between the 16th and the 18th centuries. It lies at the foot of **Montejurra**, meeting place of the Carlists for 200 years.

LA RIOJA

Logroño is the capital of the **Rioja**, the smallest region in Spain, although it is home to many treasures. Modern life has meant that almost all the ancient monu-

ments have disappeared. The town is charming, with all its lively and busy squares. The beautiful Art Nouveau market is much more than just a historic building. Its products are served as *tapas* on the counters of all the local bars. Spain's best vegetables come from Rioja; its paprika, asparagus, artichokes, Swiss chard, borage and fruit are famous throughout the world. And let's not forget the wine, originally brought here by Bordeaux vintners, which grows on the vines along the banks of **Río Oja**. It is divided into three regions of origin: *Rioja Alta, Rioja Baja* and *Rioja Alavesa*.

From the castle of **Clavijo** you can look out far across the Ebro Valley. In 844 a decisive battle was fought here against the Moors. It was here that James the Moor Killer helped out the desperate Christian army for the first time. Many later depictions show him in this blood-

Above: Rioja wine cellars. Right: The hens in the Sto. Domingo de la Calzada cathedral remind us of a miracle.

thirsty role, often with Moors' heads rolling around under his horse's hooves.

The central area of the intensively farmed and irrigated Ebro Valley stretches from Tudela to Logroño, and then further to Haro. From the north you can get to the **Conchas de Haro**, two monoliths regarded as the natural gateway to Rioja. **Haro** is the center of Rioja Alta, with the palaces of the Paternina, Tondonia or Murrieta families, where today you will find the administrative offices of the best wine cellars. Each year a wine battle takes place here on June 29. Don't attend it unless you are wearing your oldest clothes.

In **Cenicero** and **Fuenmayor** wine is at the center of everything. In **Lodosa** red paprikas dry in picturesque chains hanging outside the houses. **Calahorra** is the center of **Rioja Baja** and the national vegetable capital. It was an important town as far back as Roman times. The rhetorician Quintillianus and the poet Prudencius were born here. Despite its present splendor, the *fames calagurritana* is still remembered. This was a famine which the Roman troops suffered. In their hunger they are reputed to have even eaten salted corpses.

Tudela, the second largest town in Navarra, was founded in the 9th century by the Moors and has retained the character of a Moorish town. The **cathedral** (12th/13th century) in the middle of the crooked old town streets was built on the site of a former mosque. The **Portal of the Day of Judgment** shows sinners what awaits them after death. Near by is the Cistercian **Monastery of Fitero** (12th century) and the spa **Baños de Fitero**. At **Casacante** a gallery with 39 arches leads to the **Church of Señora del Romera** (Rosemary). **Corella** and **Cintruénigo** are also worth visiting, not only for their *bodegas*.

Nájera lies on the fluvial plain of the Río Najerilla. In the 10th century it was the capital of Navarra. Under the red

cliffs along the steep river bank is the **Monastery of Sta. Maria la Real**, with its beautiful cloister (15th century, Portuguese influence). This is where you will find the graves of the Navarrese kings and the cave in which the legend of the monastery's foundation originated, where a statue of the Virgin is said to have been discovered.

Sto. Domingo de la Calzada (of the country road) is the patron saint of construction engineers. A hermit, he began the building of the pilgrim road and the bridge. His splendid grave can be found in the town's cathedral.

This is the site of one of the many miracles which are portrayed on altars along the whole pilgrim route to Germany and Italy. The so-called "chicken miracle", which is always commemorated by a live chicken and cockerel in a Renaissance cage in the town's cathedral, is supposed to have happened to a pilgrim family traveling to Santiago from Cologne. The maid in the pilgrims inn is said to have made eyes at the son of the family. But when he rejected her she decided to seek revenge. She hid a silver cup in his luggage and sent the police after him. When the young man was captured he was hanged. His parents found him still hanging on the gallows on their return from Santiago, and they were convinced that he was speaking to them. Disturbing the mayor at his meal, they asked if they could take him down because he was still alive. The mayor joked that the young man was as alive as the chicken on his plate. At that moment the chicken rose up and ran crowing from the room. Since then it is said:

En Sto. Domingo de la Calzada
cantó la gallina después de asada.
(The chickens cackle after they're roasted.)

From Sto. Domingo it is but a short trip to **San Millán de la Cogolla** with its upper *(suso)* and lower *(yuso)* monasteries. St. Emilianus lived here in caves with a number of other hermit monks in the 6th century. They came together to pray in the church which incorporates Moz-

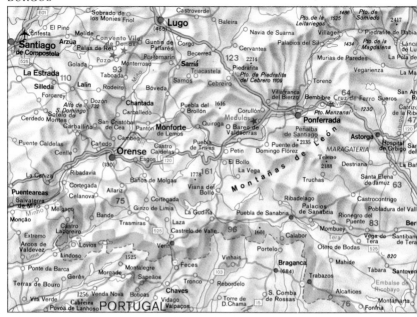

arabian and Visigoth elements. The lower monastery (12th century) was rebuilt in its present form in the 16th century, and was made famous by the *Emilian Codex,* which has the first recorded written words in Spanish and in Basque. The monk Gonzalo de Berceo (12th/13th century) went down in history as the first poet in the Spanish standard language.

The monastery lies at the foot of the **Sierra de Demanda**, a nature reserve with mountains reaching the elevation of 2.300 m, where wild boar, red deer, birds of prey and wildcats are still found. From **Ezcaray**, which is best reached from Sto. Domingo, you can take a lovely tour. A side trip from Nájera runs between the Sierra de la Demanda and the mountain valley of Urbión, with reservoirs for swimming, rivers for fishing and lovely mountain hikes.

This is where you will find **Anguiano**, which celebrates its village festival every year at the end of July when young lads dance along the steep village streets on tall stilts.

Sto. Domingo is not far from the province of Burgos. **Belorado** was the border town of Castile and was therefore heavily fortified. Convents, churches and hospitals commemorate its importance for the pilgrims, who gathered their strength here before crossing the pass in the mountains of **Oca**. The arduousness of the route is reflected in the name of its single spring: **Fuente de Mojapán** (spring to soften bread). From up here you can look out over the entire breadth of the Castilian Plain.

San Juan de Ortega is named after the saint who helped Sto. Domingo build the bridges of Logroño, Nájera and Sto. Domingo, and who is buried in the Romanesque church in the town. A little further north is the Renaissance town of **Briviesca**, built on the model of Sta. Fé near Granada, just like the Latin American towns. You can take a little trip from here to the **Bureba**. **Poza de la Sal**, **Oña** and **Frías** are all picturesque towns at the

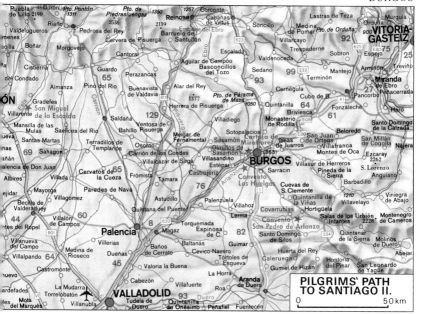

PILGRIMS' PATH
TO SANTIAGO II.
0   50 km

foot of the Cantabrian mountains. They have a number of sights, including castles, spectacular bridges and monasteries.

The towers of the Gothic **Cathedral of Burgos** can be seen from far and wide. They are very like those of the Cologne Cathedral – and this is no coincidence, for the builder Hans, his son Simon and their stonemasons all came from Cologne in the 15th century. In 1221 construction of a cathedral was begun at the site of a former Romanesque church, and was already consecrated by 1230. The two oldest portals are those of the transept in the south, the **Puerta del Sarmental** (1230), and on the north side, the **Coronería** (1250), a coronation portal through which the kings entered the cathedral. From here the first double Renaissance stairway built in Spain (1519, Diego de Siloe) takes you downstairs. The main entrance is the west portal, finished in 1440 but rebuilt in the 18th century. Here you are greeted by a strange figure with a clock, the *Papamos-*

cas (fly eater). He opens his mouth whenever the hour is struck. But, as a local saying goes, the people who stand gaping up at him open and close their mouths in the same foolish way.

The cathedral is an enormous three-aisled construction, with several chapels and a chancel in the nave enclosed by splendid iron railings. The most beautiful of the many side chapels is that behind the main altar, built on the site of a smaller one as a grave for the *Condestable* (military leader). A particularly unusual altarpiece can be seen in the **Sta. Anna Chapel**, in the northern side aisle. El Cid and his wife Jimena are both buried beneath the star-shaped memorial stone which lies under the splendid crossing tower. El Cid's famous wooden chest can also be seen here, hanging in the cloister.

The most popular chapel must be that of **Santísimo Christo**, right next to the western portal, which has an almost mummy-like figure of Christ hanging above several ostrich eggs. This figure is said to have been found in the sea and covered with real skin. Its head and limbs can move and the cloth is changed several times during the ecclesiastical year.

From the cathedral square a walk takes one through the **Arco de Sta. María**, with its figures of Charles V and El Cid, to a shady park by the river bank called **Espolón**. Long streets run through the old town with whitewashed *miradores*, glassed-in balconies that offer protection from the cold. The elegant shops show that Burgos is now gradually recovering its former medieval splendor. Behind the cathedral, in the **Huerto del Rey** and in the neighboring pedestrian zones, a number of restaurants and cafés make for a lively nightlife.

Burgos was founded in 884 inside the walls of a repeatedly destroyed fortified complex. For six centuries it was the capital of Castile, and many of its buildings still reflect its former splendor. Several Gothic churches have survived: **San Nicolás**, with a fine alabaster altarpiece; **San Esteban**, with its cloister; and the church of **San Gil**, with its beautiful side chapels. On the other side of the river, **Santa Clara** and the **Convent of Santa Dorotea** also date from this period. In the Casa Miranda you will find an archaeological museum.

To the west of the cathedral is **Santa Agueda** and the three-cornered archbishop's palace. Columbus was received by the Catholic monarchs after his second journey to America in the **Palace of Condestables**, called *Casa del Cordon* by the locals because it is decorated with giant cord reliefs. The palace was the Habsburg kings' residence, and Philip the Fair died here. He was buried in the **Cartuja de Miraflores**. From there his wife, Juana the Mad, took his corpse to Granada because she could not bear to be parted from him. It is said that Philip traveled farther through Castile when he was dead than he had when he was alive.

The significance of Burgos in the Middle Ages can only be understood when one has also seen the two famous monasteries on the edge of the city. Today they are surrounded by building sites which fill the inner town. Upstream, in the middle of a verdant countryside, stands the **Cartuja de Miraflores**, a Carthusian Monastery (15th century) begun by Hans of Cologne under Juan II and finished by his son Simon under the king's daughter, Isabel the Catholic. Isabel had an impressive stone memorial built on her parents' graves by the most important cathedral artist, Gil de Siloe. The church houses other treasures, including altar pieces by Van de Veyden and Berruguete, as well as Gothic and Renaissance pews. But everything is overshadowed by a giant main altar retable, also created by Gil de Siloe. The picture is so full of figures that it is hard at first to make anything out, but if you look more closely you will see that it is a complete composition that symbolically depicts the most important scenes and characters from the New Testament, the sufferings of Christ, the Evangelists and the Trinity. Even the king, his daughter and their patron saints are portrayed.

On the other side of Burgos is the most famous Cistercian convent in Spain: **Las Huelgas**. It was the burial place of the Castilian kings from 1187 onwards. It was founded for noblewomen and has many riches. The abbess had certain special rights and was very powerful for a woman of her time. The chapter room, the Romanesque cloister and another small cloister (*claustrillas*), the Moorish Santiago Chapel and a museum with medieval costumes are all worth a visit.

Not actually on the pilgrims' route, but only a short trip from Burgos are the towns of Lerma, Covarrubias, Sto. Domingo de Silos, Salas de los Infantes and Quintanilla de las Viñas. **Lerma** is named after the duke made famous by Schiller in his play *Don Carlos*. He was

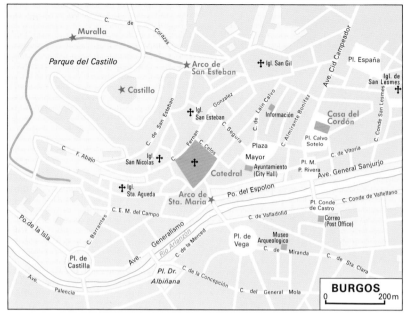

Philip III's favorite, and had six monasteries, a collegiate church and a Baroque Palace built in the town. **Covarrubias**, of Roman and Visigoth origin, is still much like a medieval village today. Besides to the village square, the many beautifully renovated houses and the **Doña Urraca Tower**, there is still the Colegiata to see here, with its graves of the founder of the County of Castile, Fernan Gonzalez and his wife. The priest is the best person to show you round the church, the cloister and the museum which has many regional treasures. A little further east along the same road you will come to the ruins of one of the richest monasteries in Castile, **San Pedro de Arlanza**. Its proportions and its significance are still obvious. Those treasures which could be saved in the period of secularization are now in museums all over the world. Shortly beyond the **Yecla Gorge** is the Benedictine monastery of **Sto. Domingo de Silos** and its much praised cloister with an ancient cypress growing in its center. This impressive Romanesque cloister (11th/12th century) is famous for its artistic capitals and reliefs in which the monsters of evil are portrayed alongside many Biblical scenes and a depiction of Christ as a the pilgrim.

On the way back to Burgos you can visit the **Salas de los Infantes**, founded by the father of the seven Infantes of Lara who were killed by the Moors. Their heads are said to be in a chest in the church. A little off the road is the village of **Quintanilla de las Viñas**, with the remains of a Visigoth church.

Further west on the pilgrims' route there are other Gothic churches worth visiting in **Sasamón** and **Olmillos de Sasamón**. The latter is dominated by a picturesque castle. In **Castrojeriz**, too, the path winds around a castle on a mountain. At the time of the pilgrimages there were seven hospitals and many churches and monasteries here. The collegiate church, which dates from the 13th century, is dedicated to the "Virgin of the Apple Tree" and contains several interesting paintings by Mengs.

LEÓN

On the bridge of Fitero, built for the pilgrims over the Rio Pisuerga by Alfonso VI, you cross to the province of **Palencia** with its Gothic Fields and more than 200 Romanesque churches. This is the typical meseta, with its harsh clay soil and wheat fields stretching all the way to the horizon. Many buildings made are of dried adobe bricks and the villages are the color of earth. There are few stones and churches such as **San Martín of Fromista** were built with stones carried by the pilgrims from the nearest quarry. This church, sponsored by Sancha la Mayor of Navarra, may be one of the most perfect examples of Romanesque architecture in Spain.

Carrión de los Condes is the home town of the dishonorable Infantes of Carrión, who married the daughters of El Cid and then insulted and deserted them. They were killed by El Cid's noblemen and buried in the plateresque **Monastery of San Zoilo**.

Right: The entrance to the León cathedral.

124

LEÓN

The first town you come to in the province of León is **Sahagún**. From the pilgrim **Church of La Peregrina** you can look out over the town with its unique Mudejar **Churches of San Tirso** and **San Lorenzo** (11th/12th century). Only the Baroque entrance arch is still left of the huge **Monastery of San Benito**. The banks of the Río Cea are overgrown with trees. According to one legend these trees are actually lances which belonged to Charlemagne's soldiers and which took root here. The soldiers are said to have stuck their lances in the soft river bank before a battle. The next morning they were shocked to discover that some of them had bent – the symbol of an imminent martyr's death. The owners of these lances were locked up and not taken to the battle with the Moors. But when the others returned they found them dead anyway.

A little further west is the town of **Valencia de Don Juan**, with a splendid castle standing guard over the Río Esla and the bridge. It has many *bodegas* buried in the soft sandstone, where you can eat and drink at modest prices.

Before you get to León, make a detour through the river valley of the Río Esla to the Mozarabian **Church of San Miguel de la Escalada**, built by monks from Cordoba in the 10th century.

The irrigation canals in this river and its tributaries now reach the whole northern part of the province, where the administration is attempting to prevent permanent poverty and subsequent emigration of its population through the promotion of intensive agriculture. The town of **León** is also included in this problem area, where modern town quarters can be found adjacent to decaying and poor quarters.

The old town begins at the square of **San Marcelo** with the **Casa de los Botines**, built more than 100 years ago

by Gaudí. It is now a bank. The town hall also stands here as well as the **Palace of Guzmanes** (both 16th century), where the provincial government meets. The town's old palaces, the cathedral and **San Isidoro** can be found in the Roman quarter. The buildings of the old quarter of **San Miguel**, called the damp quarter, are in a considerably worse state of repair. At its center is the **Plaza Mayor** (17th century), where markets and flea markets take place. The small alleyways are haven to countless little eateries and cafés where the young people of the town gather in the evenings. There are quiet spots around the old corn market, **Plaza del Mercado** and the **Calle de la Rúa**, the street which was formerly part of the pilgrims' route.

The town of León was the capital of the old kingdom. It is proud of the fact that it had 24 rulers before Castile even existed. The name does not come from the lion on its coat-of-arms, but from the Seventh Roman Legion, which erected its *castrum* here in A.D. 70, the walls of

which have survived. It achieved significance at an early date as a trading post situated along the Roman Silver Road.

The **cathedral**, *la pulcra leonina* (12th century) has the most beautiful Gothic windows on the entire pilgrims' route. The number of windows and their weight has meant that the walls have had to be reinforced several times since they were built. The 1.700 square meters of glass and the three large rose windows showing plants, ornaments, coats-of-arms and Biblical scenes bathe the church nave in color. The altar area has remains of the Gothic altar found in the attic of the bishop's palace. There is a Renaissance chancel, the chapel of the patron saint, the White Virgin, and next to it a rare pregnant Virgin and some Plateresque reliefs on the back of the chancel. Like medieval picture books, the beautiful entrance portals tell of the Day of Judgment, the story of Mary and the story of John the Baptist and Paul. The Pillar of Judgment of the *locus apellationis* attests to its former legal function.

The basilica of **San Isidoro**, the oldest church in León (12th century), was the destination of pilgrims. Those who were sick or exhausted, and who feared that they would never reach Santiago, could receive complete absolution here if they walked through the Gate of Forgiveness, the **Puerta del Perdón**. Above the main entrance, Bishop Isidoro of Sevilla is shown as a slayer of Moors. He is regarded as the most important scholar of the Visigoth period, and was certainly not a warlike man. His shrine is worshipped in the church. His bones are said to have spoken in the distant land of the Moors, and to have prayed to be transported to the north, which had already been liberated in the Reconquista. The museum next to the church takes you to a section of the building which is part of the early Romanesque church, and was destroyed by the Moors. It once formed the entrance to the royal palace. In the upper section you can see the church treasure, and in the lower the pantheon of León's kings, with some of the most beautiful paintings preserved in Spain. The entire room is painted with scenes from the Apocalypse and the Salvation, and also features folk art of the period. The hostal of the Catholic Monarchs, a pilgrims' hospice in the Middle Ages, has now been made into a *parador*. In the 17th century Quevedo was held here, and Republicans were also imprisoned within its walls after the Civil War.

The Mountains of León

Crossing the fields of **Páramo** you come upon the luxuriant river meadows of **Río Orbigo** and the pilgrims' **Hospital de Orbigo**. Its old bridge was given the name of "the honorable crossing" in the 15th century, when ten noblemen defended it against 300 attackers.

Right: Peñalba de Santiago in the Valley of Silence (León).

At the foot of the mountains of León lies the old diocesan town of **Astorga**. Towering over the Roman town walls and visible from a great distance, are the 16th century **cathedral** and the modernistic bishop's palace, designed by A. Gaudí in a curious neo-Gothic church style. It now houses an interesting museum which includes art from León, religious art, objects from the pilgrims' path and remains of Roman constructions. The Roman slaves' prison, or **ergastula**, is also worth a visit. Two figures chime the hours on the town hall. They are Colassa and Zancudo, dressed in the costume of the *Maragatos*. The **Maragatería** is the poor area to the south of Astorgas, which stretches as far as **Monte Teleno**. Its inhabitants used to travel the country as horse traders or musicians. They are a marginal group of people who lived in isolation until the 19th century, with no marriage contacts with the outside world.

One of their most amazing traditions was the *covada*, whereby the men lay in their beds in pain when their wives were giving birth to their children. Most of the villages are dilapidated, but some (**Castrillo de Polvazares**, **Sta. Colomba de Somoza**) have been lucky enough to find friends who have renovated the typical stone houses.

There is a small iron cross, the **Cruz de Ferro**, at **Rabanal Pass** (1.504 m) in the mountains of León, brought here by a pilgrim. At the foot of the cross are countless stones, also carried by pilgrims to increase their penance. Beyond the pass a road winds for 1.000 m down to the **Bierzo Basin**, which is dominated by vineyards, vegetable fields, coal hills and lovely valleys. The capital of this area, which was even an autonomous province for 11 years during the last century, is **Ponferrada**. A Templar castle guards the "iron bridge" across the **Río Sil**. Some way out of the town you will find the Mozarabian **Church of Sto. Tomás de**

las Ollas. Molinaseca, Bembibre, Ca-cabelos and **Vega de Espinareda** are all pretty towns by mountain streams, many of which have been dammed to make village swimming pools. But the most beautiful parts of the region are the **Medulas** and the **Valle del Silencio** (Valley of Silence). A breath-taking road runs through the valley to **Peñalba de Santiago**. High in the mountains you will find the remains of the **Monastery of San Pedro de los Montes**, the Mozarabian **Church of Santiago de Peñalba** and (a 45-minute walk from here) the **Cave of San Genadio**.

Beyond Lake Carucedo, the **Medulas** spread out like a miracle of nature. But they are not natural at all. For this bizarre landscape of valleys, truncated hill caves and gorges was created by the Romans while digging for gold. Their methods of extraction were strange. Water pipes were fed through many kilometers of tunnels dug into the soft earth by slaves. Within a matter of a few decades the entire mountain was washed out (300 million tons of

earth were moved) and 3 million kilogram of gold had been extracted. Today some of the caves are open to the public, and you can hike from Las Medulas through the valleys, now overgrown with chestnut trees.

The last town of the Bierzo is **Villafranca**, with the **Calle del Agua**, which unites most of the noble coast-of-arms from the pilgrims' path. The **Church of Santiago** has another Puerta del Perdón, and the **Church of San Francisco** has a very beautiful Mudejar ceiling.

Hikers will enjoy the **Sierra de Ancares**, which adjoins the Bierzo to the north in the border regions of León, Galicia and Asturias. Parts of it have been declared a nature reserve. Although many of the forests here have been burned down, this isolated mountain area has fresh mountain streams, water falls and abandoned *castillos*. Its fauna includes capercallies, wild boar, red deer and rare birds; and its flora wild orchids, heather, mountain ash and the grasses which were traditionally used by the Celts to thatch

the *pallozas*. Small roads run from **Vega de Espinareda** to **Tejedo** and the Leonese parts of these mountains, and from **Becerreá** to **Donis** on the Galician side.

LA CORUÑA

A final arduous climb awaited the pilgrims before they came to the flatter, rounder mountains of Galicia: first the **Piedrafita do Cebreiro Pass** at a height of 1.109 m, and shortly afterwards the **El Poyo Pass** at 1.337 m. Between them lay the village of **Cebreiro**, with the monastery and pilgrim's hospice given to the Cluny monks by Alfonso VI, now an idyllic mountain hotel. Surrounding it are former *pallozas*. One is a pilgrims' inn, another was inhabited until the 1950s and is now a museum. The latter gives you some idea of how people and animals used to live together under one roof. The little church dates back to the 9th century.

Above and right: On the way to church.

In the 13th century one of the most famous miracles of the pilgrims' path is said to have taken place here. An old monk was reluctantly saying mass for a pilgrim who had arrived late at night. Suddenly the wine in the chalice was transformed into real blood, and the monk's flagging belief was rekindled. Many pilgrims subsequently flocked to this place. When the Catholic Monarchs stopped here on their pilgrimage in 1496, they had the chalice and patents plated with gold, and incorporated them into the Galician flag. They also sponsored the reliquary shrines which can still be seen today.

On the journey through the mountains there is a new and breathtaking sight awaiting one round every corner. To the south, accessible by a little road between **Hospital** and **Linares**, or from **Samos**, is the **Sierra de Courel**, a natural mountain region suitable for hiking. But your enjoyment of the surroundings will probably be tempered by the almost barren landscape, burned in many forest fires. In the summer months one to two hundred fires are registered every day in Galicia, most of which are the result of arson. Disputes between towns and communes, acts of revenge, resistance to forest plantations in the areas which have traditionally been grazing areas for goats and semi-wild horses, the promotion of the timber industry and literal smoke-screens to hide illegal coastal transactions are some of the reasons behind the fires – together with the deep-seated Galician tradition of burning anything remotely undesirable. And so you will only see half of the region's beauty. But all the more surprising is the way the locals go about their daily business, apparently untouched and unworried about the billows of smoke always visible around them.

The pilgrims' path crosses Galicia by the shortest route, for after their long and arduous journey their only concern was that they should get there. They took stones from Triacastela to Casteñeda, which were then cut for the construction of the cathedral. Little has been preserved of the Mozarabian Benedictine monastery of San Julián in **Samos**, where Alfonso I spent his youth. Today's monastery, with its splendid Baroque façade, dates back to the beginning of the 17th century, but was completely rebuilt after a fire in 1951. Unlike that of the other regions, Galicia's landscape is scattered with sprawling settlements – often it is hard to tell which town you are in. The countryside is characterized by farmhouses with vegetable gardens and tiny parcels of land, the typical *horreos*, maize stores and little stone barns. Everywhere on the edge of the road you will see *cruceiros*, stone crosses decorated on both sides, and from time to time a more stately house, a *pazo*, which is sometimes decorated with a tower, more for adornment than defense.

Sarria is famous for its Augustine Convent, founded in the 13th century, but now run by the Brothers of Mercy. In the

old town center stands the Romanesque **Church of El Salvador** and a tower from the old *castillos*. Cross the Miño and you will come to **Portomarín**. The fortified **Church of San Juan** once stood, as the whole town did, on a square further down. When the river was dammed in the 1960s it was carried brick by brick to its present site.

To the north it is not far to **Lugo**, an old town with slate roofs and surrounded by a more than 2-km long Roman town wall (2nd century) along which you can walk. The Santiago town gate shows that many pilgrims also passed through Lugo. The **cathedral**, whose origins can be traced back to the 12th century, was not completed until the 18th century, and now represents a cross-section of all architectural styles. It has a beautiful Romanesque portal. Small side doors take you to the chancel with Baroque pews by Francisco Moure. Both transept ends are decorated with a curious altarpiece from the 16th century, which was cut into sections and reinstalled here. The town's saint, San Froilán, is depicted with a wolf. According to local legend a wolf attacked and ate the saint's donkey one day as he was walking through a field. Froilán was angry and he reproached the animal for its behavior. The wolf is said to have contemplated his deed for a while and then proceeded to carry the donkey's burden himself as penance. Adjoining the **Church of San Francisco** (15th century), with its beautifully preserved cloister, is the **provincial museum**. Here you can admire finds and traditional cultural artifacts from the region, which date from Roman times onwards. The magic of this somewhat forgotten town is particularly obvious when the granite stones and slates glisten, and the lights of the small busy streets glow in the rain.

The Galician knights had their headquarters in the monastery of **Vilar de Donas**. Today the Romanesque church with its frescoes and old knights' tombs appears somewhat neglected. From **Rosario** the pilgrims could already see the **Pico Sacro**, the mountain before Santiago, and it was here that they began their prayers. **Palas do Rei** is the last pilgrimage station mentioned in the *Codex Calixtinus*. Not far away is the **Pazo de Ulloa**, seat of a local aristocratic family and the title of a novel by Pardo Bazán, which describes the double standards of Galician society during the last century. **Melide** has a final gem, the Romanesque **Church of Sta. Maria**, which has some beautiful paintings. And then you are on the approach to the Mountain of Joy, the **Monte Gozo**. This is where the first person to see the cathedral of Santiago was named as the pilgrim king.

Santiago de Compostela

The pilgrims came along the **Rúa de San Pedro**, through the **Puerta del**

Right: The end of the pilgrimage – the Santiago de Compostela Cathedral.

Camino, and then entered the town with its granite houses. All too often they were welcomed in drizzling rain. They passed by the **Casas Reales**, the **Chapel of Poor Souls**, **Cervantes Square**, and the **Street of Azabachería**, where black jet stone was and still is made into jewelry and sold as souvenirs. The pilgrims could wash and change their clothes at the northern portal of the cathedral. Their old clothes were burned on the roof of the church on an iron "cross of rags". The square in front of the **cathedral**, the **Plaza do Obradoiro** is reached through the arch of the bishop's palace of **Gelmirez**, with its unique Romanesque festival halls. The large square opens out onto the Baroque western façade, with a figure of Santiago high above in the center, and two towers. Entering the church at this point you stand in amazement before yet another façade, the **Gloria Portal** by the master Mateo, from 1188. No one dared, or perhaps they were unable, to tear down this Romanesque masterpiece during the Baroque enthusiasm for renovation.

Buried deep in the pillar under the **Statue of Santiago**, you can see the five fingers of the millions of pilgrims who have worshipped the saint over the last eight hundred years. The interior of the cathedral is an overwhelming mixture of styles, in keeping with its long history. On specific feast days, at 12 o'clock during the pilgrims' mass, the holy incense burner, the *botafumeiro*, is swung at a rather dangerous speed through the cathedral. It is said that this method of cleansing the air comes from the time when pilgrims not only prayed here, but also spent the night. Apart from the church itself, the **Gloria** and **Platerías Portals**, the **Puerta Santa** (only opened in holy years) and the **Quintana Portal**, the museum also has a large number of things to see: the library in which the *Codex Calixtinus* is kept, the gobelin collection with carpets made from designs by Rubens and Goya, the church treasure

and the so-called crypt, a Romanesque basement construction beneath the west portal. Inside the church is the real crypt with a shrine and the skeleton of the saint, which has rested here since its second discovery in 1884.

The sides of the Cathedral square are formed by other imposing buildings: on the north side is the **Hostel of the Catholic Monarchs**, who gave money for it to be made into a pilgrims' hospice, and where there are four cloisters around a chapel. Today it is a *parador nacional*, but still offers genuine pilgrims free accommodation in keeping with its original purpose. On the east side, in the **Rajoy Palace**, you will find the former seminary for confessors and choirboys (18th century) and the town hall with its bloodthirsty monument of Santiago the Moor Killer. On the south side stands **San Jeronimo Seminary** (17th century), with a beautiful 15th century portal. It was a college for poor students and artists. Behind it is the **Fonseca Palace** (16th century), reserved for the better situated students.

Santiago is one of the oldest university towns in Spain. Until recently it was the only one in Galicia. There are around 40.000 students in the city and they fill the streets and bars with life. Many of the old monasteries are now student halls of residence, although most of the university buildings on the edge of the town are new. In recent years Santiago has become an important administrative center, after it was chosen as the capital of the Galician region. The enormous population pressure is reflected in the many new residential areas on the outskirts of town. Southwest of the preserved old town a new and lively town center has developed, where the best designers in Spain have their shops.

The **Galician Folk Museum** is housed in the old Dominican monastery. Around the cloister are the various rooms that can be reached by a curious treble winding staircase of granite. The museum has excellent displays of folk costumes, handicrafts, household objects and tools from Galicia.

131

PROVINCE HUESCA

(Telephone area code: 974-)

Accommodation

JACA: *MODERATE:* **Conde Aznar**, Paseo Grl. Franco 3, Tel: 361050. *BUDGET:* **Hostal Galindo**, C/Mayor 45, Tel: 363743

PROVINCE NAVARRA

(Telephone area code: 948-)

Accommodation

RONCAL: *BUDGET:* **Hostal Zaltua**, C/ Castillo 23, Tel: 895008. **OCHAGAVÍA:** *BUDGET:* **Hostal Laspalas**, C/ Urrutia, Tel: 890015. **ELIZONDO:** *MODERATE:* **Baztán**, Ctra. Pamplona- France, km 56, Tel: 580050. **LEYRE MONASTERY:** *MODERATE:* **Hospedería**, Tel: 884100. **PUENTE LA REINA:** *BUDGET:* **Puente**, Pl. de los Fueros, Tel: 340146. **OLITE:** *LUXURY:* **Parador Príncipe de Viana**, Pl. de los Teobaldos 2, Tel: 740000. *MODERATE:* **Don Benito**, Rua de Medios N 1, Tel: 740644. **CARCASTILLO:** *BUDGET:* **Hospedería del Monasterio de la Oliva**, Tel: 725006. **OBANOS:** *MODERATE:* **Hospedería Arnotegui**, C/ San Juan 1, Tel: 344208. **RONCESVALLES:** *MODERATE:* **Pension La Posada**, Tel. 760225. **SANGÜESA:** *MODERATE:* **Pension las Navas**, C/ Alfonso el Batallador 7, Tel: 870077. **JAVIER:** *MODERATE:* **El Mesón**, Pl. de Javier, Tel: 884035. **Javier**, Pl. del Santo, Tel: 884006. **TUDELA:** *MODERATE:* **Hostal Remigio**, C/ Gaztambide 4, Tel: 820850. **ESTELLA:** *BUDGET:* **Hostal Cristina**, C/ Baja Navarra 1-1º, Tel: 550772. **PAMPLONA:** *MODERATE:* **Europa**, C/ Espoz y Mina 11, Tel: 221800. *BUDGET:* **Hostal la Perla**, Pl. del Castillo 1, Tel: 227706.

Tourist Information / Post

PAMPLONA: **Oficina de Turismo:** C/ Duque de Ahumada 3, Tel: 220741. **Post Office:** Paseo Sarasate 9. **Bus Terminal:** C/ Conde Oliveto 2, Tel: 223854. **Rail Terminal:** San Jorge, Tel: 111531.

Museums / Sightseeing

LEYRE: **Church** and **Crypt** open all day. **MONASTERY OF IRACHE:** 10 a.m.–2 p.m. and 5–7 p.m., Sat and Sun 9 a.m.–2 p.m., 4–7 p.m., closed Mon. **RONCESVALLES: Colegiata**, 8 a.m.–9 p.m., in winter until 8 p.m. **Museum**, 11 a.m.–1.30 p.m., 4–6.30 p.m. **ESTELLA:** San Pedro de la Rúa, 10 a.m.–1 p.m., 5–7 p.m., on weekends open for church services only. **PAMPLONA: Cathedral** and **Museum of the Diocese**, 8–11.30 a.m., 6.30–8 p.m. **Citadel** 8 a.m.–9 p.m.

PROVINCE LA RIOJA

(Telephone area code: 941-)

Accommodation

LOGROÑO: *LUXURY:* **Gran Hotel**, General Vara de Rey 5, Tel: 252100. *MODERATE:* **Marqués de Vallejo**, C/ Marqués de Vallejo 8, Tel: 248333. *BUDGET:* **Gonzálo de Berceo**, Gran Via del Rey Don Juan Carlos I. N 37, Tel: 229612. **ANGUIANO:** *MODERATE:* **Abadía de Valvanera** (outside of town, at the monastery), Tel: 377044. *BUDGET:* **el Corzo**, Crt. de Lerma 12, Tel: 377085 (good food). **EZCARAY:** *MODERATE:* **Echaurren**, C/ Héroes del Alcázar 2 (good food). **VINIEGRA DE ABAJO:** *BUDGET:* **Goyo**, Puente del Río Neila 3, Tel: 378007 (for anglers). **STO. DOMINGO DE LA CALZADA**, *LUXURY:* **Parador Santo Domingo de la Calzada**; Pl. del Santo 3, Tel: 340300. *MODERATE:* **Hostal Santa Teresita**, Cistercian Hospedería C/ Grl. Mola 2, Tel: 340700. **HARO:** *LUXURY:* **Los Agustinos**, C/ San Agustín 2, Tel: 311308. *BUDGET:* **Hostal Aragón**, C/ La Vega 9, Tel: 310004.

Museums / Sightseeing

LOGROÑO: **Museo Provincial**, Pl. S. Agustín. **NÁJERA:** Sta. María la Real, 9.30 a.m.–12.30 p.m.; 4–7.30 p.m. **San Millán de la Cogolla**, daily 10.30 a.m.– 1.45 p.m., 4–7.15 p.m., closed Mon in winter. **STO. DOMINGO:** Cathedral, 11 a.m.–7 p.m.

Tourist Information

LOGROÑO: **Oficina de Turismo:** C/ Miguel Villanueva 10, Tel: 215497.

PROVINCE BURGOS

(Telephone area code: 947-)

Accommodation

SANTO DOMINGO DE SILOS: *MODERATE:* **Tres Coronas**, Pl. Mayor 6, 10, Tel: 380727; accommodation in the monastery for men only. **COVARRUBIAS:** *MODERATE:* **Hotel Arlanza**, Pl. Mayor 11, Tel: 403025 (good food). **LERMA:** *MODERATE:* **Hostal Residencia Docar**, C/Sta. Teresa de Jesús 18, Tel: 171073. **BRIVIESCA:** *MODERATE:* **Hostería del Santuario**, Santa Casilda, km 16, Tel: 590152. **BURGOS:** *LUXURY:* **Condestable**, C/ Vitoria 8, Tel: 267125. *MODERATE:* **España**, Paseo del Espolón 32, Tel. 206340. *BUDGET:* **Hostal Castellano**, C/ Laín Calvo 48, Tel. 205040.

Tourist Information

BURGOS: **Oficina de Turismo**, C/San Carlos 1, summer 10 a.m.–2 p.m., 5.30–8.30 p.m., Sun 12 noon–2.15 p.m.; winter 10 a.m.–2 p.m., 4.30–7.30 p.m., Tel: 203125.

Museums / Sightseeing
CLUNIA: **Roman Excavations**, in summer 10
a.m.–2 p.m., 5–8 p.m., in winter 10 a.m.–2 p.m.,
3–6 p.m. **BURGOS: Cathedral**, 9.30 a.m.–1
p.m., 4–7 p.m. **Museo Arqueológico:** 10 a.m.–1
p.m., 4.45–7.15 p.m., Sat 11 a.m.–1 p.m., closed
on Sundays and public holidays. **Monasterio de
las Huelgas**, 11 a.m.–1.15 p.m., 4–5.15 p.m.,
Sun 11 a.m.–1.15 p.m., closed Mon. **Cartuja de
Miraflores**, 10.15 a.m.–3 p.m., 4–6 p.m., closed
Mon. **Monasterio de San Pedro de Cardeña**
(outside of town), 10 a.m.–1 p.m., 4–6.30, Sundays and public holidays 12 noon–2 p.m., 4–6.30
p.m., Tel: 290033. **STO. DOMINGO DE
SILOS: Benedictine Monastery**, 10 a.m.–1
p.m., 4.30–6 p.m., public holidays 4.30–6 p.m.,
Holy Mass with Gregorian chants: weekdays 9
a.m., Sundays and public holidays 12 noon; daily
7 p.m., in summer: Thursday 8 p.m. Tel: 300768.
COVARRUBIAS: Colegiata, 10.30 a.m.–1.30
p.m., 4.30 –6.30 p.m., Sat and Sun 10 a.m.–2
p.m., 4–7 p.m., closed Tue.

PROVINCE PALENCIA
(Telephone area code: 988-)
Accommodation
FRÓMISTA: *BUDGET:* **Hostal San Telmo**, C/
M. Veña 8, Tel: 810102. **CARRIÓN DE LOS
CONDES:** *BUDGET:* **La Corte**, C/ Santa María
34, Tel: 880131. *PILGRIMS' HOSTELS:* **Par-
roquía de Sta María, Monasterio de San Zoilo.**
Sightseeing
FROMISTA: San Martín, 10 a.m.–2 p.m. and
4.30 –8 p.m., closed Mon and Tue. **SALDAÑA:
Roman Excavations** La Olmeda and Quintanilla
de la Cueza, 11 a.m.–2 p.m., 5–8 p.m., cl. Mon.

PROVINCE LEÓN
(Telephone area code: 987-)
Accommodation
SAHAGÚN: *BUDGET:* **Hospedería des
Monasterio de las Madres Benedictinas**, C/
Bermejo Caldrón 8, Tel: 780078. **GRADEFES:**
BUDGET: **Hospedería del Monasterio**, Tel:
333011. **HOSPITAL DE ORBIGO: Pilgrims'
quarters** at the school; call at the city hall for
information; Tel: 388206. **ASTORGA:** *MOD-
ERATE:* **Gaudí**, C/ Edoardo de Castro 6, Tel:
615654. *BUDGET:* **Hostal Norte**, Pl. de la
Estación 9, Tel: 616666. **PONFERRADA:**
MODERATE: **Hotel de Temple**, Avda. Portugal
2, Tel: 410058. **VILLAFRANCA DEL
BIERZO:** *BUDGET:* **El Cruce**, C/ San Salvador
37, Tel: 540185. **LEÓN:** *LUXURY:* **San Marcos**,
Pl. San Marcos, 7, Tel: 237300. *MODERATE:*
Orejas, C/ Villafranca 8, Tel: 252909.

Sightseeing
SAN MIGUEL DE LA ESCALADA: 10.30
a.m.–1.30 p.m., 4–7 p.m. closed Mon.
ASTORGA: Palacio Gaudí and **Museo del
Camino**, 10 a.m.–2 p.m., 4–8 p.m., in winter 11
a.m.–2 p.m., 3.30–6.30 p.m., closed Sun. **Cathedral**, 9–12 noon and 5–6.30 p.m. **LEÓN: Cathedral** and **Museum**, 9.30 a.m.–1 p.m. and 4–6.30
p.m., closed on Sun for tourists. **SAN ISIDORO**:
9 a.m.–2 p.m., 3.30–8 p.m., Sundays and public
holidays 9 a.m.–2 p.m. **San Marcos**, 10 a.m.–2
p.m., 5–7 p.m., Sundays and public holidays 10
a.m.–1.30 p.m. **PONFERRADA: Sto. Tomás de
las Ollas**, 11 a.m.–1 p.m., 4–8 p.m.
Tourist Information
LEÓN: Oficina de Turismo, Plaza de la Regla 4
(opposite the Cathedral), Tel: 237082.

PROVINCE LUGO
(Telephone area code: 982-)
Accommodation
CEBREIRO: *MODERATE:* **Hospedería San
Giraldo de Aurillac**, Tel: 369025.
LUGO: *LUXURY:* **Gran Hotel Lugo**, Av.
Ramón Ferreiro 21, Tel: 224152. *MODERATE:*
Portón do Recanto, La Campiña, Tel: 223445.
BUDGET: **Muralla**, Ronda Muralla 5-6, Tel:
242328.
SARRIÁ: *MODERATE:* **Londres**, C/ Sarriá,
Tel: 532456.
Tourist Information
LUGO: Oficina de Turismo, Pl. de España 27,
Tel: 231361, 10 a.m.–2 p.m., 4–7.30 p.m.
Museums / Sightseeing
**LUGO: Museo Provincial with Iglesia de San
Francisco**, Ruanova. **CEBREIRO: Museum
Palloza**, 10 a.m.–2 p.m., 3 –7 p.m., in winter 11
a.m.–2 p.m., 3–6 p.m., closed Mon; should the
museum be closed, one can usually find the
caretaker in the bar next door.

SANTIAGO DE COMPOSTELA
(Telephone area code: 981-)
Accommodation
LUXURY: **Peregrino**, C/ Rosalia de Castro, Tel.
521850. *MODERATE:* **San Lazaro**, C/ Baliño,
Tel: 584151. *BUDGET:* **Barbantes**, Rúa del
Franco 3, Tel: 581077.
Tourist Information
Oficina de Turismo, Rúa del Villar 43, Tel:
584081.
Museums / Sightseeing
Museo del Pobo Galego (Galician Folk Mu-
seum) in the Monasterio de Santo Domingo, 10
a.m.–1 p.m., 4–7 p.m., closed Sun, Tel: 583620.
Museo de las Peregrinaciones, Pl. San Miguel.

FROM GALICIA
TO MADRID

ORENSE
OLD CASTILE
SALAMANCA
ÁVILA

There is a good road from Santiago to Orense, crossing the Galician countryside and running past clean rivers suitable for swimming. The **Pazo de Oca**, a Baroque palace of the landed gentry, is open to the public and has a small church and a magical 18th- century garden with roses, myrtles and labyrinths. Beyond **Lalín**, off the main road, is the **Monastery of Sta. María la Real de Oseira**, a Renaissance masterpiece still inhabited by 15 Cistercian monks. It has three cloisters and curious playful architectural elements, such as arches of different heights, or the chapter room with its crooked, turned pillars: all "simple but elegant", as the monk proudly says when showing you around.

ORENSE

Orense was already an important town for the Celts and the Romans because of the hot springs of **Las Burgas**. Until recently, women used to come here to fetch hot water for their households. Today the fountainhead is neo-Classical in style and hemmed in by a busy road on the edge of town. The center is the sloping **Plaza Mayor**, lined with cafés and restaurants, the town hall, an **archaeological mu-**

Left: A Galician grain storage hut (horreo).

seum in the former archbishop's palace (16th century) and the onetime **Casino de los Cabelleros**.

The **cathedral**, built on the foundations of an ancient basilica, hides a Romanesque portal, the **Portico del Paraíso** (13th century), behind its new façade, which is reminiscent of that of the cathedral of Santiago. It shows Santiago surrounded by prophets and the 24 wise men of the Apocalypse. Inside is a splendid crossing cupola, a Gothic altar retable and beautiful, carved Gothic choirstalls. The cloister, a covered hall of pillars, is now a museum, but the most spectacular piece can only be seen if you book in advance: the guard on duty closes his museum and takes you to the ornate Baroque **Chapel of Cristo de la Agonía**, where he presents the figure of Christ to you with all the pathos of a Verdi opera. It is made of an unknown material, very like real skin, so they say. It is alleged that the hair and the nails actually grow.

The old town, with its typical streets and squares such as **Pl. del Cid**, **Pl. del Hierro** and **Pl. de la Magdalena** with a Galician stone cross, a *cruceiro* (17th century), have retained their old-fashioned atmosphere and traditional taverns interspersed with modern cafés. The new town, too, with its modern buildings and wide streets, is friendly and the parks, the

Jardines del Posío and San Lazaro and the Paseo have a number of shady outdoor cafés and benches where you can sit and take a rest from sightseeing.

A trip from Orense to the northeast takes you to the Tierra de Lemos. Where the Miño and the Sil join in deep gorges, lined by steep vineyards, you will find the Monastery of San Esteban de Ribas de Sil. This "Escorial of Galicia", an enormous monastery complex, is currently being transformed into a hotel with a restaurant. It has three cloisters and lies in a romantic setting in the mountains above the river. It can be reached from Luintra or from the road which runs along the Sil. On the other bank of the Sil a little road with wonderful views runs through the vineyards to the town of Pombeiro and its Romanesque church. Around Ferreira de Pantón, which has a Cistercian monastery, you will find the Pazo de Maside, a castle-like palace of

Above: The cattle market is an important event in rural Galicia.

the landed gentry (14th century), and a series of other interesting Romanesque churches, including San Miguel de Eiré, San Esteban de Atán and San Fiz de Cangas. The center of the region is Monforte de Lemos, in the valley of the Cave at the foot of a hill. This hill is crowned by the Monastery of San Vincente del Pino (16th century) and a castle. From there you can look out over the new town center, the Roman bridge and the glittering Colegio del Cardenal which has various treasures including paintings by El Greco and Andrea del Sarto.

West of Orense lies the dreamy setting of the Ribeiro wine growing area on the long, steep slopes of the Río Miño and around the town of Ribadavia and the Río Avia. The old town center of Ribadavia with its narrow alleys is hemmed in below the through street, near the ruins of a castle, and extends down to the river where the Jewish quarter was once situated. South of Orense you will find Celanova, whose wonderfully cool squares are shaded by plane trees and its enormous monastery (founded in the 10th century) in which the unique Mozarabian **San Miguel Chapel** is integrated. **Allariz** is where the Castilian Queen Da. Violante wanted to spend the rest of her days, and where she had the Convent of Sta. Clara built. The Virxen Abrideira, the nuns' treasure, is one of more fascinating displays in the convent museum. The small ivory figure of Mary can be opened to reveal a multitude of Biblical scenes.

A little further to the south the fertile Tierra del Limia begins, an area surrounded by legends. The Romans believed that the river Limia was the mythical Lethe, the river of forgetfulness. When Julio Decio Bruto conquered the country he had to first cross the river alone and then call each soldier by name, to prove that he had not lost his memory.

In the middle of maize fields, near the Lake of Embalse de las Conchas, stands **Santa Comba de Bande**, another surprising, tiny but esthetically perfect Mozarabian church. **Verín**, the old town in the south of the province, is famous for its thermal springs and its wine, and for the fortress of **Monterrey**, protected by a belt of three walls.

OLD CASTILE

In the Valley of Sanabria, the natural gateway to Castile, on a hill at the confluence of the rivers Tera and Castro, lies **Puebla de Sanabria**. A steep street with typical balconies cuts a path to the Plaza Mayor with its town hall (15th century) and church (12th century) whose entrance portal is decorated with four figures from an old pre-Romanesque church. Next to it is the recently renovated *castillo* (14th century) and a Baroque chapel in a desolate but undoubtedly picturesque state. The nicest aspect on this somewhat remote mountain is the terrace of the *cervecería*, which offers a wonderful view.

About 15 km further, south of the Sierra de la Cabrera, you come to **Lago de Sanabria**, a nature reserve lying 1.000 m above sea level, and featuring Spain's largest natural lake, many "lagoons" and smaller glacial lakes that can be reached via marked paths. The wonderful mountain area, which inspired Unamuno's philosophical comments in *San Manuel Bueno, the Martyr,* is also very suitable for fishing, swimming, hiking and camping. High above the lake is the monastery of **San Martín de Castañeda**, which has been preserved in the purest Romanesque style but has not been used since the 19th century. An information center with the most important treasures from the monastery and an exhibition on the ecology of the nature reserve has been arranged in its rooms.

The road to the east takes you through the little town of **Mombuey**, which obtained its name from the bull's head on the church tower. South of the road are the refreshing reservoirs of the Río Tera. Some 11 km before Mombuey a little road runs along the reservoir wall of the Embalse de Cernadilla and on past the Valparaiso reservoir to the **Sierra de la Culebra** (snake mountains), a low wooded mountain range which has been turned into a nature reserve. It is rarely visited. For this reason it is full of birds and animals and is wonderful for hiking.

Between the Río Esla and the Río Orbigo lies the town of the Count of **Benavente**, whose coat-of-arms with a flying eagle hangs resplendent on the "snail tower" of the *castillo* (15th century, *parador*). When the second Count of Benavente separated his county from Portugal in order to form an alliance with the stronger powers of Castile and León, the King of Portugal attempted to make him stay, alluding to the proverb that a bird in the hand is worth more than a flying eagle. As the coat-of-arms shows, the Count opted for the less certain fate. One of his descendants established the famous

fiesta of the *toro enmaromado*. After one of her sons had been killed by a bull she decided to punish all bulls once a year by tethering one on a long rope and letting the locals test their courage on it. Originally Benavente was a Celtic settlement, destroyed by Almanzor. The Templar monastery of **San Juan del Mercado**, bearing the first Gothic dome in Spain, and the Plateresque **Hospital de la Piedad** (15th century) are noteworthy sights. **Sta. Maria del Azogue** (12th century) has five impressive Romanesque apses.

If you do not drive via Benavente, but take the direct road to Zamora before the Sierra de Culebra, you encounter **Tábara,** boasting a lovely Romanesque church, and then cross the foothills of the enormous Ricobayo reservoir. The ruins of the Cistercian Monastery of **Moreruela** (12th century) can be found on its

Above: On the Plaza Mayor in Salamanca.
Right: Everything can be best seen from one of the Plaza cafés.

138

eastern shore. Further down along the reservoir is the village of Campillo, which can only be reached from Zamora. Its modest claim to fame is the small Visigoth Church of **San Pedro de la Nave** (7th century), which would have disappeared beneath the flood waters of the reservoir had it not been carried piece by piece to the edge of the village that was itself moved to the middle of the corn fields. The miniature basilica, measuring 12 by 20 meters, has a charm all of its own and is an esthetic pleasure not only for art historians.

Near **Zamora** you leave the green northwest corner of Castile and get onto the Roman Silver Road to the Duero Valley. Zamora itself, a defiant and pugnatious town with a long history, makes a good starting point for a charming trip along the Duero to the east. But you can also follow the river westwards. On the way to Portugal it is portly and generously dammed, but changes into deep gorges, the **Arribes del Duero**, where it forms the border to Portugal. A trip there takes you along small country roads in the direction of **Miranda do Douro**, which is already in Portugal, or, on the Spanish bank, Fermoselle, Aldeadávila or Salto Saucelle, towns which can be just as easily reached from Salamanca. They are closest to the 162-km **Duero Gorge**, which sometimes reaches a depth of 150 m. At some places in these parts you find yourself 500 m above the water table, which is only 200-300 m above sea level at this point. Tributaries like the Esla, the Almendra and the Tormes have also carved themselves deep, dramatic river beds. The natural power of this water has, however, been decreased by the excessive hydroelectric exploitation of these slopes, and by around a dozen dams.

This unique ravine landscape has a microclimate all of its own, caused by the differences in altitude. It also has its own flora and fauna, untypical of the overall region. Ecologists of both countries want the area to be declared an international nature reserve. Because of the inaccessibility of the area, a number of animal species have been preserved here which are rare in other places, including foxes and boar. Bird lovers in particular will enjoy the area. Various species of eagle and vulture and the almost extinct black storks nest here.

GOLDEN SALAMANCA

The road from Zamora to Salamanca is bad but straight. In **Villanueva del Cañedo** you will find the well-maintained Castillo del Buen Amor (15th century), a combination of castle and palace in the Gothic Mudéjar style – with moats and a drawbridge.

The road continues through the typical meadowlands of Salamanca, the dry Dehesas, enormous fenced-in meadows with scattered trees, usually holm oaks, where cattle and sometimes pigs are raised. The pigs eat the acorns from the trees and are the source of the dark, tasty

but expensive Belota ham. The peaceful cows on the meadows are often genuine *toros bravos*, wild fighting bulls, so it is not advisable to climb the fences in this area to have a picnic under a shady tree.

Although **Salamanca** already existed in Roman times it became particularly important only in 1200, when Alfonso IX chose the town as the seat of his court, granting it with a university that was regarded as one of the most important in Europe in the middle of the same century. Today the town has three high schools: a state, the diocesan and the Dominican school. All buildings are made of a golden yellow sandstone, which originates in the quarries of Villamayor. Words cannot describe the colors of the buildings at sunset.

Salamanca has two cathedrals. One is the old Romanesque **Catedral Vieja** from the 12th century, with a Byzantine crossing tower, the *torre del gallo*, Romanesque apses and the remains of an old portal covered by a neo-Classical portal. Inside its priceless treasures include the

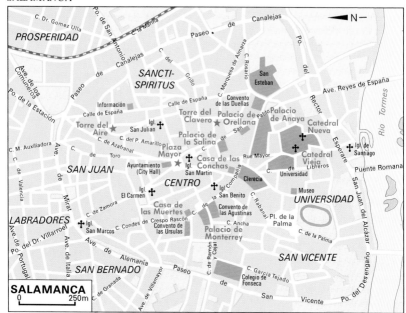

Italian altar retable (15th century) by Nicolás Florentino and the Byzantine statue of the Virgen de la Vega with eyes of pearl.

In the Chapel of Sta. Barbara (1340), opposite the grave of Bishop Lucero, stands the empty chair in which prospective doctors of the university would meditate the night before their exam, which was held in the chapel.

The construction of the **Catedral Nueva** was begun in the 16th century, next to the old cathedral, and required almost two centuries to complete. It is in the Gothic style fashionable at the time. The façades and towers are the most famous sights in the town of Salamanca today. Inside, Cristo de las Batallas, who accompanied El Cid to battle, is honored in a huge Plateresque altar by Joaquín Churriguera. The Baroque choirstalls are also interesting.

Both cathedrals have many richly decorated side chapels, and you would need more than a day to admire all the treasures in peace.

The oldest of the university colleges, the **Colegio Anaya**, renovated in its present form in the 18th century, were built right next to the cathedral complex. Today it houses the philological faculty. In the colonnade around the inner courtyard you will find the grave of Fray Luis de León, the most famous of the Salmantine professors, a religious poet and translator of the *Song of Songs* into Castilian, for which he was imprisoned for 5 years by the Inquisition. When he had served his sentence he returned to the lecture hall and began his class with words which have now become a popular saying: "As we said yesterday ...". The lecture hall where this took place has been preserved unchanged in the **university**. San Vicente Ferrer, Nebrija, Lope de Vega, Góngora, Calderón and even Charles V attended lectures in this room. Marble steps take you to the upper floor of the inner courtyard, where the library is located, the first university library in Europe. It was built from plans by Churriguera, and contains more than 13.000

old manuscripts and incunabula. Somewhere in the richly decorated façade of the building, the figure of a frog is concealed which every student must find if he wants to begin his student career successfully, according to an established tradition.

The building opposite is **Hospital del Estudio** and the **Escuelas Menores**, which has a ceiling decorated with the signs of the zodiac in one of the lecture halls. On the walls you can still make out the *vítores*, V-signs which the newly elected doctors wrote in bull's blood. Further down, on the bookseller's slope, the *cuesta de los libreros*, is **Clerecía**, now a church university. It is a solid Baroque building with 906 windows and once served as a Jesuit college. The building complex, which contains a church and a beautiful Baroque inner courtyard, was commissioned by King Philip III.

On the other side of the street you can see the famous **Casa de las Conchas** (15th century), which belonged to a nobleman from Santiago who decorated it with 300 mussel ornaments and many coats-of-arms. The **Casa de las Muertes**, or death house, takes its name from a crime of passion which made it uninhabitable until Unamuno, rector of the university until 1936, refused to take any notice of the curse. His bust by Pablo Serrano is in front of this house.

The town is dominated by the historical university colleges from the 16th, 17th and 18th centuries, a mixture of residential and educational buildings, as well as the many religious buildings and almost a dozen monasteries. The Romanesque churches of San Martín, San Julián and San Marcos are only some of the other noteworthy architectural delights. Among the nicest monasteries are the Dominican Convent de las Dueñas, the Church of the Dominican Monastery of San Esteban and the Ursuline Convent, with its fine Gothic church.

Many of Salamanca's buildings have been preserved in their original form but fulfill new purposes: the provincial government is located in the **Casa de la Sal**, the old salt store; the **Casa de los Maldonados** is a casino; the **Palace of Garci-Grande** is a bank; and the **Casa de los Abarca** is a provincial art museum. The former rectory of the university is now a museum for the poet, philosopher and university rector Miguel de Unamuno. The **Palacio de Monterrey** (16th century), opposite the Augustan Convent is one of the most splendid palace buildings of the 16th century. The **Torre del Clavero** (15th century), on Columbus Square, houses a small museum dedicated to the town history.

The Salamanca of today is the prototype of a Spanish university town. No less than 27.000 students fill the lecture halls during the winter months; in summer around 10.000 foreign students come to attend language courses. They and the tourists are the town's main sources of income, and everything is very much tailored to their requirements. For the students and tourists, the center is the **Plaza Mayor**, said to be the most beautiful in Spain. You have to stand right in the middle to get a feel of its true atmosphere. It was built from plans by Chirriguera in a unified Baroque style in memory of the War of Succession under Philip V. The town center is always teeming with young people, and the arcades of San Antonio, the Calleja and the pedestrian streets around the Pl. Mayor are full of small, quaint restaurants. Tuna groups sing here in the evenings, the former bands of the students' associations who now perform for visitors.

A Roman bridge crosses the **Río Tormes**. The stone bull was already referred to in the *Lazarillo de Tormes*, the first picaresque novel in literary history. In this anonymous work, the young Lazaro acts as a guide for a blind man. The blind man orders him to put his ear to

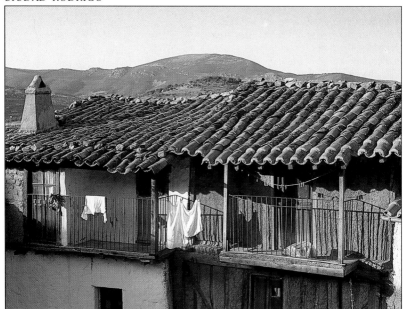

the stone bull to hear the sound it makes. The young lad does this and the beggar hits his head against the stone to give him a lesson for life: "A blind boy even has to put one over on the devil!"

On the river bank you will find the **Cave of San Cipriano**, where the black arts were taught and which was the site of various adventures in the liberary works of Cervantes, Ruiz de Alarcón and Hartzenbusch.

Through the Back Door to the South

From Salamanca well-built and fairly steep roads take you either to Portugal or to southern Spain, to the Extremadura. To the north of the road, on the way to the Portuguese border on the Tormes, is the spa of **Ledesma**, a pretty little settlement with a well- preserved wall and a fortress (15th century). Nearby you will find a

Above: La Alberca in the Peña de Francia.
Right: The women sit outside their houses in the evenings, doing embroidery.

spa with sulfurous medicinal springs. From here side roads lead to the **Arribes del Duero**, a good 60 km away. If you stay on the road from Salamanca to the border, you will soon encounter the green river oases of the Río Agueda and **Ciudad Rodrigo**, which is worth a visit and is much more than a mere stop on the way to Portugal. If you follow the road around the town, which runs along the almost 2-km long and completely preserved town wall (14th/15th century), you will get a glimpse of the entire fortified complex with its moats, the Roman bridge and the wide stretch of land extending to the mountains of the Sierra de Gata (Cat Mountains) and Sierra de Francina in the distance. Close by you can enjoy the flower gardens which the locals have lovingly planted along the fortified wall.

In 1808 the French captured the town with 50.000 men on their way to Portugal and turned the cathedral into a barracks. Many treasures were lost at this time. Wellington liberated the town and was

awarded the title of Duque de Ciudad Rodrigo for his efforts, a title he thereafter
carried with pride.

Despite all the irreverence of the
French the **cathedral** (12th century) is
still full of things to see. Its southern, Romanesque "portal of the chains" is
guarded by a row of 12 prophets. The
western entrance is a double portal and
has well- preserved Gothic archivolts on
the inner front. Inside, the choir stalls are
worth closer inspection. Like those in the
cathedrals of Toledo, Plasencia and
Zamora, they were carved by Rodrigo
Alemán and are lovingly decorated with
pictures that must have shortened the
long hours the singers had to spend in the
cathedral. The carvings show a number
of people and animals committing sinful
acts. The Gothic cloister is one of the
most beautiful of its kind. It has curious
details on the pillar capitals and plinths.
The deacon, Don Estanislao, will per-
sonally give you an interesting and enthusiastic tour of his cathedral.

The little town itself is full of old
palaces sporting pretty coats-of-arms,
and is very lively. The Renaissance town
hall seems to rule over the main square,
and you will find the post office in the
former **Casa de los Vasquez** (16th century), which has tiled pictures, Gothic
windows and a decorated coffered ceiling
which makes even the obligatory waiting
in line for the post office counter a
pleasure. The **Castillo** (14th century) of
Enrique II from the house of Trastamara
has now been transformed into a *parador.*

The southern area of Salamanca Province borders on the Castilian mountains.
Whilst the climb from the approximately
800-m high northern Meseta is relatively
easy, you have to descend on the south
side to a level of 400 m to get to the beautiful green valleys of the Río Alagón, the
Río Jerte and the Río Tiétar, in front of
the Gredos Mountains. Tobacco, cotton,
fruit and vegetables thrive in the mild climate of this area, and small white villages

nestle on the mountain slopes. Red paprikas hang out to dry from the balconies
and dates are spread out in front of the
houses. In this western area of Spain you
will still find *cañadas,* the wide cattle
driving trails along which cows and
sheep have been moved for centuries.
They are taken to the mountains in summer and to the flat plains and harvested
fields in winter. The *cañadas* are considered common land and are used by
cattle herds from the Extremadura and
from Salamanca, or wherever transhumance is still practiced. Often these
trails, which cut straight across the land,
are used as hiking treks or bridle paths.

The **Peña de Francia** is the first destination for those coming from Salamanca
to find some fresh air. From the **Mirador
de la Peña** (1.732m) you can see far
across the Salmantine Plain. The monastery and the inn up here can only be
reached in the summer.

La Alberca is the most important town
of this mountain region. It is an old settlement with dark, romantic half-timbered

houses of Moriscan origin, which have been declared national monuments. Until tourists recently discovered the town genuine traditional costumes were worn here and the old customs retained. Today the locals are proud of their heritage, and use the income they earn during the few summer weekends of their tourist season to pay for the upkeep of those areas endangered by hikers. The most famous local festivals, full of color and costumes, take place at the time of La Loa on the 16th of August and the pilgrimage to **Zarzoso** on the 8th of September. A visit to the town is particularly interesting at this time.

From **Portillo de la Reina**, between La Alberca and the **Batuecas Valley**, one has a splendid view over the hidden valley. It is full of chestnut and nut trees, prehistoric rock paintings, and it also contains the ruins of a Carmelite monastery burned down in the 19th century, and a few abandoned hermits' chapels.

Not far away, to the west of the large Gabriel y Galán reservoir on the slopes of the Sierra de Gata, is **Las Hurdes**, one of the poorest regions in Spain. It is said that the population of this isolated mountain area descended from Arabs who wanted neither to leave the country nor to serve the Christians and who lived here for centuries on the fringes of society, forgotten by the rest of the country. The barren land in the area, endogamy and isolation have resulted in glaring differences between these villages and their populations and the neighboring regions. They were portrayed in Luis Buñuel's now famous documentary of 1933 *Tierra sin Pan* (Land without Bread). When the film was finished it was banned by the government. More than 50 years later, despite various political measures and regional aid, it is still an area in which the steep, stony fields and the sturdy little villages

suggest to the observer an all too difficult existence. In the mountains to the east of Las Hurdes are the towns of Béjar and Hervás. When the Jews were expelled from Spain or forced to convert in 1492, many of them moved to the isolated region near the border with Portugal, where they were not persecuted.

In **Béjar**, which overlooks the river valley like a fortress, they created a flourishing textile industry which still makes the town famous today. The old center, which really consists only of one street that leads to the Pl. Mayor has survived the centuries well. Behind the **Palacio Ducal** (16th century) was the Jewish quarter, flanked by walls of which only ruins remain.

The most distinctive Jewish quarter from the 15th century is to be found at **Hervás**. The town is situated on a hill, crowded around a Gothic church. Below it, outside the old town, in the area around the Río Ambroz and the Roman bridge, the *judería* joins with the streets of del Rabilero and de la Sinagoga, which still have typical busy shops and where the descendants of the Jews who converted to Christianity, the *conversos*, still live today.

Candelario and **Baños de Montemayor** are to be found between the two towns. Mountain ham dries particularly well in the fresh air of these parts. The inhabitants of Madrid, Barcelona or Bilbao love to spend the hottest weeks of the summer in the thermal springs of Montemayor, in the surrounding woods and the cool mountain streams of the Sierra de Candelario.

ÁVILA

Travel west and you will come to the province of Ávila, where the high **Gredos Mountains** separate the northern and the southern Meseta. On the highest peak, the Almanzor (2.592m), snow often glistens even in the hot June sun.

Right: The city wall with its 90 towers surrounds Ávila.

El Barco de Avila, the capital on the northern side of the mountain, is a wealthy agricultural center, famous for its white beans, and the starting point for many excursions into the mountains. The town has a well-preserved castle (15th century) and town walls.

The little road along the banks of the Río Tormes and the Río Alberche slinks along the foot of the mountain to the nature reserve. The Río Alberche is loved by anglers for its trout. Near **Navar-redonda**, at an altitude of 1.600 m, is the first *parador de turismo*, opened in 1930 by Alfonso XIII. The road forks at Hoyos del Espino. One road leads high into the mountains to a serviced mountain hut and to ice-cold glacial lakes. Follow the hiking paths and you will quickly come to places where mountain goats, now found only in this area, boar, wildcats, eagles and rare species of birds such as the oriole and kingfisher can be spotted.

Further west you soon come to the area to which Madrid's inhabitants flock on days out. More and more weekend houses are being built here. It is inadvisable to risk a drive here by car on Sundays, but during the week the area is less busy and very charming. **Cerebro** is famous for its excellent wine. In **El Tiemblo**, and not, as you might think, in the pretty town of Guisando, you will find the famous *toros de Guisando*, Iberian bull figures, made of stone, who must have once borne of heathen religious significance. Similar figures were also discovered in Avila and Segovia.

Ávila, the town of St. Theresa, is best viewed from outside. From the observation point with four pillars, the *cuatro postes*, you can look down over the impressive town wall with its 90 towers and the defiant cathedral built into it. The two- and-a-half kilometer long wall, built in the 11th century and locked by 9 gates, surrounds the town completely. It is 14 m high in some parts.

The early-Gothic **cathedral** is still a veritable fortified construction with small windows and little decoration. It has grown over the centuries, particularly

145

ÁVILA

during the Renaissance, from which period the expressive choirstalls date. Pedro Berruguete's altar retable (15th century) is one of the finest pieces in the cathedral. The alabaster grave of Bishop El Tostado, who is portrayed here as a scholar, is yet another masterpiece in the cathedral museum found behind the octagonal sacristy.

Also leaning on the town wall is the medieval **Casas de los Dávilas**, belonging to the richest aristocratic family in the town. Right next to it is the **Convent of St. Theresa**. In its church you can admire the room in which the saint was born, now a chapel. Theresa of Ávila was influential in the reform of the Carmelite order during the 16th century, and was one of the few female teachers of the Church to be canonized. She replaced Santiago as Spain's most important saint, and General Franco, among others, is said to have carried her relics with him into important battles.

While the old town center was located between the Pl. de la Victoria and the Cathedral, the new center has sprung up in front of the walls and around the Pl. Sta. Teresa. In the time when Ávila was still an expanding town, various churches and monasteries were built outside the town walls. Right in front of the **Puerta San Vincente** is the church bearing the same name, a late- Romanesque building of particular beauty, with a covered colonnade which is dedicated to St. Vincent and his two sisters who died here as martyrs in the 4th century. Inside you can see the richly decorated tomb of the saint.

On Sta. Teresa Square stands the partly Romanesque, partly Gothic **Church of San Pedro**, a simple but imposing building. Almost on the edge of town is the **Monastery of Sto. Tomás**, built under the Catholic Monarchs at the end of the 15th century, who also had the tomb of their only son Juan placed here. The monastery served the Catholic Monarchs as a summer residence, and the Inquisition, too, had its seat here. In the sacristy you will find the tomb of the Grand Inquisitor Torquemada (1498). The unusual chancel and the main altar area is raised. The high altar was made by Berruguete. Along with the choir stalls which included seats for the Royal Couple, the high altar can only be reached from the Cloister of Silence. The monastery has three cloisters in all, and is one of the richest in the whide area.

In the **Casa de los Deanes**, now a provincial museum which includes exhibits of typical old furniture, you can see how the deans of the cathedral once lived, and get an idea of the importance of the town during the Middle Ages. Ávila lost much of its significance after the Reconquista and during the decline of the wool industry that lost its significance to cotton in the trading ports of the 17th century. Today it is a sleepy little provincial town with no more than 40.000 inhabitants, lying in the middle of a barren region, even though it is located no further than 100 km from Madrid.

PROVINCE ORENSE
(Telephone area code: 988-)
Accommodation
CARBALLIÑO: *MODERATE:* Arenteiro, Alameda 19, Tel: 270558. *BUDGET:* Tojo, C/ Cuesta 5, Tel: 270334.
RIBADAVIA: *BUDGET:* Evencia 2, Av. Rodríguez Valcárcel 30, Tel: 471045.
VERÍN: *LUXURY:* Parador de Monterrey, 4 km outside of town, Tel: 410075. *BUDGET:* O'Augueiro, Av. Sousas 117, Tel: 411026.
ORENSE: *LUXURY:* Gran Hotel San Martín, C/ Curros Enríquez 1, Tel: 235690. *MODERATE:* Riomar, C/ Mateo de Prado 15, Tel: 220700. *BUDGET:* Irixo, C/ Hermanos Villar 23, Tel: 220035.
Tourist Information
ORENSE: Oficina de Turismo, C/ Curros Enríquez, 1 Edificio Torre; Tel: 234717.
Museums / Sightseeing
LA ESTRADA, PONTEV: Pazo de Oca: 9.30 a.m.–2 p.m., 4–8 p.m., closed Mon.
ORENSE: Museo Arqueológico Provincial, 10 a.m.–1 p.m., 5–8 p.m., Sat and Sun 10 a.m.–1 p.m., closed Mon. Cathedral, 11 a.m.–1 p.m., 4.30–6.30 p.m.
CELANOVA: Mozarabic Chapel San Miguel, 11 a.m.–1 p.m., 5–7.30 p.m. (in the monastery San Salvador).
CARBALLIÑO: Monasterio Sta. María la Real de Oseira, 9.30 a.m.–12.30 p.m., 3.45–7 p.m., Sun 9.30 a.m.–12.30 p.m.
RIBADAVIA: Museo Etnologico, 10.30 a.m.–2.40 p.m., closed Mon.

PROVINCE ZAMORA
(Telephone area code: 988-)
Accommodation
PUEBLA DE SANABRIA: *MODERATE:* Hostal Peamar, Pl. Arabal 10, Tel: 620136. *BUDGET:* Victoria, Pl. Arabal 20, Tel: 620012.
BENAVENTE: *LUXURY:* Parador Rey Fernando II. de León, Paseo Ramón y Cajal, Tel: 630300. *MODERATE:* Hostal Bristol, C/ General Mola 16, Tel: 631032.
Nature Reserve Lago de Sanabria
Visitors' Information Center, summer 10 a.m.–1 p.m.; 5–7 p.m., information pavilion at the road turnoff to Vigo and San Martín.
Sightseeing
PUEBLA DE SANABRIA: Castle, 11 a.m.–2 p.m., 5–9 p.m.
CAMPILLO: San Pedro de la Nave, 10 a.m.–1 p.m., 5–8 p.m. closed Sunday afternoon.
BENAVENTE: Fiesta del Toro enmaromado, one day prior to Corpus Christi Day.

PROVINCE SALAMANCA
(Telephone area code: 923-)
Accommodation
CIUDAD RODRIGO: *LUXURY:* Parador Enrique II., Pl. Castillo 1, Tel: 460150. *BUDGET:* Pension Paris, C/ Toro 10, Tel:461372.
ALBA DE TORMES: *MODERATE:* Benedictino, C/ Benitas 6, Tel: 300025.
LA ALBERCA: *MODERATE:* Paris, C/ La Chanca, Tel: 437056.
BÉJAR: *MODERATE:* Blázquez Sánchez, Travesía Santa Ana 6, Tel: 402400. *BUDGET:* Comercio, Puerta de Avila 5, Tel: 400219.
CANDELARIO: *MODERATE:* Hostal Cristi, Pl. Béjar 1, Tel: 413212.
SALAMANCA: *LUXURY:* Monterrey, C/ Azafranal 12, Tel: 214400. *MODERATE:* Oriental, C/ Azafranal 13, Tel: 212115. *BUDGET:* Valencia, Paseo San Antonio 5, Tel: 269864.
Museums / Sightseeing
SALAMANCA: Cathedral and Museum, 10 a.m.–1.30 p.m., 5–8 p.m., closed Sun, Mon and public holidays. Museo de la Historia de la Ciudad (town history), Pl. Episcopal. Museo Provincial, Pl. Patio Escuelas Menores 2, 9.30 a.m.–1.30 p.m., 2.30–4.30 p.m., closed Sun, Mon and public holidays.
Tourist Information
CIUDAD RODRIGO: Oficina de Turismo, Pl. de Amayuelas 5, 10 a.m.–2 p.m., 4.30–7 p.m. Tel: 460150. SALAMANCA: Oficina de Turismo, C/ España 39; Tel: 243730.

PROVINCE ÁVILA
(Telephone area code: 918-)
Accommodation
EL BARCO DE ÁVILA: *MODERATE:* Manila, on the road to Plasencia, km 69,3; Tel:340844. PIEDRAHITA: *BUDGET:* La Casona, C/ Calleja, Tel: 360362.
NAVARREDONDA DE GREDOS: *MODERATE:* Parador de Gredos, 2 km outside of town, Tel: 348048.
ÁVILA DE LOS CABALLEROS: *LUXURY:* Palacio Valderrábanos, Plaza de la Catedral, 9, Tel: 211023. *MODERATE:* El Rastro, Pl. del Rastro 1, Tel: 211219.
Museums / Sightseeing
ÁVILA: Museo de Arte Oriental in the Real Monasterio de Sto, Tomás. Cathedral and Museum,10 a.m.–1.30 p.m., 3 –7 p.m., in winter until 5.30 p.m. Museo Provincial in the Casa de los Deanes, C/ de Nalvillos 3, 10 a.m.–1 p.m., 5–8 p.m., on weekends sometimes 10 a.m.–2 p.m. Museo Teresiano in the Convento de San José, 10 a.m.–1 p.m. and 4–6 p.m.

ANCHA CASTILLA
The Duero Basin

ZAMORA
VALLADOLID
PALENCIA
SORIA

The region lying between Zamora and the hills on the edge of the Ebro Basin is hallmarked by the Duero River Valley and the flatlands of the Meseta. Its first inhabitants were the Celtiberians. The Romans spent 200 years overcoming the hardiness of the natives and the rough climate, and thus to conquer the region. Their settlements were founded on existing villages: La Olmeda (Palencia), Clunia (Burgos), Tiermes and Numancia (Soria). Later, after the Visigoths moved to the area, the region between Palencia and Portugal came to be known as the *Gothic Fields.*

For many centuries, the Duero River constituted the main battle front between Christians and Moors, until Toledo was captured in the 11th century. At the same time, a number of territorial skirmishes were fought out between the newly created Christian realms. The epic poem *El Cantar de Mio Cid* is not only dedicated to El Cid, but also bears testimony to the resistance exercised by the Castilian people against León, Aragón and Navarra. In the ensuing *repoblación* (repopulation) not only Christians from the north but also those who had been living among the Arabs in the south, the so-

called Mozarabians, were resettled in the area. The churches which they built in their settlements represent today's wealth of monuments from the Romanesque period. New monasteries were generally established by monks from France, first from the Benedictine, later from the Cluny and Cistercian orders. The many castles situated along the banks of the Duero all date from this period. They were built to defend the area from the Moors and other enemies. Little more than ruins remain of many of these, but the spirit of the age survives in numerous poems, romances and in legends which have been passed down from this time.

After the Reconquista had moved on southwards, the area became Spain's breadbasket. From the 16th century onwards the lands around Valladolid began to export agricultural produce. Santander, which became the coastal center of Cantabria, witnessed a flourishing trade in wool, wine and grain, notably with Flanders. The tradition of wine growing in the region and its most famous dish, *codero asado,* or baked lamb, prepared to this day in the *hornos* (clay ovens), date back to this time. Four of the wine-growing regions in the Duero Valley have been declared *Denominación de Origen.* The region of **Toro** is famous for its rich red varieties. The largest region, **Rueda**, pro-

Preceding pages: Evening chat in the main square of Soria.

duces light, fruity white wines. Then there is the *Ribera del Duero,* with its red and rosé wines and the exquisite *Gran Reservas* from the **Vega Sicilia**. And finally, the **Cigales**, which is the origin of the famous rosé wines, the *Claretes.*

ZAMORA

On the right bank of the Duero, situated between the corn-growing and wine-producing sierras on the Roman *Via Argentii*, lies the well-fortified town of **Zamora**, called *samurah* by the Arabs. Heavily disputed by Christians and Moors, it saw a succession of different rulers during the 9th and 10th centuries. In 893, under Alfonso III, it was resettled by Mozarabians from Toledo. In the 11th century it was accorded special rights (*fueros*) by Fernando I on whose death his daughter, Doña Urraca, became queen of the principality. Her story is celebrated in traditional romances. On his deathbed, Fernando divided his kingdom among his three sons. His daughter Urraca, already much in love with her childhood friend El Cid and hoping to win him over with a substantial dowry, appeared at her father's deathbed and threatened, were she to be left out of his will, to sell herself for love or money to Christians and Arabs respectively. And so she was promised the stronghold of Zamora, while her sister was to have Toro. Wishing to unite the kingdom, her brother Sancho II, King of Castile, and his *caballeros*, El Cid among them, captured Zamora in a siege which lasted for 7 days. To this day a proverb warning against impatience says *no se ganó Zamora en una hora*, which translated means: Zamora was not conquered in an hour. It was through the arch at San Isidoro, the *Portillo de la Traición,* or Gateway of Treason, that Bellido Dolfos fled, having feigned allegiance to, and then killed King Sanchez. Alfonso VI, the murdered monarch's brother, became king while El Cid agreed to remain in his

service on condition that he swear to having had no part in his brother's killing. Reluctantly, the king agreed to do so, but soon afterwards exiled the Cid in revenge for his humiliation. Thus began the famous and much celebrated adventures of El Cid.

From the walls of the **castillo**, you can look down over the fertile river valley and onto a small church, **Santiago de los Caballeros**, in which El Cid was made a *caballero*. 100 meters from the church, in the direction of La Hiniesta, stands a stone cross which marks the place where the king was wounded. A second stands two kilometers further, marking the spot where he died. The site is visited each year by pilgrims. In the late Middle Ages, Zamora benefited from the general revival of Castile. The 15th century saw the beginnings of the textile industry in the wool sector and in the 18th century there were no less than 70 mills here, producing blankets for the military.

The **cathedral** in Zamora, which is, along with those in Salamanca and Toro, one of the finest examples of Romanesque architecture in Castile, dates from the 12th century. It has a strange crossing cupola, clearly inspired by Byzantine architecture. Inside, one is immediately struck by the immense walls and the majestic Gothic confessionals. The left one of the two crossing altars is dedicated to the bald virgin, *La Virgen de la Calva* (13th century). The cloister is Baroque in origin, but in tune with the Renaissance style of Herrera. Of considerable interest as well, is the much revered recumbent figure of Christ of the Flesh. It is made of real human skin, hair and blood. Behind the gridiron one can see the choir stalls attributed to Rodrigo Alemán (early 16th century). The ornamental carvings on the fold-up seats intended for the tired, elderly members of the chair feature satirical representation of vices to which the monks and nuns of that period were prone.

151

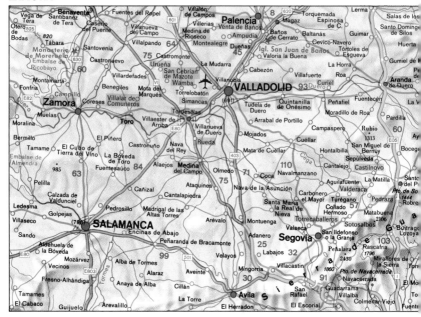

Zamora has numerous noteworthy Romanesque and Gothic churches. There is, for example, the Iglesia de la Magdalena, San Ciprione, Santiago de Burgo and Santo Tomé. The oldest, **Maria de la Horta**, dates back to the 8th century and was the site of the "Mutiny of the Trout". When, in the 12th century, a fisherman refused to cede his catch to a nobleman, a meeting of the aristocracy was held in the church to discuss what should be done about such rebelliousness. Hordes of local people gathered outside, locked the doors and set fire to the church and its occupants. As though by a miracle, the Hosts flew to a convent in the neighboring town of Dueñas through a crack near the chancel, which is still there today.

Regardless of its well-preserved medieval foundations and city walls, the town now has a modern, partly pedestrianized centre. The modernistic market is as much worthy of a visit as the Plateresque **Palacio de los Momos**. The Renaissance palace of the Condes of Alba and Aliste has been converted into a *parador*, whose terrace looks out over a pool and onto the river plain.

Zamora's Holy Week festivities are among the most interesting in Spain, and are attended by many people. Scenes from the Stations of the Cross (*pasos*) are, however, better viewed in the **Museo de la Semana Santa** (next to Sta. Maria la Nueva), than in the huge crowds which make up the Good Friday procession. Some of the statues are very old (17th century), while others were made at the beginning of this century by Mariano Benlliure, a contemporary of Gaudí, including his first piece, made at age 15.

Former Royal Residences

The small town of **Toro** takes its name from the Celtiberian bull, a model of which stands at the end of a crossroads on the edge of town. Through the clock gate (by Churriguera, 1719), along the main road and across the plaza with its many shops and street cafés, is the church of **Sta. María la Mayor** (12th-13th cen-

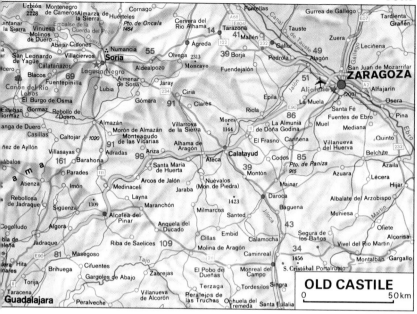

tury), which seems far too large and imposing for such a small town.

Whilst the nave and the transept of this church still have Romanesque barrel vaulting, the side aisles were already constructed with Gothic ribbed vaults. Here, as in Zamora, the most striking feature of the edifice is its crossed tower. Light streams in through the cupola. Inside, one finds a variety of fine Baroque altars and a painting by the Dutch artist Gerard David (1520), depicting the *Virgen de la Mosca*, which takes its name from the fly on the coat on Mary's knee.

The **Espolón**, a park at the rear of the church, looks out over the valley with its irrigated vineyards where the famous Toro wines are produced. The houses all have *bodegas*, or cellars, some of which function as the area's typical taverns. At the end of August, during the fiesta, a wine fountain is installed in the bullring for the young men to drink from while the bulls run around them.

The town became known not only as the residence of the king's daughter, El-

vira, but as the site of the battle between Hannibal and the Romans (220 B.C.) and as the theater of the Wars of Succession between Isabel the Catholic and Juana la Beltraneja of Portugal, which took place in 1476.

Walking through Toro one should note diligently the anecdotal streetnames: *Calle Abrazamozas* (Maidens Embrace); *Calle Buenaguia* (Good Guide), along which the Catholic Monarch's army was led through the town by a shepherd; *Calle Rejadorada* (Golden Gate), where Doña Elvira's palace stood; *Calle Miraflores* (Flower View), which leads to the *vega*, the river banks; *Calle Salsipuedes* (Get-out-if-you-can).

The residence of Juana la Loca, **Tordesillas**, and its adjacent 16th-century Mudéjar-style Monastery of Sta. Clara, where she also died, can be seen from afar, as it stands high above the Duero Valley. On display in its museum are a clavichord given by Charles V to his mother and the portable relic and lantern which accompanied Philip's funeral pro-

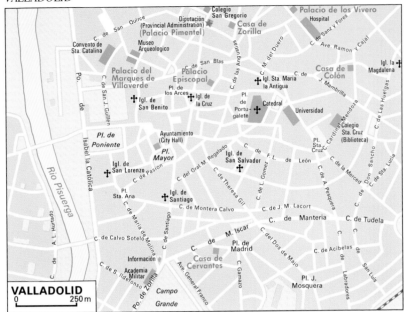

cession. The ritual was repeated each year by his wife, who was rendered mad by his death, hence the nickname the Demented, *la loca* .

Rueda, a wine-producing region, lies south of Tordesillas. The rather dusty town itself is full of *bodegas*, which surround the huge church with its Gothic cloister. In the 15th century, **Medina del Campo** was the venue of important markets for trade in livestock, and the **Castillo de la Mota** was a major meeting place of the *Cortes* under the Catholic Monarchs. After the expulsion of the Jews, the town experienced economic decline, accelerated by its support of the *Comuneros* in their uprising against Charles V. The castle was used as a state prison in which César Borgia and other members of the nobility were once held captive.

The Castillo of **Simancas** can be seen from a distance. It is Arabic in origin

Right: Valladolid has got a famous museum with religious sculptures.

154

(14th century), and has housed state archives since the time of Philip II. One of the old palaces displays the town's coat-of-arms: seven hands. Prior to the Reconquista, the Christians of the region were obliged to provide the Arabs with 100 maidens each year. In a gruesome form of retaliation, Simanca's residents cut off the hands of the seven maidens required of them.

VALLADOLID

With the *repoblación* in the 11th century, the town of **Valladolid**, or Arabic *Vela Baled*, passed to the Count of Carrión and became the most important town in Castile. The Church of **Sta. Ma. la Antigua**, rebuilt in the 13th century, dates from this time. Its Romanesque spire is typical of those found in Castile. In the 13th century, the town became crown property and Spain's administrative center. The university of Palencia moved here in the 14th century. The town gained even greater significance under the

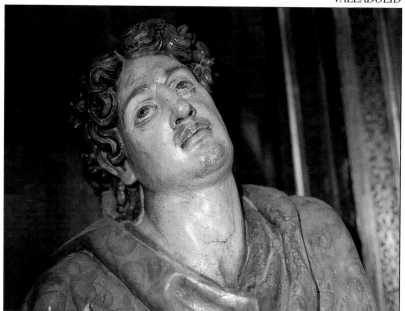

Catholic Monarchs, whose marriage took place in the secrecy of the **Palacio de los Vivero**. The town's most important monuments were built during this period and are in keeping with the late Isabelline Gothic style. The façades of San Pablo and San Gregorio are most impressive as they were constructed just like Plateresque altar tops.

The **Colegio San Gregorio** was built by Juan Guas and Diego de Siloé. It has an inner quadrangle which is regarded as one of the finest examples of Isabelline architecture to be found in Spain. Today, the building is a national museum of sculpture and home to an extensive collection of religious sculptures from the Middle Ages to the Baroque, with works by Alonso Berruguete, Juan de Juni and Gregorio Fernández. Alonso Berruguete (1489-1561), son of the Renaissance artist Pedro, studied in Italy and came to Spain with Charles V. The Frenchman Juan de Juni (1507-1577) worked in Valladolid all his life and established the foundations of Castile's tradition of religious sculpture. Both greatly influenced the prolific Baroque artist Gregorio Fernández (1576-1636), many of whose works relate closely to the Holy Week processional scenes and have had an important influence on religious artforms.

The **Colegio Sta. Cruz**, now the university library, has a quadrangle with three stories. Its chapel houses the *Cristo de la Luz*, a masterpiece by Gregorio Fernández. The **Palacio Pimentel**, birthplace of Philip II, now serves as the seat of the regional parliament.

When the uprising of the *Comuneros* was crushed under Charles V, Valladolid, their former headquarters, was stripped of its privileges. It was at this time also that the first attempts were made to build a cathedral in there. Its history reflects that of the town itself, whose many attempts to become Spain's capital remained without enduring success. Charles V commissioned the work to begin, but Philip II ordered court architect Herrera to alter the plans. Following his death, the work was not continued

155

until much later, under the Bourbons, when Churriguera completed the façade in 1729. To this day it bears a single tower, finally built in the 19th century. Of particular note inside are the especially fine altarpiece by Juni, which was originally planned for Sta. María La Antigua, and the Diocesan Museum with a monstrance by Juan de Arfe.

The Renaissance buildings of La Magdalena, the Palacio del Marques de Villaverde, Las Angustias and the Palacio of Fabio Nelli, now the Museo Arqueológico, all date from the time of Charles V and Philip II. The magnificent **Plaza Mayor**, built by Philip II, was destroyed in a blaze along with another 440 buildings, but work was already begun on the existing plaza with its beautiful arcades soon after in the 16th century.

For 20 years under Philip III, Valladolid was the capital of Spain. Many of the Baroque buildings of the time can still be seen today. The most significant of these are the university, the church of La Pasión, now a museum for 16th-18th century painting, the convent Las Agustinas and the Church of Porta Coeli.

Court was held once again in Valladolid under Philip V at the time of the Wars of the Succession (1781). In the 19th century, Napoleon's troops made Valladolid their headquarters, and today it serves as the capital of the *Comunidad Autónoma de Castilla y León*.

However, it was not only its rulers who left their mark on the town. The **Casa de Colón** (Columbus) is a museum to the great discoverer who died here, embittered and impoverished, in 1506. Cervantes also lived and wrote two of his works here: *El Licenciado Vidriera* and *El Coloquio de los Perros*. Another museum is devoted to the Romantic writer José de Zorrilla, the third famous prodigy of the town. His is the most

Right: The scattered oaktrees in Castile are characteristic of this part of Spain.

popular version of the drama *Don Juan Tenorio*. Also living in Valladolid is Miguel Delibes, author of perhaps the finest contemporary depictions of life in the villages of Castile.

We recommend a trip into the province of Segovia to see the pretty villages of Cuéllar, Coca, and Sta. María la Real de Nieva, the latter with its magnificent Gothic church. All have well-preserved old walls, **Coca** being the birthplace of Roman Emperor Theodosius. Its 13th-century fort is one of the finest in Spain. It is built from clay bricks and offers a picturesque sight at dusk. **Cuéllar** also has a fine castle which belonged to Don Beltrán de la Cueva and served as a bastion of the Beltraneja faction during its disputes with Isabel the Catholic. In the 19th century it was Wellington's residence during the war of independence with France, and later still it was used to incarcerate the romantic revolutionary Espronceda.

PALENCIA

The village of **Cigales**, with its excellent *Clarete* wine, lies just off the expressway to Palencia. It forms the gateway to the open **Tierra de Campos**, where the villages scattered throughout the area bear names of historic significance. The adobe or half-timbered houses merge with the very terrain on which they are built, the streets converge at the Pl. Mayor, with its arcades and timber balconies. While most of them have been simply modernized, each village still bears some hallmark from its according past: the burial chamber in the church in **Wamba**; the stocks, *rollo,* at **Villalón**; the battle of **Villalar de los Comuneros**; the splendid and well-preserved fortresses of **Montealegre, Ampudia** and **Torremormojón**; the cattle markets at **Medina de Rioseco**; the walls of **Urueña**, and the Mozarabian church of **San Cebrian de Mazote**.

About 20 km away, across the expanse of cornfields which seem to still reverberate with the cries of battle, where the Gothic kings lie buried somewhere, one can see the church spires of the next village. "Its a long way to Castile", is a popular saying in these parts. There are few occasions for the villagers to get in each other's ways.

Dueñas is the place where Isabel of Castile and Fernando of Aragón met for the very first time. Such was their overwhelming passion for one another, that they were married within the week so that they could enjoy the pleasures of married life as early as possible.

On the outskirts of **Venta de Baños**, a suburb of Palencia and site of a large chocolate factory run by Trappist monks, stands the 7th-century basilica **San Juan de Baños**, one of the few remaining monuments from the Visigoth past. Visitors are advised to drink from the abundant waters of the spring beside it, to benefit from the allegedly wondrous healing powers it is said to have.

On the distant hills stands a larger than life statue of a benificent Christ, the *Christo*, by Antonio Macho (1930), emblem of **Palencia**. The town, situated above the River Carrión, shows few signs of its history. We know that there was a university here in the early 13th century, but the Palentinians expelled the students for their scandalous behaviour. The two most notable monuments are the cathedral and San Miguel.

The Gothic **cathedral** was built in the 14-16th century. Its name is "the unknown beauty", not so much   for its rather stolid outer appearance than for its numerous interior features: the Plateresque retable of the high altar; the Flemish altarpiece, *Trascoros,* depicting Mary's suffering; the curious relief in the Chapel of San Gregorio portraying the divine medics Cosmas and Damian after having transplanted the leg of a black slave onto a white nobleman. The mysterious 11th century crypt is also worth a visit. A precious and enormous silver altar is displayed in a side chapel, while

the cloister is hung with Flemish goblets dating from the 16th century. Paintings by El Greco and Berruguete are exhibited in a small cathedral museum in the sacristy, along with a Mannerist portrait of Charles V painted by Lukas Cranach, which can only be seen through a hole in the side of the picture frame. A 13th-century painted wooden chest containing the mortal remains of Doña Urraca is displayed in the Santuarium Chapel.

El Cid and Doña Jimena were betrothed in the church of **San Miguel**, with its noteworthy Gothic spires and merlons. Those with a taste for the macabre can, provided they are let into the chapel of the church of **San Fransisco**, just off the Plaza Mayor, see the skulls which cover its walls. The rather strange mummy of the *Christo de Tierra* (Christ of Earth), in the church of **Sta. Clara**, already provided Unamuno with sufficient horror to dedicate a sonnet to it.

Above: The quainter the restaurant is, the better the roast lamb tastes.

Palencia, with its inviting park "El Salon", is a peaceful and affordable provincial town. Its climate makes it a pleasant place even at the height of summer season and it is recommended to tourists, sightseers and those interested in Gothic architecture alike.

The Cordero Asado Route

Between Valladolid and El Burgo de Osma lie the wine gardens of the *bodegas* of the Vega Sicilia in **Quintanilla de Onésimo**, the finest on the **Duero river**. The wine cellars are immediately adjacent to the church, itself famous for an anonymous altar retable which is reputed to be the finest Renaissance work in Spain. In **Peñafiel**, which lies between the rivers Duero and Duratón, at the foot of a bow-shaped fort, lived Don Juan Manuel. He is the author of the *Conde Lucanor*, the great tome of stories from the 14th century.

The popular *bodega* in the next village, **Curiel**, has a *horno* or oven, used to bake lamb, kid or sucking pig. The **Duratón Valley** is truly the kingdom of the *horno*. In the past every village had at least one such brick oven which every household made use of for baking bread. Since then it has become customary in many restaurants to use them to roast meat. Such places are called *horno, fogón, posada* or *mesón*. A valley of gastronomic superlatives and Romanesque villages, the Duratón also has pleasant surprises in store for nature lovers. Lying on a hill is the area's most important town, **Sepúlveda**. The ancient town center, which has three churches of pure Segovian Romanesque origin, is surrounded by walls and overlooked by a fort. Neighboring **Castilnovo**, too, has a 15th-century fort that has survived the years rather well.

The area between Sepúlveda and the Embalse de Burgomillodo is a nature reserve. At the center of this nature reserve park you will find a Romanesque church which was consecrated to S. Frutos, a Visigoth saint who is said to have confronted the attacking Moors brandishing a cross. As he rammed the cross into the ground, a 100-m chasm opened up, the *hozes* of the Río Duratón. The dense vegetation growing there today offers an ideal habitat for birds and small mammals. In addition to foxes and nutrias, there are vultures, falcons and owls which have made their nests on the steep cliff face.

Pedraza is the birthplace of the Roman emperor Trajan. It has a fort and a Plaza Mayor typical of old Castilian urban architecture. **Turégano** lies in the valley of the Río Pirón, at the foot of a well-fortified 13th-century castle. It is renowned for its numerous Romanesque churches and tasty honey. A Gothic church with a tall bell-tower rises above its ruins.

Sotosalbos, while small, has a fine Romanesque church with valuable capitals. It is even given mention in the clerical-picaresque poems of the *Libro del Buen Amor*, written in the 14th century by high priest Hita. It is thought that he was born in nearby **Valdevaca**.

Of **Torrecaballeros**, it is said that, whilst otherwise unremarkable and lacking in sights to see, its wealth of *hornos* qualifies it for entry into the Guinness Book of Records. Another center of Lucullan culture, and a significant town on the banks of the Duero, is **Aranda de Duero,** in the province of Burgos. Its bridge has been immortalized in a famous nursery rhyme. Although the town is now heavily industrialized, it also has a pretty church with Plateresque portals, and its restaurants enjoy a good reputation for their lamb specialities, delicious dishes which have become famous throughout Spain.

A detour into some of the villages south of Arandas, in the direction of Madrid, would be very rewarding. They have cobbled streets and plazas surrounded by archways. On each plaza there are restaurants offering outdoor seating. Best known of these are **Riaza** and **Ayllón**, the latter of which has a Gothic palace and a Romanesque church as well as a museum of modern art. Both lie just north of the **Sierra de Ayllón**, not far from the beechwoods of **Tejera Negra**.

SORIA

Traveling eastwards along the Duero Valley you will come across another group of Romanesque villages, which have narrow alleyways and plazas surrounded by nice arcades. **Peñaranda de Duero** has a fort, a church and an apothecary museum dating from the 17th century. Not far away you will find the convent **La Vid** (12th-16th century). **San Esteban de Gormaz** has the oldest Romanesque churches in the region – San Miguel and Sta. María de la Ribera –, as well as a medieval fortress and a bridge which plays an early role in the *Cantar*

parklands and Templar church of **Cañón del Río Lobos**, ideal setting for walks, for resting in the shade of the pines or for watching the vultures, who nest on the rock face. The river, however, does not live up to its wild name, being more like a stagnant pool than a rushing torrent. South of Burgo de Osma lie **Gormaz**, with its impressive 10th-century Arab fort, everything in ruins save for twenty-four towers and 10-m high walls; and **Berlanga de Duero,** which is less famous for its 15th- century castle or richly furnished 16th-century church, than for the Chapel of **San Baudelio de Berlanga**, in nearby **Casillas**. It represents a unique example of 11th-century Mozarabian architecture. Although its Romanesque frescoes have been dismantled and moved to the Prado and the History of Art Museum in Boston, its structure remains essentially unchanged. The Mozarabian arches descend from a central pillar like palm leaves. No one knows what the secret chamber at the head of the stairs was for. It may have served either as a monk's hiding place from the Arabs or as a confessional.

For the mere thirty inhabitants of **Calatañazor**, a medieval village in the heathlands of the **Sierra de Cabrejas**, north of the Duero Valley, time seems to have stood still. Visitors attracted by the church with a small museum and the ruined fortress with a balcony looking out over the valley will also find board and lodgings here. Excursions can be made to the source of the Río Avión, for bathing at **Cuerda de Pozo Reservoir**, and from there on via **Vinuesa** into the **Sierra de Urbión** for hiking on the shores of the **Laguna Negra**, a deep and mysterious glacier lake 1.780 m above sea level.

Soria, with its 31.000 inhabitants, is Spain's second-smallest provincial capital. It was founded near the Iberian town of *Numancia*, 8 km further north, which its inhabitants so courageously defended

del mío Cid. Finally, in the tributary valley of the Río Ucero, **El Burgo de Osma,** Iberian in origin and a trade center since the 11th century, has romantic alleys and nooks and crannies in the typical Castilian style. The town also has a **cathedral**, the construction of which began in the 12th century. By the time its cloister and façade were built, the style had changed to Gothic. The cathedral contains an interesting parish museum. There was a university here in the 16th century, the Renaissance building still exists. In more recent times the town has achieved fame for its culinary specialities derived from pork dishes and the specialties produced during the slaughtering. Up to thirty-two variations of different dishes are available in the many restaurants at reasonable prices.

About 17 km further north along the Río Ucero, at the end of the gorge, are the

Above: Roman cloister San Juan de Duero in Soria. Right: The wines from the Duero Valley have a longstanding tradition.

against the conquering Romans and finally destroyed themselves. Archaeological finds from the region, of central importance to Celtiberian culture, can be seen in the **Museo Numantino** in Soria.

After Fernan González had taken Soria from the Arabs, the town underwent a period of resurgence in the 13th century under Alfonso VIII. It became the capital of the Extremadura, as the front region of the Duero was then known. The Romanesque churches of Santo Domingo, San Juan de Rabanera, parts of the cathedral of San Pedro and a convent on the banks of the Duero – San Juan de Duero – of which only the cloister remains, all date from this time.

Today, Soria is not a wealthy but a lively town with its own unique flair. The park of **La Dehesa** is an attractive place to take a stroll, drink a beer in one of the many bars around the *Tubo*, or go to a tavern for a *tortilla española* or grilled lamb chop. Or one might explore the surroundings immortalized in ink by Bécquer in his romantic legends, *The Mount*

of Restless Souls or *The Moonbeam*, in which the soul of the unhappy lover is ever present; and by two great writers of the '27 generation, Gerardo Diego and Antonio Machado.

Machado, born in Seville, was a master in the art of landscape descriptions. As a highschool French teacher in Soria in 1911, when it had 7.000 inhabitants, he fell in love with his landlady's thirteen-year-old daughter, Soledad, who died soon after he married her, aged fourteen. Her memory lives on in his lyrical works. Antonio Machado has captured like no other the atmosphere along the promenade from **San Polo** to **San Saturio**, on the edge of town "where the Duero draws its crossbow". Young lovers still stroll along the banks of the Duero to **San Sorio** and carve hearts, names and dates in the poplars along the way. When they grow too tall, the inscriptions of undying love, which form a chronicle of the towns happy couples, have become illegible.

Soria's **fiesta** to celebrate St. John's Day in June is no longer typically Castil-

161

ian and tends to resemble those of Rioja or Navarra. The five days of ritual center around the figure of the bull. On Thursday, *La Saca*, the bulls are brought from their pastures to the outskirts of town; on Friday, *de Toros*, there are morning and afternoon bullfights; on Saturday, *Agés*, the better parts of the twelve bulls are distributed among the citizens of the twelve *peñas*, or parts of town, while the inedible parts, like ears, tails and hooves are auctioned off to the highest bidder. On Sunday, *Calderas*, the twelve *peñas* display their decorated cooking pots in a carnival procession.

The route from Soria towards the Ebro Valley girds the mysterious conical mountain, the **Moncayo**, which, with an attitude of 2.316 m, is the highest of the Iberian foothills and remains snow-covered almost all year round. A road leads from **Agreda** to an *Ermita*, which is a popular spot for family picnics and out-

Above: The Tarazona Cathedral – characteristic of the Arab Mudéjar architecture.

ings. The mountain itself, which lies at the center of Rioja, Navarra, Zaragoza and Soria, is the leitmotiv of local folklore and of the songs and dances, the *jotas*, originally inspired by the Moors. From Tarazona you can get to the **Monastery of Veruela**, which was built in 1146 by Cistercians based on the model of Poblet. There is also a 13th-century church there, built in a transitional style between Romanesque and Gothic. While recovering from a severe illness, the Romantic poet Bécquer spent a period of convalescence here, during which he wrote a number of legends and his *Letters from my Cell*.

Tarazona itself lies at the foot of the Moncayo and is the commercial center of the area around the Río Queiles. The Moorish architect Aragón has left his mark everywhere in this place. On one side of the river stands the Gothic **cathedral** with a brick *cimborio* and a portal by Juan de Talavera. Inside one should view the chapel of the *Calvillo*, with its altar by Juan Levi, and the Arabian-style Renaissance cloister. The curiously shaped octagonal *bullring*, surrounded by 32 houses, was built in the 18th century after consultation with the locals. Situated on the other side of the river El Cinto, the medieval quarter which grew from a Celtiberian settlement has steep streets spanned by archways, sections of the old boundary wall and the handsome spires of the churches of Magdalena and Concepción. Both are built of brick, are decorated with tiles, and, having single aisles, serve as excellent examples of Aragonese architecture. The town hall is the former 16th-century stock exchange building. Its façade is richly decorated with the shields of Tarazona, Aragín and Charles V, who brought the Fugger bankers here.

Leaving Tarazona behind, you come to the Ebro Valley, from where you can continue on the motorway towards either the Mediterranean or the Basque region.

PROVINCE ZAMORA
(Telephone area code: 988-)
Accommodation
TORO: *BUDGET:* **Hostal Doña Elvira**, C/ Antonio Miguélez 47, Tel: 690062. **ZAMORA**: *LUXURY:* **Parador Condes de Alba y Aliste**, Plaza Viriato 5, Tel: 514497. *MODERATE:* **Hostal Sol**, C/ Benavente 23, Tel: 533152.
Museums / Sightseeing
ZAMORA: **Museo de la Semana Santa**, 10.30 a.m.– 2 p.m., 4–7 p.m. **Cathedral, San Cipriano, La Magdalena, Sta.M. de la Horta, Santo Tomé**, (June–Oct) 10 a.m.–1 p.m., 5–8 p.m., Sun 10 a.m.–1 p.m. **Cathedral Museum**, 11 a.m.–2 p.m., 4–8 p.m.
Tourist Information
ZAMORA: **Oficina de Turismo**, C/Sta. Clara, 20, in summer 8 a.m.–3 p.m.

PROVINCE VALLADOLID
(Telephone area code: 983-)
Accommodation
TORDESILLAS: *MODERATE* **Juan Manuel**, Burgos–Portugal road, km 151, Tel: 770951. VALLADOLID: *MODERATE:* **Hostal de la Torre**, C/ Alcalleres 1, Tel: 350213. **Imperial**, C/ Peso 4, Tel: 330300.
Tourist Information
VALLADOLID: **Oficina de Turismo**, Pl. Zorrilla 3, Tel: 351801.
Museums / Sightseeing
VALLADOLID: **Casa-Museo de Cervantes**, C/ Rastro 7, 10 a.m.–6 p.m., Sun 10 a.m.–2 p.m., closed Mon. **Casa-Museo de Colón** (Columbus), C/ Colón, 11 a.m.–2 p.m., 4–7 p.m., Sun 11 a.m.–1 p.m., closed Mon, public holidays. **Casa-Museo de Zorrilla**, C/ Fray Luis de Granada 2, 10 a.m.–1.30 p.m., 5–9 p.m., Sun 10 a.m.–1.30 p.m. **Museo Oriental**, Paseo de los Filipinos 7. **Museo de Pintura**, C/ Pasión, 10 a.m.–1.30 p.m., 4–7 p.m. **Museo Arqueológico Provincial**, Pl. Fabio Nelli, Mon–Fri 9 a.m.–2 p.m., 4–6.30 p.m. **Museo Nacional de Escultura**, C/ Cadenas de San Gregorio, 10 a.m.–1.30 p.m., 4–7 p.m., closed Sun afternoon, Mon and public holidays. TORDESILLAS: **Monastery Sta. Clara**, 11 a.m.–2 p.m., 4–7 p.m., closed Mon. SIMANCAS: **Castillo**, 9.30 a.m.–12.30 p.m., 4–6 p.m.

PROVINCE PALENCIA
(Telephone area code: 988-)
Accommodation
MONZÓN DE CAMPOS: *LUXURY:* **Castillo de Monzón.**
PALENCIA: *MODERATE:* **Roma**, C/ Alonso

Fernández de Madrid 8, Tel: 745700. **Rey Sancho de Castilla**, Av. Ponce de León, Tel: 725300.
Museums / Sightseeing
PALENCIA: **Cathedral**, 10 a.m.–1 p.m. and 4–6 p.m. **Museum of the Diocese**, weekdays 10.30 a.m.– 1.30 p.m.
VENTA DE BAÑOS: **Iglesia de San Juan Bautista**, Tue–Sun 9 a.m.–1 p.m., 5–7 p.m., closed Mon.; 24.6. Holy Mass with visigothic rites.
Tourist Information
PALENCIA: **Oficina de Turismo**, C/ Mayor 105, Tel: 740068, Mon–Sat 9 a.m.–2 p.m., 4–9 p.m., Sundays and public holidays 10.30 a.m.–2 p.m., 5–8 p.m.

PROVINCES BURGOS AND SEGOVIA
Restaurants
ARANDA DE DUERO: **Rafael Corrales**, C/ Obispo Velasco 2; **Mesón El Roble**, Pl. Primo de Rivera 7.
TURÉGANO: **Casa Holgueras**, Pl. de España.
PEDRAZA: **Bodegón de Manrique; El Yantar de Pedraza; Corral de Joaquina.**
RIAZA: **La Taurina; Casaquemada.**
SEPÚLVEDA: **Casa Paulino**, C/ Calvo Sotelo 2, **Figón de Ismael.**
TORRECABALLEROS: **Mesón de los Caballeros: Posada de Javier, Horno de la Aldegüela. BURGO DE OSMA: Virrey Palafox**, C/ Universidad.

PROVINCE SORIA
(Telephone area code: 975-)
Accommodation
CALATAÑAZOR: *BUDGET:* **Casa Ondategui**, Meson, Tel: 340928.
BURGO DE OSMA: *MODERATE:* **Virrey Palafox**, C/ Universidad 7, Tel: 340222.
SORIA: *MODERATE* **La Posada**, Pl. de San Clemente 6, Tel: 223603.
Tourist Information
Oficina de Turismo, Pl. Ramón y Cajal, Tel: 212052.
Museums / Sightseeing
CALATAÑAZOR: **Church** and **Museum**, 10.30 a.m.–1.30 p.m., 4.30–7.30 p.m.
MONTEJO DE TIERMES / NUMANCIA: **Museum**, Roman excavations, 10 a.m.–2 p.m., 5–9 p.m., spring and autumn 4–7 p.m., Sun 10 a.m.–2 p.m., closed Mon. **San Baudelio de Berlanga**, 10.30 a.m.–2 p.m., 4–7 p.m., Sun 10.30 a.m.–2 p.m., closed Mon and Tue.
SORIA: **Museo Numantino**, Paseo del Espolón 8, 10 a.m.–2 p.m., 5–9 p.m., Sun 10 a.m.–2 p.m., closed Mon.

MADRID

MADRID

THE METROPOLIS
THE NORTH AND SEGOVIA
THE SOUTH AND TOLEDO

This city, with its four million inhabitants, welcomes its many visitors with a mixture of people, traffic, noise and activity which hardly allows time and space to breathe. You can look for the heart of the city for hours and never find it, for the whole city is a great, throbbing center. There are crowds and construction sites everywhere. Madrid seems to be a city in upheaval, a city at the forefront of economic development, decadently full of the declining splendor of the '20s, ahistorical, modern, oblivious of the past and yet at the same time full of history.

Historical Madrid

In the 11th century the Moorish community of *Mayrit* was conquered by Christians. This little village stood on the two hills above the Manzanares River. The Moorish castle, the Alcázar, and the outer walls as far as the Puerta del Sol were extended under Alfonso VI. An attempt by the Moors to reconquer the town foundered on the Campo del Moro, which is today the park behind the royal palace. From the 14th century onwards the *Cortes* met sporadically in Madrid.

Preceding pages: The city as seen by the artist Anatonio López. Left: All the houses in Madrid have balconies.

This was the itinerant Diet and City Parliament. In 1561 Philip II made it into the capital of the whole country, for geopolitical reasons really, as Madrid is situated right in the center of the Iberian Peninsula. At this time the place was an agglomeration of one- storied clay houses with about 25.000 inhabitants. Under Philip II the population grew to 100.000; larger houses were built, and the aristocracy began to erect their palaces near the Alcázar. The court architect, Juan Herrera, built the Escorial and the bridge which led from the castle to the Escorial, the **Puente de Segovia**. When Philip III subsequently transferred the court back to Valladolid, the town of Madrid sought, for purely material reasons, to recover its privileges. The **Plaza Mayor** was built at this time. In what was in fact rather rugged terrain, the narrow streets of the old town were dissolved to form the parade grounds, which were designed according to the "Golden Mean". The parade grounds were officially opened in 1620 with the canonization of the patron saint Isidro. It was given the self-contained shape it has today by the architect of the Prado, Villanueva, in 1790, after the parade grounds had been destroyed by fire for the third time.

Under Philip IV the town, which had long been bursting at the seams, was en-

larged for a third time. Its new boundary ran where the large peripheral roads run today, and can be identified from the two Baroque gates, the **Puerta de Alcalá** and the **Puerta de Toledo**. The 17th century was the Golden Age for artists and writers. Cervantes, Lope de Vega, Quevedo, Velázquez, Ribera and Murillo all pursued their creative life in the vicinity of the court. The town grew unchecked; the dirt, overcrowding and hygienic conditions must have been indescribable. The court issued a declaration stating that in every house, where more than one family lived, half the living space should be given up to government officials. As a result the *malicia* houses were created. These looked from the front as if they had only one storey, whereas in fact there were a number of small apartments at the back. The reign of King Charles II saw the building of the Buen Retiro folly, the Palacio de Sta. Cruz, to house the lawcourt and prison, today the Foreign Ministry; and the palace of the Duque de Uceda, now housing the offices of the army administration.

The Bourbons did not like the austere style of Habsburg architecture or the military-looking Alcázar. Philip V was therefore not in the least perturbed when it burnt to the ground in 1734. Many treasures were actually retrieved; among them the *Meninas* painted by Velázquez. The 18th century brought the *Illustración*, the Enlightenment, and the heyday of Madrid. Today Charles III is still remembered as having been the best mayor the city has ever known. He established a land register, had s sewage system and street lighting installed, and ordered that *serenos* should keep watch over the various districts of the town. Until only a few decades ago it was still possible to hear people come home and clap in order to hail the *sereno*, who would come out of a side-street and open the front door. Art and literature were encouraged with the establishment of royal academies.

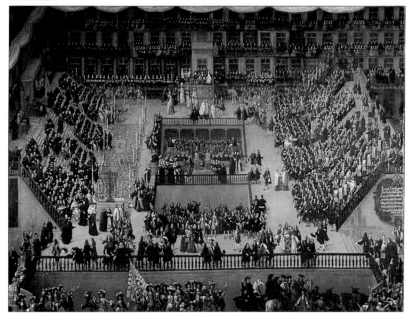

The royal carpet-weaving factory and china factory set about competing with the French importers. The sciences were promoted by the sponsorship of the botanical gardens – where you may still pick up curative herbs once a week – and by the establishment of the observatory and the science museum. The court architect was Ventura Rodríguez, and, after his death, Juan del Villanueva. The era was brought to an end by the French invasion. On May 2, 1808, the city put up a fierce, but unsuccessful resistance. This day has since been declared a holiday for Madrid. Goya cast the gruesome executions of that night on canvas. Napoleon's brother, Joseph, was King of Spain for six years. He was popularly known as *Pepe Botellas*, since he was very partial to wine. In the name of the French Revolution he began to expropriate and pull down monasteries. As a result a series of

squares was created in the environs of the royal palace; the church in which Velázquez was buried also fell victim to demolition. Cemeteries and slaughterhouses were removed to the outskirts of the town. Under Isabel II secularization was continued: 60 monasteries were pulled down, ecclesiastical and military buildings were converted into housing. Altogether 500 buildings came down setting freeing up 20.000 square meters of land. The town had 280.000 inhabitants, and the walls built by Philip IV proved to be too narrow. In 1857 Carlos Maria de Castro drew up a plan for the extension of the town, the *Ensanche*, according to which there would be strict segregation of the classes. The university was transferred from Alcalá to Madrid.

About a million people lived in Madrid at the beginning of the Civil War. The city defended itself to the bitter end from takeover by the nationalists and many buildings were destroyed in the battle. After the war Madrid experienced a huge increase in immigration. Industrial areas

Above: An autodafé on the Plaza Mayor in 1680 (Francisco Rizi). Right: Present day Plaza Mayor with Philip III's monument.

grew up freely and sordid housing compounds sprang up overnight. From the 1960s onwards these buildings were gradually demolished and replaced by more pleasant highrises.

The Castellana

The **Paseo de la Castellana** is the large road forming the north-south axis of the town. At the northern end is the business district, known as the Azca, and the area where Franco established his ministeries, the *Nuevos Ministerios*. As long ago as the 18th century the section between Colón and Atocha was, however, enlarged from a meadow into an avenue, the **Sálon del Prado**. Also dating from this period are: the grand lawns, the magnificent fountains dedicated to Cybele, Neptune and Apollo, the Prado Museum, planned as a science museum and the botanical gardens. The **Plaza de Colón** was enlarged by having its houses pulled down and a modern cultural center built instead. The next stretch is called the **Paseo de Recoletos**, where the most expensive cafés in Madrid are to be found. Many of the old aristocratic palaces, which lined the Paseo, disappeared as a result of speculation. In the 20th century the **Plaza de la Cibele** became the hub of the city's traffic. The Patisserie-style post office, the military headquarters, the Banco de España and the Linares Palace stand at its four corners. A little further on, at **Lealtad Square,** are the stock exchange and the war memorial. The **Glorieta Emperador Carlos V** forms the end of the Paseo with the Reina Sofía cultural center, in what was the San Carlos Hospital, the Ministry of Agriculture and both the new and old Atocha trainstations. The **Royal Carpet Factory** is in a street behind the station. Here carpets and Gobelin tapestries are made, as in Goya's days.

A Tour of the City

The **Puerta del Sol**, the square at the Gate of the Sun, behind the city's second wall, is the heart of the city. The uniform architecture of the houses dates from last century. The provincial administration building was formerly the post office, and later became the headquarters of Franco's security police. Opposite stands the sculpture of Madrid's coat-of-arms, a bear nibbling the strawberry plant which have long since ceased to grow in the mountains. If you look east you can see the **C/Alcalá**, the most magnificent of the old Madrid streets, dominated by huge bank buildings, on which brass billboards display the day's rate of exchange.

Our route takes us south to the **Pl. Pontejos** with its haberdashers' shops. Finally, on the **Pl. Sta. Cruz**, is the Ministry of Foreign Affairs, in the building which used to house the state prison. From there the route passes through an archway onto the **Plaza Mayor**.

The buildings there today are those which were rebuilt after the fire of 1790. The **Casa de la Panadería**, where bread was once distributed, bears the royal coat-of-arms on the balcony, from which the king would watch the spectacles in the square below. Some of the symmetrically constructed entrances have only false arches. You can see here how a Renaissance square was incorporated into an already existing street. The monument in the middle bears the name of the founder of the square, Philip III. There used to be room for 50.000 people to watch the autodafés, bullfighting, jousting or theater. Today musical and folkloric events are performed here. The Christmas market, and on Sundays the stamp-collectors' market take place here too. On the south side you can look down the **C/Toledo**, which is one of the oldest artisan streets in the whole city. Cloth manufacturers and ropemakers all set up businesses here. On the left hand side stands the **Church of San Isidro**, which functioned as the city cathedral until the new building was completed. A long flight of steps leads from the exit at the southwestern corner. This indicates the difference in levels which had to be overcome when the square was constructed. Some of the buildings backing onto the **Cava de San Miguel** have as many as ten stories, which is unusual for 17th-century buildings. The damp cellars are used for storing wine, which is one of the main reasons for their popularity today as *bodegas*, *mensones*, and restaurants.

If you go along the cutlers' street, **C/Cuchilleros**, you reach the **Puerta Cerrada** where there used to be another gate in the second city wall. In the **C/ de la Pasa**, not far from the **C/Panacillo,** the poor used to be given bread on their way out of church. They could get raisins at the monastery round the corner. On the squares **Conde de Barajas** and **Conde de Miranda** are several noble palaces from the Habsburg period. If you go along the **C/ del Codo** (Elbow Street), you get to the Town Hall Square, the **Plaza de la Villa**. The town hall was built in 1644 and is like a Herrera, but in Baroque style. Its interior resembles that of a palace. The house next door, the **Casa de Cisneros**, is the home of the present mayor. On the other side, the square is surrounded by aristocratic palaces and the **Torre de Lujanes**.

We leave the square along the **C/Cordón**. The **C/del Rollo**, the pillory, derives its name from the court of the Inquisition, which met on the **Plaza del Cruz Verde**. From here you have a view of the viaduct, which links the hills of Moorish Madrid.

On the other side of the **C/Segovia** is the old Moorish quarter, the Aljama. The **Plaza de la Paja** was long a grain market and it has indeed retained its onpaved form of yore. Beyond this square are the Wagon (*carros*) and Barley (*cebada*) Squares, which lead into the **Rastro** district and to the Madrid flea market, which, in keeping with old traditions, fills this whole quarter of the city every Sunday. If you cross the **Costanilla San**

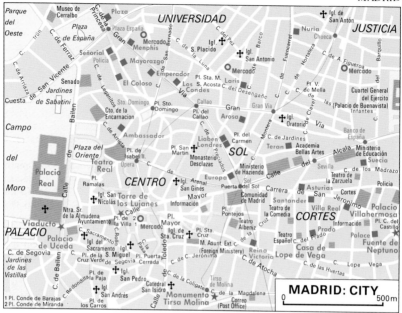

Andrés here you arrive at the **C/Bailén** and the **Viaducto**, which you have already seen from below. Here you find the **Jardines de las Vistillas** with their shady outdoor cafés and distant views. To the south lies **San Francisco el Grande**, the most beautiful Baroque church in Madrid, with paintings by Goya, in which the *Cortes* are shown meeting under Bonaparte. To the north rises the rear of the **Almudena Cathedral** which was built in 1883, and for which an old church had to be demolished. Beside it lies the **Palacio Real**, a grandious building with over 2.000 rooms. You can visit the throne room, the porcelain collection, the royal apothecary and the chapel. Until Alfonso XIII left the country in 1931, the Spanish kings lived here. Since Franco's time, however, these rooms are only used for show. The stables of the magnificent mounted guards were situated in the huge basements. Under the forecourt are the royal archives. The **Sabatini Garden** and the **Campo del Moro** park below spread out in the other direction.

The semi-circular **Plaza de Oriente**, where the royal theater stands, is in front of the palace's main entrance. The statue of Philip IV on a horse was made by four artists: the model for the king's bust was made by Velázquez; Galilei did the calculations necessary to ensure that the full weight of the statue could be borne by the hind legs of the horse; Montanes made the sculpture; and Piero Tacca cast the whole statue in bronze. The **Pl. de Ramales**, on which the old church stood where Velázquez was buried, and the **Pl. Santiago** are two of the squares constructed by Bonaparte. By going along the C/Conde Lemos and the C/Espejo you come back to the royal theater, the **Opera**, and from there onto the C/de Arrieta to the royal convent, **Real Monasterio de la Encarnación**, which was founded by Philip III's wife, Margaret of Austria. The C/Encarnación ends at the **Senate**, the provincial parliament, which on account of its newly-acquired functions, recently underwent an extension. If you go along the C/del Reloj and the

C/del Río, you come out onto the **Plaza de España**, the large square established in the 1950s with two sky-scrapers, the Edificio de España and the Torre de Madrid, and the Cervantes Memorial in an olive grove. The **C/ de la Princesa** leads out of the square in a northwesterly direction, past the Palace of the Duke of Alba and onto the university campus. Parallel to it is the Parque del Oeste (the western park), with the Egyptian **Temple of Debod**, which Spain received as a gift in return for its help during the flooding of the Aswan region. The most important street in Madrid, the **Gran Vía**, runs eastward. At the turn of the century it sliced through the back-streets of the old city. In the 1920s it was the smartest address in Madrid. The local population used to wander along it on Saturday evenings, awestruck by the bright lights and big cinemas; later on the street went through a decadent period which is now only gradually being checked by the renovation of the buildings. But the queues in front of the cinemas remain.

At **Callao** square the pedestrian streets, lined by large department stores, fork. Right next to the square is where the Carmelites still have their convent, **Las Descalzes Reales**, with its large garden in the midst of the milling crowds. It was a palace which Carlos V's wife picked up for the birth of their youngest daughter, Juana de Austria, who later endowed the convent which she entered as a widow. The **C/Arenal** brings us back to our point of departure, Puerta del Sol.

Museums in Madrid

Many travelers to Spain come to Madrid just to see the **Prado**. Nowhere are the works of the great Spanish painters (El Greco, Murillo, Velázquez and Goya) and of their Italian peers (Titian, Tin-

toretto) exhibited together in a greater number. Besides these artists, who mainly worked at the Madrid court, there is also a considerable number of paintings by Dürer, Rembrandt, Bosch and Rubens. One day is hardly enough to appreciate all the treasures. The famous picture of the horror of the war, *Guernica*, which Picasso painted for the world exhibition in Paris in 1937, is kept in a building a little further away, but affiliated to the Prado, the **Cason del Buen Retiro**. Opposite the Prado is the Palacio de Villahermosa, currently being built for the Thyssen collection. Along with this Collection, and besides the fine specimens of the old masters, works by little known Central European artists from the beginning of the 20th century are exhibited.

Madrid also has other museums besides the great art complex of the Prado: the **Archaeological Museum** with valuable finds from all over the world; the **Science Museum**, which also gives you something to do with the children on a rainy day; and finally the **Centro Reina Sofía**, which has a huge exhibition area, and houses the gallery of modern art. Malicious critics maintain that Madrid has tried to ape Paris, and that is how the word *Sofidú* (a play on Paris' Centre Pompidou) got into the language. The **National Gallery of the Decorative Arts** shows everything in ceramics, furniture and fabric that has made the Spanish style what it has been for centuries. In the **Ethnological Museum** there is a collection from Spain's former colonies. As well as its extensive art collections, the **Real Academia de Bellas Artes de San Fernando** has recently put the copper plates from which Goya's etchings were taken on display. The exhibition is in Goya's study; he himself was the gallery's director for many years. The art on show in the **Sorolla Gallery** is quite different. It is a collection of Sorolla's Impressionist paintings.

Right: Tourists in front of the Velázquez entrance to the Prado Museum.

Other than the large, famous galleries there are also a number of pretty, small ones in which you can be almost the only visitor. The two private collections of **Galdiano** and the politician **Cerralbo** show impressive collections of art treasures and portraits in the palaces of each of the founders. You can also stroll through the **Museo Romantico** as if it were just a well-furnished house. In the **Museo Municipal**, in what was formerly the hospital, there is a chapel, newly renovated by Pedro Rivera. The model of the city made in the last century is especially interesting. The **Railway Museum**, in the old Delicia Station; the **Naval Museum**, with models of ships and old maps from the time of Columbus; and the **Museo Taurino** in the Las Ventas bullfighting arena are other alternatives.

Madrid still has a little way to go before it can be considered the cultural capital of Europe, though. For example, there are no buildings at all for folkloric, architectural, and theatrical museums, although there are some splendid collections. Entrance into other museums, such as the Pharmaceutical Museum, is by special arrangement only. In order to get into the exhibition at the Banco de España you must first write a letter to the person in charge of the bank's social events. Several museums have long been closed for renovation, so that it is impossible for the time being to count on visiting the **Museo de America**, the **Goya Pantheon**, with the painting of San Antonio on the cupola, or the **House of Lope de Vega**.

Going Out in the City

You may not always feel like visiting a museum. There are cool parks outside the city center, which may be reached on foot. To the east is the **Retiro**, with its romantic crystal palace, exhibition pavilions, the artificial lake in front of the statue of Alfonso XII, many fountains and inviting outdoor cafés. To the west, behind the Royal Palace, lie the Royal Gardens, and to the north the **Parque del**

Oeste, which extends down to the university campus. You can get a cable car out of this park over the valley of the Río Manzanares to the huge Royal Game Park, the **Casa del Campo**. Even if you only go for a cup of coffee, the trip is worth it, just for the view of the palace. You glide over the Northern Station into a green oasis and you can see the leisure park, the lake with people boating on it, the garden cafés and the **Zoo**.

During hot nights, when it is difficult to sleep, it is pleasant to stroll through the streets of the old quarter of the city. All the doors and windows are open and you can savor the feeling of beeing a voyeur as you walk along, witnessing family scenes, television programs and the smell of the food being cooked that night.

To the southwest of the Plaza Mayor lies the oldest district of the city, the **Habsburg Quarter**. Further south, on

either side of the C/Toledo is the **Latin Quarter** and on the other side of the Pl. Tirso de Molina is the old Jewish Quarter, **Lavapiés**, with its hallmark houses, the *corralas*. The **Barrio Maravillas** is another old artisan quarter to the north of the Gran Vía.

A visit to the church of San Sebastian in the C/Atocha provides a taste of the artists' quarter, the **Barrio de las Musas**, as it was in the 16th and 17th centuries. The church is a neo-Baroque reconstruction from the period after the Civil War, but the artisans and artists who built it were clearly not influenced by tradition in their work, as you can see from the paintings of paint-brushes, hammers and compasses on the altars. Plaques in the architects' chapel remind one of the famous people who have been members of the community: Cervantes, Valle de Inclán and the architects Juan Villanueva and Ventura Rodrigue, to name a few of the most famous. A special altar with lighted candles reminds the visitor too, that the immortal Lope de Vega is buried here. No

Above: Many shops and pubs still have traditional facades. Right: In a Madrid café.

one knows exactly where. The old cemetery on C/Huertas has been replaced by a flower shop. Artists did not enjoy high social status in the 17th century, and actors were not even allowed to be buried in consecrated ground. These people are only remembered through their works and a few modest memorial plaques. One of these may be found, for example, at the **Quevedo House**, on the corner of C/Quevedo and C/Lope de Vega. The house used to belong to the Andalusian poet Góngora, who does not appear on the memorial plaque due the narrow-mindedness prevalent in Madrid. There is also a plaque on the corner of C/Lope de Vega and C/Léon on the house where Cervantes used to live. His mortal remains lie in the **Convent of the Trinitarians** in the C/ Lope de Vega. If you ask politely, you may visit the church there. Once past the plain façade the noise of the traffic gives way to an ambiance from the late Middle Ages. Beside the altar hangs a memorial plaque to Cervantes, his wife and Lope de Vega's daughter.

Madrid by Night

The *movida* was the scene, a place, where beer still cost less than a dollar and a tumbler of whisky under two, where the bars never seemed to close and the people streamed onto the streets with their beers in the heat of the summer. This was at the time when Tierno Galván was mayor. He was the philosophy professor who had come out of exile and let street culture come to life again, who always spoke in Latin when someone struck him as stupid, and issued decrees ironically through "his Highness the Municipal Magistrate", and never missed a local festival. Customs were revived; *majos* (young men) and *majas* (young women) danced to the music of the barrel- organ playing the Melonera or Palomera. All this made Madrid stand out as a good tip for investment among other European cities whose atmosphere had become stale in the 1980s. Meanwhile the prices here rose to a European level, people began to complain, the initial euphoria which had

177

greeted the end of the long and oppressive years of the Franco regime having subsided. And yet every other house seems to be a bar, and at weekends the city is still full of people at times of the day when well-behaved and law-abiding Central Europeans are already in bed. The people of Madrid simply have to go for a *paseo*, an evening walk, go to the cinema, or drop in at a café or bar. It is impossible to count the bars, and it would not be fair to recommend individually any of the endess little stand-up places, *cervecerías*, *sidrerías*, *güiskerías*, cafeterías or simple bars; there are the Manilas, Nebraskas and Düsseldorfs run by emigrants who left to work abroad in the 1950s and 1960s and who have returned home. The same goes for the many Galician, Basque, Extremaduran, Andalusian and Castilian restaurants, who proudly present their regional cuisine and preserve the memory of their

village. The same provincial regulars of these restaurants will meet up again in their Galician village, just to check that it is still the best place in the world.

Live Music is offered by many bars; in La Fidula you can hear classical, and in La Taberna Encantada folk music. Jazz lovers especially seem to have a good time in Madrid. But you can also get to see a genuine *Flamenco*. The famous Café de Chinitas or the Arco de Cuchilleros are far from cheap, however, and their main acts do not start until midnight. Over the last ten years disco-fever has brought a vast number of expensive discos into existence. There are discos with swimming pools or converted theaters, like the Pacha, for example, where you can dance about in the aisles.

Until the **Royal Opera House** – its 3.000 seats making it the largest theater in the city – has actually been rebuilt, the little **Zarzuela Theater** will continue being used for operatic performances. Its design is exactly the same as that of the Scala in Milan. The **Comedy Theater**

Above: The Lope de Vega comedies are still popular today.

178

and the guest theater, the **Albéniz**, always have a good selection of shows. The **María Buerro**, a small theater where quality performances are offered, is always good for a surprise. And then there are the avantgarde studio theaters like the **Alfil**, the **Pradillo**, the **Sala Olimpia** or the **Ensayo 100** which are always causing a stir. Street theaters enjoy great popularity with the people who visit the city from the provinces weekends; a show by Lina Morgan has been filling the house for over a year now. But the **Summer Festival** in Madrid is unique; it is meant for all those who can stand heat of over 40 °C. Every night the Summer cinema shows films in the park; in the *corralas* of Lavapiés, light musicals, *zarzuelas*, are being performed on the balconies; classical concerts take place in the Retiro and the young people of Madrid gather in the bullfighting arena for rock concerts. At night this place becomes a seething mass of gyrating bodies.

We only have space here to mention a few of the best places to visit on an evening pub-crawl. You just have to let the atmosphere pull you through the streets, like the Spaniards, who prefer to stroll into several pubs, rather than one, for a quick glass of something and a bite to eat before setting off again. Young people tend to go to pubs in the streets around the Dos de Mayo Square, near the Plaza Mayor and Cava Baja. Snacks can be bought in the area around the Pl. Olavide. Atmospheric and slightly more elegant bars and pubs are located in the backstreets between the C/Mayor and the Opera Square.

Madrid's Real World

Madrid is situated in the middle of Spain. The six large national roads converge on the city in a star shape and bring thousands of trucks full of goods and hundreds of thousands of commuters into the center from the suburbs. The traffic already swamps the city, in spite of the massive ring-roads and arterial roads built in and around Madrid. The number of cars is still on the increase and the suburbs are served by a scanty and inefficient railway network. More and more people are moving to the constantly expanding satellite towns around the city. Madrid itself has a population of 3 million; another 200.000 live in the wealthier suburbs to the north of the city, but the large satellite towns in the south and southeast are home to yet another million inhabitants. For them the journey to work can often take an hour and a half each way; there is a shortage of educational and social facilities, and unemployment among the young population stands at 50%. The problems which result, such as delinquency, drug-abuse, illiteracy and vandalism are always making the news. At the same time all the international banks, large insurance companies and multinational companies want to open offices there. In the Azca business district and all along the motorway to the airport, modern office blocks are shooting up like mushrooms; it is more expensive to buy or rent a house in Madrid than in Paris or Munich; 40% of foreign investments floods into Madrid, which houses 10% of the Spanish population, while producing 15% of the gross national product. As a result of the rising prices, however, there is also a continuous rise in the numbers of unemployed, homeless, beggars and people living on housing estates on the outskirts of the city. The barely controllable growth of the city extends into the sparsely populated surrounding areas and divides the country sharply in two: in the south and east there are all the industries and huge housing estates, while in the north and west you find the wide open green spaces and residential district, which seamlessly merges into the neighborhood where people have their second homes and there are golf-courses at the foot of the mountains.

MADRID

(Telephone area code: 91-)

Accommodation

LUXURY: **Gran Hotel Reina Victoria**, Pl. del Angel 7, Tel: 5314500. **Hotel Tryp Ambassador**, Cuesta de Sto. Domingo 5, Tel: 5416700. **Ritz**, Pl. de la Lealtad 5, Tel: 5212857.

MODERATE: **Ramón de la Cruz**, C/ Don Ramón de la Cruz 94, Tel: 4017200. **Nuria**, C/ Fuencarral 52, Tel: 5319208. **Tryp Asturias**, C/ Sevilla 2, Tel: 4296676. **Londres**, C/ Galdo 2, Tel: 5314105. **Los Condes**, C/ Libreros 7, Tel: 5215455. **Embajada**, C/ Sta. Engracia 5, Tel: 4473300. **Laris**, C/ Barco 3. *BUDGET:* **Teran**, C/ Aduana 19, Tel: 5226424. **Europa**, C/ Carmen 4, Tel: 5212900. **Santander**, C/ Echegaray 1, Tel: 4296644.

Tourist Information / Post

Oficina de Turismo, Pl. Mayor 3, Mon–Fri 10 a.m.–2 p.m., 4–8 p.m., Sat 10 a.m.–2 p.m., closed Sundays and public holidays, Tel: 2665477. At the **Airport Barajas** and the **Chamartin Rail Terminal**, weekdays 8 a.m.–8 p.m., Sat 8 a.m.–1 p.m., **Plaza de España** in the Torre de Madrid, Tel: 5412325, weekdays 9 a.m.–7 p.m., Sat 9.30 a.m.–1.30 p.m., **Duque de Medinaceli 2**, Tel: 4294951, weekdays 9 a.m.–7 p.m., Sat 9 a.m.–1 p.m. **POST**: Pl. de Cibeles. **Telefonica - Locutorio**: Gran Vía 30 u. Paseo de Recoletos, 41 (9 a.m.–midnight).

Transportation

Metro–Underground: Your ticket is valid for travel on all underground routes; a *diez viajes*, – a multiple-ride ticket (10 rides on one ticket) – is a real money saver: buying ten separate tickets would cost you about double the price! All metro stations offer 3- or 5-day tickets (Metrotour) too.

Bus: Buy your ticket for a single ride in the bus; the *Estancos* (tobacco shops) sell *Bonobus* multiple- ride tickets (10 bus rides on one ticket at a reduced price); the network of buses is a closed book to outsiders, route-maps and timetables being virtually non-existent.

Rail Terminals: Estacion del Norte for short-distance trains to the north and east; Atocha, for long-distance trains to the south and west; Chamartín, for long-distance trains to the north, east and southeast; the rail terminals Charmartín and Atocha connect with an underground train. RENFE-information, Tel: 4290202.

Taxi: The fastest way to get a taxi in town is to wave one down in the street. Watch out for a sticker on the inside of the rear window, listing (in Spanish and English) the various supplementary charges which may be added to the fare displayed on the taxometer.

A motorway runs straight to the **Airport Barajas**. Taxis are allowed an extra charge for the ride to and from the airport. The **Airport Bus** runs from/to the basement garage on Pl. Colón, every 15 minutes, 200 Pts. Airport information, Tel: 4112545, Iberia National, Tel: 4111011, international, Tel: 4112011, Iberia flight confirmation, Tel: 4111895. **Town Buses**: Estación Sur de Autobusses: C/ Canarias 17, Tel: 4684200.

Teleferico: (Cable railway to the Casa del Campo) Paseo del Pintor Rosales on level C/ Marques de Urquijo; runs during daylight hours only, daily in summer, weekends only in winter.

Car Hire / Automobile Club

Hertz, Gran Vía 88, Tel: 2485803. **Avis**, Gran Via 60, Tel: 2472048. **American Express**, Pl. de las Cortes 2, Tel: 4295775. **Rentalauto**, C/ García de Paredes 57, Tel: 4413602. **Unión Rent a Car**, General Margallo 29, Tel: 2796317. **Real Automobil Club de España**, C/ José Abascal, 10; Tel: 4473200/4779200.

Museums

Circulo de Bellas Artes de San Fernando, C/ Alcalá, Mon–Fri 7 a.m.–7 p.m., Sat–Mon 9 a.m.–3 p.m. **Museo del Prado**, Paseo del Prado, and Cason del **Buen Retiro**, C/ Alfonso XII 28, 9 a.m.–7 p.m., Sun and public holidays 9 a.m.–2 p.m., closed Mon. **Museo Nacional de Artes Decorativas**, C/ Montalbán 12, Tue–Fri 9 a.m.–3.30 p.m., Sat, Sun 10 a.m.–2 p.m., closed Mon. **Museo Naval**, C/ Montalbán 2, 10.30 a.m.–1.30 p.m., closed Mon. **Museo de la Real Academia de Bellas Artes de San Fernando**, C/ Alcalá 13, Tue–Fri 9 a.m.–7 p.m., Sat–Mon 9 a.m.–3 p.m. **Museo Nacional de Ciencias Naturales**, C/ José Gutiérrez Abascal 2; Tue–Sat 10 a.m.–6 p.m., Sundays and public holidays 10 a.m.–2.30 p.m., closed Mon. **Museo Nacional de Etnología**, C/ Alfonso XII 68, 10 a.m.–6 p.m., Sun 10 a.m.–2 p.m., closed Mon and public holidays. **Museo Nacional Ferroviario**, Paseo Delicias 61, 10 a.m.–5.30 p.m., Sundays and public holidays 10 a.m.–2 p.m., closed Mon. **Museo Romántico**, C/ San Mateo 13, 9 a.m.–3 p.m., Sundays and public holidays 9 a.m.–2 p.m., closed Mon. **Museo Sorolla**, Paseo General Martínez Campos 37, 10 a.m.–3 p.m., closed Mon. **Museo Taurino** (Museum of Bullfighting), Plaza Monumental de las Ventas, Tue–Fri 9.30 a.m.–1.30 p.m., Sun 10 a.m.–1 p.m. **Museo Thyssen-Bornemisza**, Paseo del Prado 8 (from autumn 1991). **Museo Arqueológico**, C/ Serrano 13, Tue–Sat 9.30 a.m.–8.30 p.m., Sundays and public holidays 9.30 a.m.–2.30 p.m., closed Mon. **Casa de Lope de Vega**, C/Cervantes 11. **Centro de Arte Reina Sofía**, C/ Sta. Isabel 52, 10 a.m.–9 p.m., closed

Tue. **Museo Cerralbo,** C/ Ventura Rodríguez 17, 10 a.m.–3 p.m., closed Mon. **Museo Lazaro Galdiano,** C/ Serrano 122, 10 a.m.–2 p.m., closed Mon. **Museo Municipal,** C/ Fuencarral 78, 10 a.m.–2 p.m., 4.45–8.45 p.m., Sun 10 a.m.–1.45 p.m., closed Mon.

Sightseeing

The **Palacio Real** is open from 9.30 a.m.–5.15 p.m., Sundays and public holidays 9 a.m.–2.15 p.m. (closed during state visits). **Monasterio de las Descalzas Reales,** Plaza de las Descalzas 3, weekdays 10.30 a.m.–12.30 p.m., 4–5.30 p.m., Sundays and public holidays 11 a.m.–1.30 p.m., closed Mon. **Real Monasterio de la Encarnación,** Plaza de la Encarnación 1, 10.30 a.m.–1 p.m., 4–6 p.m., Sun 10.30 a.m.–1 p.m., closed Mon, Fri. **San Ginés,** side chapel, 10 a.m.–1 p.m. **Panteon de Goya,** Paseo Florida. **Panteon de Hombres Ilustres,** C/ Gayarre 3, weekdays 9 a.m.–2 p.m. **San Francisco el Grande,** C/ San Buenaventura 1, Tue–Sat 11 a.m.–1 p.m., 4–7 p.m., in summer 5–8 p.m. **Botanical Gardens,** 10 a.m.–8 p.m. **Templo de Debod,** 10 a.m.–1 p.m., 4–7 p.m. **Museo Colon de Cera,** Museum of Waxworks, Paseo Recoletos 41, daily 10.30 a.m.–2 p.m., 4–9 p.m. **Real Fabrica de Tapices,** C/ Fuenterrabía 2, weekdays 9.30 a.m.–12.30 p.m. **Parque Zoologico,** Casa de Campo, open all day, Metro: Batán. **Sala de Exposiciones del Canal Isabel II,** C/ de Sta. Engracia 125, temporary exhibitions with varying opening hours.

Restaurants

CASTILIAN: **La Bola,** C/ La Bola 5; **Casa Lucio,** Cava Baja 35; **Casa Paco,** Puerta Cerrada 11; **La Cacharrería,** C/ Morería 9; **Mi Pueblo,** Costanilla de Santiago 2; **Posada de la Villa,** Cava Baja 9; Aroca, Pl. de los Carros 3; **Botin,** C/ Cuchilleros 7; **La Fuencisla,** San Mateo 4; **L'Hardy,** Carrera de San Jeronimo 8; **Carmencita,** C/ Libertad 16; **Taberna de Antonio Sanchez,** Mesón de Paredes 13; **Le Chataubriand,** C/ Peligros 1; **Hilogui,** C/ Ventura de la Vega.
FISH: **El Boñar,** C/ Cruz Verde 16; **Aymar,** C/ Fuencarral 138; **Korynto,** C/ Preciados 36; **Tres Encinas,** C/ Preciados 33; **El Pescador,** Jose Ortega y Gasset 75; **Casa Rafa,** Narváes 68; **Bajamar,** Gran Vía 78.
VEGETARIAN: **Casa Marta,** C/ Sta. Clara 10; **Restaurante Vegetariano,** C/ Marqués de Santa Ana 34; **La Biotika,** C/ Amor de Diós 3; **El Granero de Lavapiés,** C/ Argumosa 10.
NORTH COAST DISHES: **Peña Arriba,** Francisco Gervás 15; **Moaña,** C/ Hileras 4; **Casa Gallega,** C/ Bordadores 11; **La Quintana,** C/ Bordadores 7.

BASQUE: **Jai-Alai,** C/ Valverde 2; **Irizar Jatetxea,** C/ Jovellanos 3; **Pagasarri,** C/ Barco 7; **Guria,** C/ Huertas 12; **Balzac,** C/ Moreto 7.
ANDALUSIAN: **Los Borrachos de Velazquez,** Principe de Vergara 205; **Berrio,** Costanilla de los Capuchinos/Ecke San Marcos; **Don Paco,** Caballero de Gracia 36; **Jose,** Castelló 61.

Madrid Specialities

The typical dish of Madrid, the *cocido,* is only served at lunchtime. This tasty casserole, prepared with a multitude of ingredients, gets its unique flavor from stewing for hours over a charcoal fire. Don't make the mistake to wolf it down in one go: according to local custom, the stew's sauce is served as an appetizer, followed by the vegetables and chick-peas as a first course, and the meat as second course.

Festivals / Public Holidays

The public holiday on May 2 celebrates the resistance against the Napoleonic Army. Second week in May: *San Isidro.* Second week in August: *San Lorenzo, San Cayetano* and *La Paloma.* October 12 – *Virgen del Pilar,* military parade to the Dos-de-Mayo-Monument on the Paseo de Prado. November 9: public holiday in Madrid in honor of the *Virgen de la Almudena.*

Bullfighting

Every Sunday from March to October, usually at 5 p.m., in the bullring of Las Ventas; in May during the Festival of San Isidro every day for ca. 24 days; advance booking C/ Victoria 9.
At the Casa del Campo (Metro-Station Batán) the bulls are paraded during the morning preceeding the fight; at 12 noon lots are drawn to decide which *torero* is going to fight against which bull.

Shopping

Department Stores and clothing stores in the city cluster around Gran Vía and Puerta del Sol; look for shoes, handbags and furs at bargain prices on the C/ Fuencarral; department stores and more elegant fashion shops around the metro-station Goya. **Boutiques:** On the C/ Almirante and vicinity, also on C/ Conde de Xiquena, around C/ Ayala; creations of well-known fashion houses on C/ Serrano; genuine Spanish *capa:* Seseña, C/ Cruz, 23. Discover **old-fashioned, traditional middle-class shops** in the city center on the streets C/ del Pez, Corredera Baja, Alta de San Pablo and Santi Espiritus; or in Lavapiés on the streets Mesón de Paredes, Valencia, Lavapiés. **Antiques:** C/ del Prado around the Plaza de las Cortes; in the Rastro-Quarter around the Square Grl. Vara del Rey and in the two courtyards on the right and left hand side half way up the Ribera de Curtidores; market at the Puerta de Toledo.

VICINITY OF MADRID

0   40km

NORTH OF MADRID AND SEGOVIA

The **Guadarrama Mountains** to the north of Madrid are also favorite places for outings. Numerous reservoirs, woods and rivers have created cool high valleys. In spite of the floods of visitors from Madrid desperate for some fresh air, there are still quiet spots to be found, especially if you can make your visit on a week-day. Also on the northwest edge of the city stands the **Puerta de Hierro** isolated between motorways; this is the entrance gate to the huge hunting grounds of the royal hunting castle, **El Pardo**. The route today leads past expensive leisure clubs, race tracksand golf courses, bypasses the royal residence, the **Palacio de la Zarzuela**, and finally brings you to the palace itself, where important guests reside when they visit. The well- attended park, with firs and oak woods, suggests

Right: The courtyard of the kings in San Lorenzo del Escorial.

the importance of the local dwellers. The hunting palace, built by Charles V, has undergone many alterations. In the reign of Charles III, Sabatini carried out a symmetrical extension, which doubled the size of the building; Philip V had a church added on. The kings increasingly enjoyed coming here from Madrid. The consumptive Alfonso XII lived in El Pardo for a long time and even died here. General Franco also decided to live here with his family. They had a private living area as well as using the historical rooms as official reception rooms. You will notice the great difference between the simple rooms in the Habsburg part and the rather grandiose rooms of the Bourbons. Some of Goya's most beautiful wall tapestries hang here; countless clocks, which the Bourbon kings, Charles III and IV used to collect, adorn the walls. Goya's paintings of Charles IV and his wife, Maria Luisa, are early versions of those exhibited in the Prado. Although it is possible to visit it – when no official guests are staying – the building is by no means a museum. Nowadays the room where Gorbachev or Queen Elizabeth might once have watched television, is shown to the public just as the covered courtyard, in which great banquets are held for 200 guests.

El Pardo village, which is full of tourist establishments and military and police barracks, conceals another little castle, **Casita del Principe**, a pleasure seat with ceiling frescoes by Bayeu and paintings by Lucca Giordano. Before you reach the village, a little way off the road, there is another hunting manor, the **Quinta**.

Further north the magnificent fort of **Manzanares el Real** shimmers far off on the bank of La Santillana reservoir; it dates from the 15th century. The fortress is fully equipped with crenels, battlements and galleries, and has been well-renovated; the three towers and the barbican are in good repair. There is a museum with models of fortresses and old documents. Just outside the grounds, to the west, a road forks off into the valley of **La Pedriza** in the regional park along the upper course of the Manzanares. Another, unmarked road takes you on a 20 kilometer tour of the park, and brings you right back to the entrance again. The road involves a steep climb in places, but the view of the valley below makes it rewarding. Some very strange rock formations with great blocks of weathered granite create the effect of a moonscape.

El Escorial

"The **El Escorial** castle stands for all to see at thirty miles to the northwest of Madrid against the dark background of the Sierra Guadarrama. It is a huge imposing mass of stone, cold and magnificent, dark and hostile." That is how the chapter in Lion Feuchtwanger's novel *Goya* opens, in which the painter is introduced to the court for the first time. At this point he is living in the Escorial, which he is required by court etiquette to do for 63 days of the year. The monumental building reflects all the solemnity and grandeur of its owner, Philip I. The monastery was dedicated to Saint Lawrence as compensation for another church to this saint, which was destroyed in a battle. It is shaped like a grill, the instrument upon which he suffered his martyrdom. Philip II wanted to have a residence for his old age made for himself so as to satisfy his father's command that he should have a proper place of burial. And so the building serves the purpose of a monastery, palace and mausoleum all at the same time. It is set out symmetrically around the largest of the 16 inner courtyards, the king's courtyard. To the right and left lie the monastery buildings which are partly used as a boarding school today; straight ahead lies the entrance into the huge basilica. Bronze sculptures of Philip II and Charles V and their families look with

awe at the altar piece. In one chapel you can see the breath-taking figure of Christ made by Cellini. The monks only opened it to the public a few years ago, after they had wrapped a piece of silk around that part of the body which shows that Christ, too, was a human being.

Directly beneath the main altar is the solemn and majestic mausoleum for the Spanish kings, in which all the Spanish monarchs from Charles V onwards and all their wives who gave birth to kings are buried. Two marble coffins are still empty and you can appreciate the light shudder experienced by Charles IV, according to Feuchtwanger, when he stood here and saw where he would one day lie himself. In extensive underground rooms the other members of the royal families were buried in stately fashion. On the grave of Don Juan de Austria, the illegitimate son of Charles V, there is an extremely beautiful sculpture, while for the many children who were stillborn, there is a strange monument looking like a wedding cake.

To the right and left next to the church are the private rooms of Philip II and his daughter, in simple Castilian style, with tiles and terracotta floors, and sober pictures on the walls. From his bedroom the king, who suffered from gout, had access to and a view of the chancel. The rooms of the Bourbon kings on the floors above are quite different; they are decorated with everything one associates with wealth. The tapestries on the walls are modeled on those by Rubens and Goya.

The **Escorial Library** is situated on the passage into the part of the monastery closed to visitors. It is by far the most beautiful room in the building, and contains priceless treasures. Several of the most valuable books are often put on display, such as the *Codex Aureus*, for example, which has gold-plate letters. The rest of the books are kept in book-cases, with their spines to the wall, which is unusual, and yet a rather good idea: the gold-plate on the edge of the pages reflects the light so that the books are not so badly damaged by the sun.

The Escorial was designed by Juan de Herrera and was built in less than 20 years. For this building Herrera used that Renaissance style which was then named after him. Its simplicity distinguishes it from the versions built under Isabel.

Villanueva also built a **Casita del Principe** in the park for the young Charles IV. It was decorated by Ribera, Caravaggio, Lucca Giordano, Dürer and Goya, among others. Also in the park is the little **Casita de Arriba**, built for Charles IV's younger brother.

Valle de los Caídos

It is not totally coincidental that an entire valley not too far from the Escorial was dedicated to the memory of those who died in the Civil War, and specifi-

cally to its victors. José Antonio de Rivera, founder of the Falange and the son of the dictator of the 1920s, shot by the Popular Front in 1936, lies under a simple stone slab as does Francisco Franco Bahamonde, who ruled the country single-handedly for almost 40 years. Both died on the 20 November. Since then every year on the anniversary of the deaths of both dictators, their supporters gather on the enormous parade-ground in front of the monument.

A church is built into a 150-m high hill, surmounted by a concrete cross that also stands 150 m high. At the foot of the cross are gigantic stone figures depicting the Evangelists. A wide stairway leads to the basilica, which is cut into the mountainside like a huge tunnel. 260 meters long. Its walls are hung with 16th century tapestries depicting the Apocalypse, and there are oversize statues of the Virgin Mary and reliefs, portraying her as protectress of all the various parts of the army. At the end of the church is a round chancel containing two gravestones and a Byzantine-style cupola on which the dead soldiers are depicted with their flags as they strive up towards God at the center. The earthly reality of this "striving" is to be found in the form of umpteen thousand dead bodies in the side-chapels.

The whole building was planned at the end of the Civil War. The quarrying was carried out by Republican prisoners and was completed in 1959. The attractive thing about the church is its position among wooded mountains and overlooking the valley as far as Madrid.

SEGOVIA

A skiing region, where the snow sometimes remains well into the spring, has developed further up in the mountains in the area around the passes of the Guadarrama range, called Fuenfría, Guadarrama and Navacerrada, which are between 1500 and 1860 meters high. The scenery

Right: The "skyline" of Segovia with the "Queen of Cathedrals".

and views from here are wonderful, and it is cool even in midsummer. It is a steep climb, though. If you want to go to Segovia without stopping off, it is much quicker to take the highway through the mountain.

On the hill above where the Clamores runs into the Río Eresma stands the majestic Alcázar of **Segovia**, which is the town's landmark, as well as being the prototype castle for Walt Disney films. The town is accessible from the other side, from Azoguejo Square, which is crossed by the 700-m long Roman **Aqueduct**, Segovia's second most famous piece of architecture. With its 119 arches, built on two levels in some places, it is one of the most impressive Roman constructions to have been preserved in Spain. It dates from the 2nd century when the Spanish-born Trajan was Roman Emperor, and it provided the town with water from the mountains to the south.

The actual lay-out of the old town, somewhat like a cul-de-sac, provides visitors with a natural touring program up

the pedestrian Cervantes and Juan Bravo Streets, past the squares and cathedral right up to the **Alcázar**, and back along the small streets running parallel to it. All along the route are restaurants with solid local flavor, the most famous of which, El Candido and El Duque, have virtually become institutions. They offer local specialities, like baked sucking-pig (*cochinillo*) or lamb (*cordero*). The uncooked meat and the pure white, milk-fed sucking-pig are displayed in the window. It is as though the restaurant wants to show the freshness of its fare. In the better establishments, when the number of guests eating the *cochinillo* allows for a whole animal to be used, the chefs themselves appear to carve the meat, and in order to demonstrate how tender the meat is, they use the edge of a plate as a carving-knife!

The route takes you past numerous nobles' palaces, which all indicate how significant Segovia was in the Middle Ages. The most peculiar of these is most certainly the **Casa de los Picos**, with its

principal nave. This also serves as a roof for market-stalls. There is also a rectangular tower which, for reasons of statics, has fake arches painted onto the lower rows of windows. Alongside the church is the ex-prison – today a library – in which Lope de Vega was imprisoned for his provocative writings.

The old synagogue, which retains its Moorish style and is situated in the Santa Clara Convent, is today named **Corpus Christi**, after a 15th-century legend. It was at the end of that century that the Jews were driven out of Spain, and the story reflects the age-old religious hostility. A sexton needed some money badly, and was lent some by a Jew on the condition that he bring him a consecrated wafer. When the Jews assembled in the synagogue to burn the wafer, it miraculously floated away. The Jew who was purified as a result of this, cried out, "Jesus Christ, come down to us and you will come to no harm." The wafer obeyed did so. When the Christians heard about this miracle, it was declared that the town's 14 parishes in turn should be responsible for making good the insult to the holy sacrament every 14th year. To this day each of Segovia's parish churches celebrates *Catorcena*.

On the Plaza Mayor are the town hall, the Juan Bravo Theater and the church in which Isabel I was crowned Queen of Castile in 1474. Behind this is the **Lady of the Spanish Cathedrals**, so- called because it was the last of Spain's many Gothic cathedrals. Charles V had it built after everything but the cloister and the iron gates of the old cathedral succumbed to the *comuneros* uprising. It is, in fact, a magnificent example of late-Gothic style, with impressively high naves, powerful latticework, a big Baroque organ, large choirstalls and a beautiful cloister. Among other exhibits at the cathedral museum are tapestries, a reliquary made by Cellini and paintings by Van Eyck, Berruguete and Alonso Cano.

sharply protruding stones. The Palaces of **Quintana** and of the **Marqueses de Moya** also have lovely entrances. Particularly noticeable are the towers on one row of palaces, which look as though they are meant to demonstrate power rather than to serve any particular defensive purpose. The most distinctive examples of these are the towers belonging to the noble families Lozoya, Arias Dávila, Don Alvaro de Luna, Diego de Rueda, Juan de Cascales and the Hercules Tower.

The first of these towers on the **Square of the Sirens** form the background to the Monument to Juan Bravo, the Segovian hero of the *comuneros* uprisings against Charles V. On the other side of the square stands the **Church of San Miguel**. It is one of the town's many Romanesque churches which are all beautiful and well-preserved. Most of them are built in the same style with an arcade added onto the

Right: Autumnal mood in the La Granja Park (Philip V's seat of pleasure).

The little streets beside the cathedral near the Socorro Square mark out what was once the Jewish quarter, and beyond them is the *La Claustra* district which used to be closed up at night by gates. It belonged to the parish and granted asylum to anyone staying there. Finally at the end of the street you come to an exposed crag on which there were fortifications from the Celtic period onwards. Since Alfonso VI liberated the town in the 11th century, the **Alcázar Real** has been located here; it was later chosen by the royal house of Trastamara as its official residence and was extended considerably. After a fire in the 19th century it was rebuilt in its original form and looks today just like a fairytale castle with its arms' exhibition, armaments, throne room and towers, which visitors may climb.

The journey back along the C/Velarde takes you past the erstwhile headquarters of the Inquisition, past the house in which Antonio Machado lived for many years and also past the most beautiful of the town's Romanesque churches, **San Esteban**, as well as the Hercules Tower, and finally past the museum of the province. Tucked away, in the corner by the town's wall stands the Church of San Juan de Caballeros, which forms the grand setting for the gallery devoted to the painter Zuloaga. Besides the many palaces, churches and squares making the old town something of an open-air museum, there are several places worth visiting in the lower part of the town. The Gothic **Parral cloister**, and the 12-cornered church of the Templars, **Vera Cruz**, from which the best photographs of the Alcázar may be taken, are the most important of these.

La Granja de San Ildefonso

After his victory in the War of Succession, Philip V had a French-style summer residence built for himself on the grounds where his hunting manor had previously stood. San Ildefonso or **La Granja** – after the farm which formerly stood here

The Poor Mountainous Regions

To the east of the Guadarrama, due north of Madrid following the N1 road, lies the **Sierra Pobre**, the "Cinderella" of the region around Madrid.

Many of the villages here are completely cut off and do not feature in tourist guides. They are too far away from the capital for commuting to be possible and in winter it is too cold for the people here to survive without electricity and a good infrastructure. The area is mostly higher than 1.000 meters and is to be recommended for weekend outings. Slowly leisure facilities are being built up to satisfy the requirements of holiday-makers. The Río Jarama and its reservoirs provide refreshing swims and the many woods and meadows, lined with brambles, sloes and whitethorn, are perfect for walks. The **Hayedo of Montejo**, the southernmost beechforest in Europe, is well worth a visit. It is to the north of the road running from Montejo to **Hiruela**, which had only 30 inhabitants in the 1980s, but which since then has been discovered by people seeking an alternative lifestyle. It even has a bar again, the cornerstone of any Spanish community.

A pleasant five-hour walk takes you from **Horajuelo de la Sierra** through Horcajo and Madarcos along roads which were once used solely by cattle drovers. From here the road leads along the river to the Pradena del Rincón and back to the point of departure. The paths are neither well marked nor well maintained.

The small holiday resort of **Buitrago del Lozoya** has a population of 1200, making it the largest village in the area which is situated between the main road and the reservoirs. It has an old, walled, semi-derelict town center and one of the region's most interesting museums. **Picasso's barber** bequeathed the village his art collection and now several rooms in the town hall are filled with gifts from the great artist to his hairdresser!

and belonged to the Parral cloister – has several well-preserved rooms with beautiful ceiling-frescoes and numerous Gobelin tapestries, Empire furniture and a great variety of ornamentation using motifs from Japan or from Greek mythology.

Philip V and his wife are buried in the cathedral, as he considered the place to be more suitable than the Habsburg family vault in the Escorial. What makes a visit here on a summer day really pleasant are the complex water-works and the many fountains in the extensive park with its magnificent gardens and countless sculptures. After Philip V's death a large hunting castle was built for his wife, Isabel. This is situated to the south of Segovia in **Riofrío** in the middle of an evergreen oakwood, which has been a wildlife park ever since and where stags and roes roam freely. The palace is now a hunting museum.

Above: In the mountain villages, very often only the old people remain.

PROVINCE MADRID (North)

(Telephone area code: 91-)

Accommodation

SAN LORENZO DE EL ESCORIAL: *LUXURY:* **Victoria Palace**, C/ Juan de Toledo 4, Tel: 8901511. *MODERATE:* **Jardín**, C/ Leandro Rubio 2, Tel: 8961007. *BUDGET:* **El Escorial**, C/ Arias Montano 12, Tel: 8901462.

NAVACERRADA: *MODERATE:* **La Barranca**, Valle de la Barranca, Tel: 8560000.

RASCAFRÍA: *LUXURY:* **Santa María del Paular**, at the monastery, Tel: 8691011. *MODERATE:* **Los Calizos**, Crtra. Rascafría-Miraflores, at km 22,8; Tel: 8691112.

ROBLEDO DE CHAVELA: *MODERATE:* **Las Golondrinas**, Tel: 8995252.

MANZANARES EL REAL: *BUDGET:* **Hostal El Tranco**, C/ Tranco 4, Tel: 8530063.

BUITRAGO DE LOZOYA: *BUDGET:* **Hostal Jubel**, José Antonio 39, Tel: 8680067.

SIERRA DE GUADARRAMA: Holiday- and weekend-cottages for rent in the villages Horcajuelo, La Hiruela, Montejo, Puebla and Prádena: Tel: 8697058.

Museums / Sightseeing

El Pardo, weekdays 10 a.m.–12.15p.m., 3–5.30 p.m., Sundays and public holidays 10 a.m.–1.40 p.m. **La Quinta**, Sat 10 a.m.–12.45 p.m., 3–6 p.m., Sundays and public holidays 10 a.m.–2.10 p.m. **Casita del Principe**, weekdays 10 a.m.–12.40 p.m., 3–5.55 p.m., Sundays and public holidays 10 a.m.–2.05 p.m.

Monasterio de San Lorenzo de el Escorial, 10 a.m.–1 p.m., 3.30–5.30 p.m. **Santa Cruz del Valle de los Caídos**, 10 a.m.–6 p.m., in summer 10 a.m.–7 p.m., closed Mon.

MANZANARES EL REAL: **Castle**, 10 a.m.–1.30 p.m., 5–8 p.m.

BUITRAGO DE LOZOYA: **Museo Picasso**, 11 a.m.–1.30 p.m., 4–6 p.m., in summer 5–7 p.m., Sat 10 a.m.–2 p.m., 4–7 p.m., in summer 5–8 p.m., Sun 10 a.m.–2 p.m.

Restaurants

EL ESCORIAL: **La Cueva**, C/ San Antón 4; **Fonda Genara**, Pl. de San Lorenzo 2; **Parrilla Príncipe**, C/ Floridablanca 6. **NAVACERRADA**: **La Fonda Real**, Highway N-601. **RASCAFRÍA**: **Don Lope**; **Mesón Trastamara**; **Los Calizos**.

PROVINCE SEGOVIA

(Telephone area code: 911-)

Accommodation

SEGOVIA: *LUXURY:* **Parador Nacional de Segovia**, on the highway in the direction of Valladolid ca. 2 km outside of town, Tel: 430462.

Los Arcos, Paseo Ezequiel González 24, Tel: 437462. *MODERATE:* **Los Linajes**, Doctor Velasco 9, Tel: 431201. **PEDRAZA**: *LUXURY:* **Posada de Don Mariano**, C/ Mayor 14, Tel: 509886. **SAN ILDEFONSO**: *MODERATE:* **Roma**, C/ Guardas 2, Tel: 470752.

Restaurants

SEGOVIA: **Mesón de Cándido**, Pl. de Azoguejo 5; **Duque**, C/ Cervantes 12; **La Cocina de Sant Millán**, C/ Sant Millán 5; Tel: 436226 (with garden); **Tasca La Posada**, Judería Vieja 5; **TURÉGANO**: **Casa Holgueras**, Pl. de España 11, Tel: 500028; open weekends only outside the tourist season.

PEDRAZA: **Hostería Pintor Zuloaga**, Tel: 504088, (four-star); **El Jardín**, C/ La Calzada 6; **El Yantar de Pedraza**, Plaza Mayor.

Museums / Sightseeing

SEGOVIA: **Alcázar Reál**, 10 a.m.–7 p.m., in winter until 6 p.m. **Museo Catedralicio**, C/ Marqués del Arco 1, weekdays 10 a.m.–7 p.m., Sat, Sun and public holidays 9.30 a.m.–6 p.m., in winter 9.30 a.m.–1 p.m., 3–6 p.m. **Museo Provincial de Bellas Artes**, San Agustín 8, 10 a.m.–2 p.m., 4–6 p.m., Sun 10 a.m.–2 p.m., closed Mo and public holidays. **Museo Antonio Machado**, C/ Desamaparados 4, 4–7 p.m., in winter 4–6 p.m., closed Mon. **Museo Zuloaga**, Jardines de Zuloaga, **San Ildefonso**, La Granja, 10 a.m.–1.30 p.m., 3–5 p.m., Sundays and public holidays 10 a.m.–2 p.m., closed Mon. **Palacio y Museo de la Caza Bosque de Riofrío**, 10 a.m.–1.30 p.m., 3–5 p.m., Sundays and public holidays 10 a.m.–2 p.m., closed Tue.

Post / Information / Transportation

SEGOVIA: **Oficina de Turismo**: Plaza Mayor 10, Tel: 430328, 10 a.m.–2 p.m., 4.30–7 p.m. **Post**: Correos y Telégrafos, Pl. Doctor Laguna 1. **Rail**: RENFE Obispo Quesada 1. **Bus**: Plaza de Estacionamiento de Autobuses, Tel: 427725.

Festivals

SEGOVIA: Passion week is celebrated ceremoniously, followed by a procession on Good Friday; June 24–29: *San Juan* and *San Pedro* – town festival; on February 5 the Festival *Santa Agueda* with its ancient, traditional ceremonies takes place in the village of Zamarramala a few kilometers north of Segovia.

LA GRANJA: Fiesta on August 25 with extraordinary display of waterworks in the castle park.

Excursions on horseback

Rutas a Caballo – Collado Hermoso, Molino del Río Viejo (old mill) – on Highway 110 from Segovia to Soria, km 172, Tel: 401159; bookings can also be made from Madrid: C/ Juan Bravo, 21, Tel: 2767629.

SOUTH OF MADRID AND TOLEDO

Toledo is the crossroads for all cultures from Europe to Africa. Its Roman relics include the ruins of a circus and the statue of the patron saint Santa Leocadia, a martyr during Diocletian times. During the 6th century, Toledo was the capital of the empire under the Visigoths. It was the seat of many councils and its archbishop was from then on up to 1979 the primate of all Spain. The Virgin Mary is said to have appeared to one of the bishops, San Ildefonso, and presented him with the mass vestments. Its disorderly network of streets and cramped alleyways, barely spacious enough to give access to the windowless houses, are the inheritance of the Moors who ruled here for 300 years. The Jewish quarter, which can be traced back to Roman times, was all but destroyed in the pogroms. A few street names and palaces serve as a reminder of their Jewish past but the houses themselves were built much later. After the *Reconquista* in 1086 for a period of 200 years, Toledo flourished under three coexisting cultures. An analogy of the situation can be found in Judah Ha-Levi's Jewish legend in which a king had a precious ring which was to be inherited by the favorite of his three daughters. However, not wishing to arouse any jealousy, he had exact replicas made to be given to the other two daughters. Each was content in the firm belief that she had the original. What a wise man!

In the 13th century, Alfonso X founded an institute for translation which made Toledo the cultural center of the age. Aristotle's ideas were first propounded from here throughout Europe at a time when only 60.000 people inhabited the town center. Toledo remained the capital of Spain until Philip II made Madrid the capital in 1561. In the 18th century Charles III had a weapons factory built to try to reverse the process of depopulation and to revive the town. He was supported

in his efforts by Cardinal Lorenzana who undertook renovations and founded a university that still functions to this day. The **Alcázar** represents the spirit of the 20th century. Arabian in origin, it was destroyed many times and is seen today in the style of Charles V. In 1936, emulating the heros of Numancia, the nationalist followers of General Moscardó; barricaded themselves in for seventy-two days. Today, having been rebuilt in its original form after the Civil War, it is a museum documenting the art of survival during the fascist resistance.

The 16th century **Hospital de Afuera**, originally an orphanage built by Cardinal Tavera, lies just outside the town limits. The cardinal's own magnificent tomb is

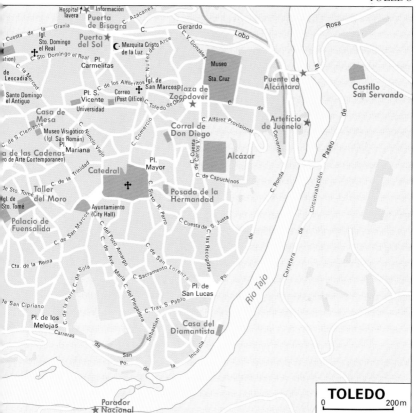

in the church, while the museum houses pictures, goblets and Ribera's painting of a strange, bearded women. The **Puerta de Bisagra** (1550), bearing the double-headed eagle, the emblem of Charles V, forms the gateway to the town. A little to the right stands the old portal of Bisagra, built by Arabs in the 9th century, through which El Cid and Alfonso VI rode in 1085. This is the entrance to the **El Arabal** quarter with the Church of Santiago founded by Alfonso VI. A statue of S. Vincente Ferrer is a reminder of the pogrom in 1405 which he initiated.

Further up stands the **Puerta del Sol**, the gate of the sun, which shows two women bearing the head of the man who raped them on a tray, and the presentation

by the Virgin of the Holy Robes to San Ildefonso. The best view of the gate is from the gardens of the miniature mosque of **Christo de la Luz**. It was built in the 9th century on the site of a Visigoth church of which a number of capitals remain. When Alfonso VI rode victorious into the town, it is said that his horse halted and knelt down on this spot: a white paving stone marks the place. A statue of Christ was retrieved from its hiding place in the church after 300 years of Arabic rule, with a candle still burning before it.

The Arabian horsemarket, the **Zocodover**, is the main square and focus of urban life in Toledo, with its street cafés, banks, shops and confectioners where

you can buy the excellent Toledo marzipan. Through the **Arco de la Sangre** you reach the Plateresque **Hospital de Santa Cruz** (16th century), now a museum. The two stories of the inner quadrangle are linked by a stairway created by Covarrubias. The building is as impressive as its exhibits: ancient paintings, 19 paintings by El Greco and Goya, works by Ribera, numerous sculptures, goblets, fabrics and documents.

The **cathedral**, work on which started in 1226, occupies the town center. The shortest route from Zocodover to the **Pozo Amargo** is through the **Puerto del Reloj**, the oldest of the cathedral's portals. In earlier times abandoned children were brought here and placed in the care of the church. Tradition demands that the stone on the altar, upon which the Virgin Mary appeared to present the robes to San Ildefonso, be kissed before leaving

Above: El Greco's Toledo; his son is showing the map. Right: Present-day Toledo – the cathedral and Alcázar in the distance.

by the **Puerta Llana**. The latter was added in the 19th century to create a ground level exit for the monstrance carried by the procession on Corpus Christi Day, a 16-century work of art created by Juan de Arfe, which is 2.5 m high and weighs 200 kgs. It is made up of 5.000 pieces of silver and the first gold brought back by Columbus from America.

The cathedral's main façade is of 15th century Gothic origin; however, the upper part was renovated in the 18th century. Also dating from this period is the painting of the *Last Supper* above the king's entrance. The latter consists of three portals: the **Puerta del Perdón**, which is used only by heads of state or religious dignitaries. Popular belief has it, that whoever passes through it is absolved for ever of all sin. To the left, like all evil, is the Gate of Hell, the **Puerta del Infierno** and, to the right, the **Portal of the Last Judgment** used by the notaries of Toledo when they went to take the oath of office. On either side are high towers. The left, at 96 m, is widely visible

with its three crowns of thorns, while the right one was never completed and was eventually covered by a dome by Jorge Manuel Theotokopoulos, son of El Greco. He also built the town hall building which is in keeping with the architectural style of the cathedral opposite. To one side, underneath the passage linking the archbishop's palace and the cathedral, is the commoners' entrance, the **Puerto del Mollete** (bread roll), where beggars used to go to receive bread.

In the 14th century, Archbishop Tenorio planned for the cloister to be built on a bothersome Jewish market. Its upper stories constitute the *Claverías*, or apartments of the cathedral's vergers. They provided the backdrop for a novel by Blasco Ibañez about an anarchist who, fleeing from the authorities, seeks refuge with a relative living here, thus abusing the sanctity of the church. For a long time, the work was banned in Spain.

The sheer expanse of the interior is itself very impressive. The caps of cardinals interred here hang from the ceiling.

It is said that when one falls down the soul of the deceased leaves purgatory. The church's valuables, which include the monstrance and a number of other precious effects, are kept in the tower. Masses following 10th century rites are still held under the unfinished tower in a Mozarabian chapel. This chapel was built by *Moriscos* and displays the coat-of-arms of the Cisneros. The interior walls are covered with scenes depicting the battle of Oran.

The center of the cathedral is dominated by the altar area and the chancel. The screen, or *trascoro*, was designed by Berruguete for the benefit of the general population who would stand behind it and would only participate acoustically to the service. Access to the choir stalls is through a gate by Domingo de Céspedes (1548) whose bill, it is said, the church refused to honor. Artistic pride drove him to complete the work at his own expense and, financially ruined, he ended up selling religious miniatures at the Puerto del Mollete. The chancel offers the greatest variety of styles. The upper choir stalls with carvings by Berreguete and Felipe de Borgoña date from the Renaissance. The lower choir stalls are by Maistro Alemán. All in all it is a masterful representation of the wars of Granada, each seat depicting the *Reconquista* of a different town. The *misericordias*, small supports beneath the folding chairs for the meary derrières of the choir, show entertaining, though not always decorous scenes.

The retable in Flamboyant style behind the Plateresque lattice of the main altar was created by 27 artists under the direction of Cisneros. On the outer side is the tomb of Cardinal Mendoza, father confessor of Isabel the Catholic, and statues of Alfonso VIII and of Alfaquí, the Moor, who helped Alfonso VI out of a politically difficult situation. The back of the altar is lit up by a lantern by Narciso Tomé, the so-called *El Transparente*.

Portraits of every archbishop of Toledo hang on the wall of the chancel with the decorative artesonado ceiling. El Greco, Goya and Velazquez are supposed to have painted their respective contemporaries. The sacristy is a museum dominated by El Greco's *Expolico.* Its walls are covered from floor to ceiling with paintings by Luca Giordano, Titian, Raffael, van Dyck, Goya and Caravaggio.

Behind the cathedral is the **Barrio Pozo Amargo**, or bitter well. This genuinely Toledan quarter owes its name to a pair of unhappy lovers who committed suicide in the well, thereby spoiling its waters. Beyond this quarter and through the Calle de la Ciudad one arrives at the Jewish quarter, worth a visit for its rich concentration of monuments. The **Taller del Moro** used to be an Arabian palace which served the Christians as a stonemason's workshop for the cathedral. El Greco's showpiece, the

Funeral of the Conde Orgaz, is exhibited in the church of **Santo Tomé**. The neighboring **Palacio de Fuensalida** has become the seat of the regional government and the guards outside prevent one from even looking into its courtyard. Its stables are, however, accessible and house a very recommendable café. The **House of El Greco**, the town's most famous personality, displays some of the artist's works. This palace orginally belonged to a Jewish doctor, Jehuda Ha-Levy, later passing into the ownership of a Christian magician who dreamed of defying the passage of time by having himself shrunk and preserved in a test tube for posterity. The building was restored in the last century as a model example of 16th- century architecture. If ever El Greco did live there then it was only for a short period during 1565.

Two of the synagogues have been rebuilt: the 14th-century **Sinagoga de Tránsito** with its museum of the *Sefardís* and the **Santa María la Blanca** (12th century), which still bears the hallmarks of its unusual and colorful past as a barracks, granary and Christian church. The latter dates from the time when Raquel, known as the Jewess of Toledo and mistress of Alfonso VIII, lived here. The affair and the existing tensions between Jews, Christians and Arabs have been unmortalized in works by Lope de Vega, Franz Grillparzer, Racine and Leon Feuchtwanger.

San Juan de los Reyes was built by Juan Guas and Covarrubias in 1475 to celebrate the victory of the Catholic Queen over the *Beltraneja* in Toro, a victory that earned the queen the Castillian crown. The church was intended as a burial place for the Catholic Monarchs, however, they later elected Granada, the site of their common victory. The chains worn by Christian prisoners prior to their liberation at Granada hang outside on the church walls. Having been destroyed by Napolean's troops, little now remains of

Right: This souvenir kiosk pays abundant tribute to El Greco.

the church's former splendor. However, the heraldic shields of the Catholic kings and their initials, symbolized by the yoke (*yugo*) and arrows (*flechas*), which represent both unity and steadfastness, adorn the building, along with the motto of the edifice itself: *Tanta monta, monta tanto*, this one is worth as much as the next. The cloister, spared by the French, has two stories. The first floor is lavishly decorated with plant motifs, monkeys, monsters and pomegranates. For the Christians of the time, the fruit was symbolic of the town of the Alhambra and, according to whether it was occupied or not at any given time, the fruit would be shown open or shut. The symbols of the monarchy are repeated in the artesonado ceiling of the upper story. Noteworthy, too, are the rather entertaining gargoyles.

The road back to the Zocodover through the Jewish quarter and over the hill of the *Virgen de Gracia* leads over untrodden paths. One should allow oneself the pleasure of following the alleyways at random, of climbing the steep paths and take a breather to look down and admire the views. A museum of modern art has been established in the **Casa de las Cadenas**, in the **Calle de las Bulas**. The very tranquility of its streets helps explain how the town came to cast its spell on the numerous artists who came here.

It is in the Convent of **Santo Domingo el Antiguo**, the oldest in Toledo, that El Greco lies at rest. The church for which he himself completed a number of paintings, was built by Juan de Herrera. Also in this area are the foundations of the house of Garcilaso de la Vega, the first Renaissance poet in the Italian style. He depicted the river populated by nymphs embroidering the town's silhouette on a spider's web, using dew drops. Here too lie the origins of the picaresque, those classic mischievous tales with their ironic depictions of the adventures of the Spanish cavaliers, the *caballeros*. Mystics made the town into a metaphysical fortress and the best of them all, the diminutive poet San Juan, was forced to flee from the Inquisition by lowering himself in a basket from the window of a convent of the barefooted Carmelite nuns down to the River Tajo. The journey now leads from Sto. Domingo el Antiguo on to **Sto. Domingo el Real**. The convent was founded by the daughter and mistress of Pedro I of Castile. If you are fortunate enough to arrive during a church service, you can enter through a portal flanked with the Doric columns to bathe in the overwhelmingly beautiful, decorative art work of Churriguera.

The square at the front is dedicated to Bécquer. Writers of Baroque drama and 19th century Romantics have often made use of the town as an atmospheric backdrop in their works. The history of Toledo, handed down through the centuries, is rendered by Zorrilla and Bécquer in works of verse or ornate prose. There is, for example, the story of a woman who, before the magistrates, called upon the *Cristo de la Vega* as witness to her husband's infidelity. The crucified Christ was said to have raised his arms and to have given testimony in her favor. Or the many variations on the theme of the Jewess who loved a Christian and whose father preferred to decapitate her, than to see her betray her religion. The streets and squares along our way are the very scenes of such tales. In a secess in the street of the little needle (*Alfileritos*), you will find a small statue of the Virgin Mary. A seamstress, having been miraculously cured of her illness, brought her a sewing needle each day in thanks. One day, a nobleman, having observed this ritual for some time, approached her on the subject. Thus the good woman was also rewarded with a good spouse.

The Church of **San Román**, formerly a mosque, houses a museum devoted to Toledo's Visigoth history. Beside it are the Plateresque buildings of the convent

Right: A pittoresque detail – a putto head in a Mudéjar wall.

of **San Clemente** and, opposite, the **Casa de Mesa** with its splendid ornaments. The way to the cathedral leads by the Jesuit **Church of San Juan**. During the period of secularization, the monastery was converted for use by the Ministry of Finance. Walking through the alleys one arrives at the **Hombre de Palo**, the man of wood where Charles V's Italian architect Giovanni Turiano, popularly known as Juanelo, lived. Legend has it, that he built a wooden automaton to go out and get him bread and wine.

The road of the *circunvalación* is a 10 km marked stretch which bypasses the town on the other side of the Tajo meander. Below the **Puerta del Cambrión** and the **San Martín bridge** are the baths of **Florinda Lacava** where, according to legend, Don Rodrigo, the last of the Gothic kings, saw a young girl bathing and took her against her will. Her father avenged the deed by ordering the Arab invasion into the Visigoth realm. In truth, the edifice is probably the remains of the old Arabian bridge. But there is another story behind the new 16th century bridge: on the night before its inauguration, the Moorish engineer noticed that some of his calculations regarding statics had been wrong. Thereupon his wife secretly set fire to the bridge in order to safeguard her husband's reputation. A little later she gave herself up and confessed to Cardinal Tenorio who had financed the bridge. He rewarded her love with an official pardon.

Beyond the bridge the road winds its way through the *cigarrales*. No one knows whether these old country houses, that do the entire hill and belong to Toledo's bourgeoisie, owe their name to the cigars smoked by passing clergy or to the deafening noise made by the innumerable crickets of the region. Further along the road is the *parador*. Its terraces offer panoramic views over the town.

Opposite the chapel **Ermita del Valle**, on the banks of the river, stands the house

of *diamantista*, the Jewish jewel merchant. His daughter is said to have loved a Christian and to have drowned herself in the river. The **bridge of Alcántara**, originally a Roman aqueduct, reinforced in the 15th century, is on the other side of the town. Maintaining a water supply for locals has always been a problem. In the 16th century, Juanelo developed a complex system of bringing water up from the Tajo to the Alcázar, but the construction did not hold for long. Its remains can be seen near the bridge, next to the Arabian town gate, **Los Doce Cantos**.

Life in a Museum

The town's undisputed beauty seems to have done little to nurture the esthetic sensibilities of its representatives. Many of its sights are either closed to the public or have inconvenient opening times. This means that tours are often over-attended and conducted by local guides whose overriding concern is their commission, and whose comments seem generally restricted to historic dates, artists' names, styles and the category "artistically significant", which has a rather negative effect on the enjoyment of the town's treasures.

The local people have an ambivalent attitude to their town. Many of them make their living from tourism or are employed in the workshops which produce ceramics or gold ware, yet have little contact with foreigners. They live mainly in the modern quarters, in the *vega* of the River Tajo. Those 16.000, about a quarter of the population, who inhabit the eight thousand or so houses of the old center, have to put up with the roads overflown with traffic and pedestrians. Because of historic preservation laws, the remains of an ancient Arabian bath in the cellar may make renovations impossible, while the presence of an old Mudéjar beam in the sitting room may prohibit expansion.

Many buildings now stand empty and delapidated. Those which can be saved are often turned into apartments. The council has developed the prototype of a

Toledan house which has become mono-tonously predominant amongst the new buildings in the Old Town. Judging from the interior design, the houses could as well be in Barcelona as in Toledo. In some cases old remains, exposed by demolition work are integrated into the new façade, so that a Gothic fresco here or a Romanesque statuette or Arabian or-namentation there suddenly appear among the pseudo-Mudéjar brickwork. Only in the older houses are inner court-yards with fountains surrounded by flower pots still to be found.

Aranjuez, Chinchón, Nuevo Baztán

On the left bank of the Tajo in the fer-tile river meadows of **Aranjuez**, stands the third royal summer residence after La Granja and the Escorial, which has been here since the time of the Catholic

Above: On the Eve of the Feast of Corpus Christi, the streets of Toledo become ban-quet halls with canopies.

Monarchs. Work on the palace was started under Philip II by Juan B. de Toledo, continued by Juan de Herrera and completed under the Bourbon King Charles III. The palace is open to the pub-lic. The town as seen today was planned by Fernando VI who kept a big flotilla of pleasure steamers on the Tajo and was re-sponsible for enlarging the gardens, adding numerous fountains and statues. The palace was rebuilt after several fires in the 18th century and was stormed in 1808 during a popular uprising. It was during this uprising that Godoy was deposed, an event that is still locally com-memorated in annual celebrations. The palace is surrounded by three parks: the **Paterre**, established by Philip V, the **Jar-dín del Príncipe**, created by Charles IV around the hunting lodge, the **Casita del Labrador**, and the **Jardín de la Isla,** on an island on the Tajo, which was a pleasure garden already in the time of the Catholic monarchs.

Chinchón is 19 km from Aranjuez. It is thanks to the Duchess of Chinchón that quinine became widely known in Europe. Today, Anis, another kind of medicine, is produced in her castle. Chinchón is a pic-turesque place with an enchantingly ir-regular town square. The restaurants on the balconies offer the best of local spe-cialities. Bull fights are still held here during the fiesta. A converted 17th cen-tury monastery now serves as a *parador* and has a shady quadrangle.

The village of **Nuevo Baztán** was planned in the early 18th century by Churriguera. Little more remains of it today than the square, a church and a palace. According to the banker Goy-eneche's plans, it was to become a settle-ment for farmers and artisans from the Baztán Valley, the *Argotes*, the descen-dants of lepers who remained marginal-ized for centuries. The town never quite developed as intended and serves only as scenery for Zorro films and for weekend outings.

PROVINCE MADRID (South)

(Telephone area code: 91-)

Accommodation

CHINCHÓN: *LUXURY:* **Parador Nacional de Chinchón**, Tel: 8940836.
ARANJUÉZ: *MODERATE:* **Infantas**, C/ de las Infantas 4 Tel, 8911341. **Mercedes**, Highway Madrid-Cádiz at km 46, Tel: 8910440.

Restaurants

CHINCHÓN: **Café de la Iberia**, Pl. Mayor 17, **Mesón la Virreina**, Pl. Mayor 29, **Mesón Cuevas del Vino**, C/ Benito Hortelano 13.
ARANJUÉZ: **La Rana Verde** (with balcony overlooking the river); **Casa Pablo**, C/ Almibar 42, **Chirón**, C/ Real 10, **El Castillo**, Jardines del Principe.

Museums / Sightseeing

COLMENAR DE OREJA: **Museo Municipal Checa**, C/ Costanilla de los Silleros 1, Fri–Sun 10 a.m.–2 p.m., Tel: 8943030.
ARANJUÉZ: **Palace and Gardens**, Palacio Real and Jardín de la Isla. **Casa de Marinos**, **Museo de Falúas Reales**, museum exhibiting the launches used for pleasure cruises on the river Tajo, including a cradle-shaped launch for the infant Fernando VI. **Casa del Labrador**, hunting seat (1803), C/ Reina, 2 km from the palace, exhibits paintings from the 17th – 19th century, 10 a.m.–1.30 p.m., 3.30–7 p.m., in winter 10 a.m.–1 p.m., 3–6 p.m.

TOLEDO

(Telephone area code: 925-)

Accommodation

LUXURY: **Beatriz**, C/ Highway in the direction of Ávila, at km. 2,75; Tel: 222211. **Parador Conde Orgaz**, Paseo de los Cigarrales, Tel: 221850 (outside of Toledo, on the opposite bank of the Tajo). **Maria Cristina**, C/ Marqués de Mendigorría 1, Tel: 213202. **Carlos V**, C/Trastamara 1, Tel: 222100. **Cardenal**, Paseo de Recaredo 24, Tel: 224900. *MODERATE:* **Santa Isabel**, C/ Santa Isabel 24, Tel: 253136. **Labrador**, C/ Juan Labrador 16, Tel: 222620. **Los Cigarrales**, Ctra. de Circunvalación (ring road) 32, Tel: 220053. *BUDGET:* **Las Armas**, C/ Armas 7, Tel: 221668. **Imperio**, C/ Cadenas 7, Tel: 227650 **Youth Hostel** in the Castillo San Servando.

Tourist Information / Post / Transportation

Oficina de Turismo: P² Merchán, in front of the city wall, opposite the *Puerta de Bisagra*. Opening times: 10 a.m.–2 p.m., 4–6 p.m., Sat 9a.m.–3 p.m., 4–7 p.m., Sun and public holidays 9 a.m.–3 p.m.; Tel: 220843. **POST**: C/ de la Plata. **Railway Station**: Paseo de la Rosa, on the river plains outside of town; trains to and from Madrid (travel- time ca 1 1/2 hours) depart or arrive between 8 a.m. and 9 p.m. at irregular intervals. Information: Tel: 221272. **Bus Terminal**: Crta. de Circunvalación; buses to Madrid depart every half hour, Tel: 215850.

Museums / Sightseeing

Hospital de Afuera/Tavera, 10.30 a.m.–1.30 p.m., 3.30–6 p.m. **Museo Santa Cruz**, 10 a.m.–6.30 p.m., Sun 10 a.m.–2 p.m., Mon 10 a.m.–2 p.m., 4.30–6.30 p.m. **Synagogue Sta. M. la Blanca**, 10 a.m.–2 p.m., 3.30–7 p.m., in winter until 6 p.m. **Synagogue Tránsito y Museo Sefardí**, 10 a.m.–2 p.m., 4–6 p.m. **Santo Tomé**, 10 a.m.–1.45 p.m., 3.30–6.45 p.m., in winter until 5.45 p.m. **Cathedral**, 10 a.m.–2 p.m. and 3.30–7 p.m. **Taller del Moro**, 10 a.m.–2 p.m., 4–6.30 p.m. **Alcázar**, 10 a.m.–1.30 p.m., 4–6.30 p.m., in winter until 5.30 p.m., closed Mon. The **Posada de la Hermandad**, used as a courthouse and dungeon by the inquisition in the 15 th century, has been converted into an exhibition hall.

The **Mezquita del Cristo de la Luz** has no official opening times; however, the caretaker lives a bit further up the same road – if you give him a tip he will let you visit the place. There is a mosque, paintings in the apsis (added in later christian times), a garden with a marvellous view and the inner side of the *Puerta del Sol*.

Visigothic Museum, Museo de los Concilios y Cultura Visigotica (in the church of San Román), 10 a.m.–2 p.m., 3.30–7 p.m., in winter until 6 p.m., closed Sun afternoon and Mon. **Museo de Arte Contemporáneo**, 10 a.m.–2 p.m. 4–6.30 p.m. **Sto Domingo el Antiguo**, 11 a.m.–1.30 p.m., 4–7 p.m., in winter only on Sat afternoon and Sun. **San Juan de los Reyes**: 10 a.m.–1.45 p.m. 3.30–6.45 p.m., in winter until 5.45 p.m. **Casa de El Greco**: 10 a.m.–2 p.m., 3.30–7 p.m., in winter until 6 p.m., cl. Sun afternoon and Mon.

Restaurants

Hostal El Cardenal, Paseo de Recaredo 24 (at the old Bisagra Gate); **El Tropezón**, Trav. Sta. Isabel; **La Venta de Aires**, C/ Circo Romano 19, **La Tarasca**, C/ Hombre de Palo 8; **La Botica**, Pl. de Zocodover 13.

Festivals

If you don't want to miss out on Toledo's famous **Corpus Christi Procession**, you should arrive in town the night before. All decorations for the procession are up by then, the streets are lined with chairs, and lanterns, swaying underneath the sun canopies, bathe the surroundings in mellow light. Inhabitants of the surrounding villages flock into town, and there is dancing on the plazas until the early hours of the next morning.

THE MOUNTAIN VALLEYS OF NEW CASTILE

GUADALAJARA
ZARAGOZA
CUENCA
TERUEL

To get to Zaragoza from Madrid you need to take Spain's busiest road, route 6, which has now been extended to an Autovia. If you have some time to spare you can turn off the Autovia beyond Guadalajara and follow the picturesque country roads on either side of the main road towards Catalonia or the Basque provinces. The two routes are described separately below.

GUADALAJARA

Alcalá de Henares, *Complutum* to the Romans, is surrounded by an Arabic wall. Today this ancient, venerable town has almost become a suburb of Madrid. The Universidad Complutense, founded here in 1506, became part of the University of Madrid in the 19th century. It had almost 12.000 students, and under the direction of Cardinal Cisneros produced such important works as a multilingual translation of the Bible and Nebrija's grammar of the Spanish language, the first of its kind. There are still a number of period student residences which have retained the atmosphere described in the works of Mateo Alemán, Espinel and

Preceding pages: Royal celebrations in the castle grounds of Aranjuez (Luis Paret: The Royal Couple).

Cervantes, who was born here in a house on the Calle Mayor. The main building of the old university is the **Colegio de San Ildefonso**, which has both a Baroque and a Renaissance courtyard and a splendid Plateresque façade. The university buildings here recently resumed their function due to overcrowding at the main university of Madrid almost burst at the seams. Other places of interest include the archbishop's palace and the 16th century **Church of San Ildefonso** where Cardinal Cisneros is buried.

The town of **Guadalajara** takes its name from the Arabic for "stone river". All that remains of the medieval town wall are the towers of Alvar González and Alamín. The *Cortes* met here a few times in the 14th century. In 1444 the town became the property of the Dukes of the Infantado named Mendoza whose presence can still be felt all over the province. The Mendoza family graves, though now in bad repair, can be seen in the **Church of San Ginés**. The tomb of Iñigo López de Mendoza, the Marquis de Santillana, is one of the earliest Gothic graves with a reclining sculpture of the deceased on it. Other masterful examples of such graves can be seen in Sigüenza. The House of Mendoza was once so powerful that it was served by 80.000 soldiers. The Mendoza residence at the

Palacio del Infantado is today the seat of the provincial government and without doubt the most impressive building in town. The wedding of Philip II and his third wife Isabel de Valois took place here. The Isabelline façade and the richly ornamented courtyard, built in the transitional style between Gothic and the Renaissance, are all that remain of the original architecture, for most of the building was destroyed by fire in 1936. The **Instituto** in the old Jewish quarter, former convent and palace of the omnipresent Mendozas, is an attractive Renaissance building with a double gallery in the courtyard. The **Urbino Chapel** (16th century) is a fine example of Mudéjar brick architecture.

The Mountains Region

A left turn shortly beyond Guadalajara leads to a more scenic route than the Autovia. It crosses the town of **Hita**, which has lovingly preserved its 14th-century architecture. The mystery play about Don Carnal and Da. Cuaresma, a literary poem written by a local priest in the 14th century, is performed here every year. In the distance stand the castles of **Torija** (13th century), close to the main road, and of **Jadraque** on a cone-shaped hill planted with olive trees. In **Cogolludo**, too, there is an attractive town square and a Renaissance palace. From here on northwards stretches the region known for "black architecture", referring to the slate roofs of the houses of the area. The reservoirs of Beleña Alcorlo and Palmaces mark the southern boundary of this isolated mountainous region, rich in wildlife and refreshing streams. To the north you will also find the **Sonsaz National Park** and the beech woods of **Tejera Negra**.

Atienza has a well-preserved old town center. The tower is all that remains of its castle, which dates from the time of El Cid's liberation of the country. You enter the town through the **Puerta de Arrebatacapas**. Atienza has characteristic squares and colonnades, a number of Gothic churches and the museum of San Gil. Every Whit Sunday since 1162 the locals have celebrated the festival of La Caballada, which commemorates the rescue of the young King Alfonso VII from the hands of his uncle Fernando II of Leon. Imprisoned by Fernando in the castle, the rightful heir to the throne was rescued by local noblemen who dressed him as a beggar.

On the border between Castile and Aragón, in the town of **Sigüenza**, old fortifications still stand guard. The castle has been converted into a magnificent *parador*. Almost every style of architecture is represented here: Romanesque by the churches of Sta. María, San Vicente and Santiago, Renaissance by the Ermita del Humilladero and the bishop's palace, and Baroque by the Colegio de Infantes and the San Fransisco building.

But the pride of the town is the **cathedral**. Construction began in 1124, but the walls show traces of all three of the centuries it took to complete it. The late Gothic cloister signalled completion. Inside is the altar built by Covarrubias in the Chapel of Sta. Librada and the sacristy *de las cabezas*, with a ceiling decorated with 304 heads in medallions. A number of the graves in the cathedral have become famous, including the tomb of Doncel de Sigüenza, a nobleman who died in 1486. The stone figure of the young man reclines on the grave, book in hand, a symbol of the Renaissance ideal of intellect and chivalry.

From Sigüenza we recommend a short detour to the wild mountain scenery of the **Río Dulce Gorge**. The curious house set deep in the cliff face at **Alcolea del Pinar** was still home to a large family until recently. High above the Río Jalón valley in the province of Soria, a Roman triumphal arch and the ruins of the Arabic castle of **Medinaceli**, *medina selim* in

Arabic, seem to beckon from afar. Medinaceli was a kind of melting pot for several different cultures: it was once ruled by the Arabian poet and commander Galib, the famous Almanazor died here, and the poet Per Abat is said to have written his *Mío Cid* here in the middle of the 12th century. Beyond Medinaceli the road runs through the picturesque but narrow Río Jalón gorge. At the other end in the river valley is the 12th century Cistercian monastery of **Sta. María de Huerta**.

Moorish Traces in Aragón

Mudéjar is the architecture which takes its name from the Arab *mudéjares* or *moriscos* who settled in Christian regions. It is a reminder of the Moorish minority who lived in the period between the Reconquista, which reached this area in the year 1118, and the expulsion of the Moors by Philip III in 1610. Characteristic of the Mudéjar architecture of the lower Aragón are the beautiful brick church towers, often decorated with tiles. The towers usually stand apart from the nave and can be Romanesque, Gothic or Renaissance, according to the period in which they were built. An enchanting example of the style is the church at **Utebo**, an otherwise colorless and unattractive modern town where the tapered stories of the church tower rise majestically above the factory chimneys.

Southwest of Zaragoza, the Río Jalón flows through a rich fruit- and wine-growing region, originally cultivated by *moriscos*, most of whom were farmers. **Calatayud** is the main town in this region and has three Mudéjar churches, San Andrés, San Pedro de los Francos and Sta. María la Mayor. Calatayud was the Roman town of *Bílbilis*, the remains of which can still be seen today, and home to the Roman poet Marcial. Under the Arabs the town was called *Kalat Ayub* (Castle of Ayub). The church tower at

Ateca is one of the finest examples of Aragonese Mudéjar. The thermal springs of **Alhama de Aragón** were famous in Roman times and the town has been a spa since the turn of the century. **Cetina** and **Ricia** lie at the foot of the mountains, while **Ariza**, built entirely of adobe, seems an integral part of the red earth of the steep slopes to which it precariously clings. Not far from Alhama, on the other side of the Tranquera reservoir, signs point you in the direction of the **Monasterio de Piedra**, near the small town of Nuévalos in the middle of a desolate landscape. The monastery was founded in the 12th century by the Cistercians and has now been transformed into a hotel. But it is not only the monastery which

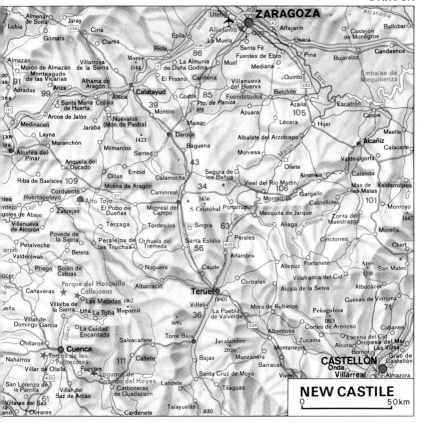

visitors come to admire. The magnificent gardens through which the streams of the Río Piedra run are also an enchanting sight to behold.

South of Catalayud in the valley of the Jiloca river lies the town of **Daroca**. It is encircled by a 3 km long wall with over a hundred towers in Morisco style. The town gate, the **Puerta Baja**, was not built until the time of Charles V. Two Romanesque churches, San Juan and San Miguel, have been preserved, as has the old Jewish quarter. There are also a number of attractive houses on the Calle Mayor which once belonged to the nobility. Daroca has a Colegiata, with a Byzantine exterior and Gothic altars where the *Corporales* are worshipped. Accord-

ing to legend, the church was attacked by Moors during mass, just as the priest was celebrating the Eucharist. The priest hid the consecrated host between the altar cloths, and as the Moors were searching for it the cloths became soaked with blood. The holy relic was wisely claimed by three towns: Calatayud, Teruel and Daroca, and a bitter dispute ensued. Finally it was tied to the back of a donkey who chose to stop right in front of the Colegiata, where the relic remains today.

Before embarking on the 400 m descent into the **Ebro Valley** towards Zaragoza, you might like to make a short detour to **Cariñena**, a town famous for its wines. **Fuendetodos** is the birth place of Goya, and some of his etchings hang

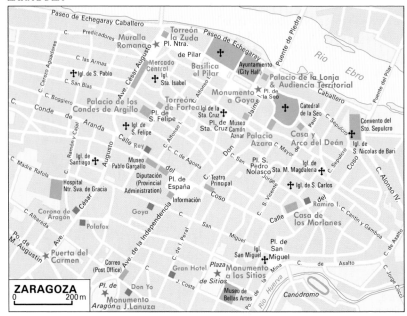

in the museum there. Gruesome relics of the Spanish Civil War have never been cleared from **Belchite** and were used as a backdrop for scenes in the film *Baron von Münchhausen*.

ZARAGOZA

Aragón's capital is one of the largest cities in Spain, with a population of 570.000. It is a center of trade and industry for the entire Ebro Valley and has attracted many immigrants from the surrounding countryside. Its influence extends from Soria to the border of Catalonia and from the Pyrenees to the Basque Country. People come here from Moncayo, the Rioja, the lower Navarra, the Pyrenees, Cinco Villas and the countryside around Teruel on business, or just to go shopping. They all meet, too, every year on the 12th October for the festival of the *jotas*, a famous music and

Right: A the Virgen del Pilar procession in Zaragoza – women in gala costumes.

dance competition which falls on the same day as the national holiday of the *Hispanidad* and the religious festival of the *Virgen del Pilar*.

Zaragoza went by many different names before it became the capital of the kingdom of Aragón. There was a town here in Iberian times, known as *Salduba*, to the Romans it was *Caesaraugusta* and the Arabs called it *Sarakusta*. Its history has been far from peaceful. The marriage of the Catholic Monarchs caused unrest between the Aragonese nobility and Castile ending with the guarantee of special privileges or *fueros* for Aragón. When Antonio Perez, the secretary of King Philip II, fled from the king to Zaragoza to seek the protection under the *fueros* in 1590, he was taken prisoner by the omnipotent Inquisition. The people of Zaragoza rose up in his defense, challenging the might of a 12.000 strong army which had been sent to capture the town. But they were defeated and Lanuza, the mayor whose name had become synonymous with the struggle for justice, was publicly beheaded in the town square. During the War of Independence it twice resisted a siege under its brave and skilled leader Palafox. The French were only able to conquer the town after it had been completely destroyed. In the final battle one townswoman named Agustina de Aragón became a local heroine after taking over a cannon from a gunner who had been killed.

Christian legends link Zaragoza with Santiago, who is said to have passed through the region as an apostle in the year 40. Exhausted and despondent at his lack of success as a preacher, he lay down to sleep on the banks of the River Ebro. The Virgin appeared to him in a dream, standing on a pillar (*pilar*) and encouraged him to continue his teaching. The truth of this episode may be disputed, but it is interesting to note that Pilar is just as common a girl's name in Spain as Carmen. On the banks of the Ebro is the basilica of **El Pilar** which commemorates the event. The present building was constructed in the 17th century on the site of various predecessors. Inside the basilica there are three naves and countless cupolas and frescoes by the young Goya and his brother-in-law Bayeu. In the center is a chapel dedicated to the Virgin. A comparatively small (38 cm) statue of the Virgin stands on a pillar of jasper, two meters high, and surrounded by flickering candles. Every day of the year the pillar is covered with a new cloth to enhance the statue's presence. Behind it is the stone said by some to be the one on which Santiago slept, but by others to be the place where the Virgin stood. Thousands of reverent hands have left deep traces in the stone.

Zaragoza's real cathedral is, however, not the basilica but the old Visigoth Church of **La Seo**, originally a cathedral, then a mosque, and now a cathedral again. It has in the meantime a total of five aisles and represents fusion of all ar-

chitectural styles from the Romanesque apse to the Gothic chapel of San Agustín and the Mudéjar walls of the Luna. The chancel dates from the Renaissance, as does the chapel of San Bernardo. The church tower is Baroque. In addition, a fine collection of Gothic and Flemish tapestries can be seen in the **Diocesan Museum**. Other churches of interest are the Gothic San Pablo, and the churches of St. Gil, La Magdalena and San Miguel, all of which have interesting Mudéjar towers. Sta. Engracia is dedicated to the Roman martyrs.

There are two attractive Renaissance palaces: the **Audencia Territorial**, with its paved inner courtyard and artesonado ceilings, is the former residence of the Count de Luna, and now houses the law courts. The **Palacio de la Lonja** used to be the town's stock exchange. On the outskirts of the city is the **Aljafería**, pleasure palace of the local Moorish rulers. It was later rebuilt by the Catholic Monarchs who took up residence in the second floor. One small mosque remains. It was once the headquarters of the local Inquisition, and provides the setting for part of Verdi's opera *Troubadour*, which is based on a play by the Spanish author Garcia Gutiérrez.

Zaragoza has many museums, but a visit to the **Museo de Bellas Artes** is especially recommended. It has an excellent archaeological exhibition and rooms devoted to the works of Goya, El Greco and Sanchez Coello. The **Camón Aznar Museum** in the Palacio de los Pardo, with its Plateresque courtyard, is dedicated to the historian and critic who left his home town a valuable collection of paintings. A further museum has an exhibition of elegant, mostly metal sculptures by **Pablo Gargallo**, an artist from the '27 generation.

In Zaragoza's colorful streets the visitor's eye is drawn more to the people than to any particular features of the town, although there are many attractive parks and gardens, particularly the **Jardines del Torero** near the exhibition center. The picturesque area around the Lanuza market in Zaragoza is known as **El Tubo**. People come here in the morning to the market and return in the early evening to the resaurants, bars and taverns in the little winding streets around the market place. Here, too, are the few remaining places which cater entirely to local tastes, **La Plata**, a café with singing and striptease acts in the afternoons, and the variety theater **El Oasis**.

Remote Regions of New Castile

The direct route from Madrid to the Mediterranean provides a small detour beyond Guadalajara, through some of the little-known parts of New Castile. To the east spreads the **Alcarria**, famous for its honey and the setting for the first novel (1948) of Camilo José Cela, who won the Nobel Prize for Literature in 1989. Today

Right: A shepherd in the remote mountains.

the inhabitants of these small mountain villages are just as friendly and eager to chat with visitors as they were when Cela wrote about them, and although some villages are now deserted or, in particular around the reservoirs, have been converted into holiday resorts, the area has lost little of its natural beauty.

The medieval town of **Pastrana** has had a long history and still has many a story to tell. Originally the property of the Order of Calatrava, Charles V gave it to Ruiz Gómez da Silva, who had come from Portugal with the court of Queen Isabel. The town owed its early wealth to da Silva, who built a palace here and founded a silk factory, establishing a plantation outside the town, and bringing skilled Morisco workers from Valencia. Da Silva married the famous Mendoza Princess de Eboli from Guadalajara who was much younger than he. Together they had thirteen children. De Eboli has gone done in history as a kind of Mata Hari of the Renaissance. Her one-eyed beauty is the center of the legend surrounding Philip II who, so the story goes, is supposed to have been her lover. That she was simultaneously the mistress of Antonio Pérez, the elegant secretary of the monarch, is certain. Her downfall came when the king and Pérez had the advisor to Juan of Austria assassinated. When the family of the dead man demanded justice, the king disguised the political murder as a crime of passion, planned by Peréz and de Eboli. For fear that they might betray his state secrets, he had them placed under house arrest. The Da Silva fortune was confiscated by the Inquisition and the estates ruined. The Princess de Eboli was allowed to leave her room for only an hour a day to sit on her balcony overlooking the village square, still called the **Plaza de la Hora** (of the hour) today. Antonio Pérez managed to escape to Zaragoza and from there to France.

Opposite the town's old silk factory is the **collegiate church** where the pink

marble tombs of the Princess de Eboli and her family can be seen in the crypt. The church museum contains an unexpected treasure, a collection of 15th-century Flemish tapestries which depict the conquest of Tangiers and Arzila by Alfonso V of Portugal, splendid colorful works in almost perfect condition. Outside the town in the **Convento del Carmen**, founded by the Princess of Eboli, you will find a curious museum of natural history, whose exhibits include a number of stuffed animals brought back by missionaries from the Far East.

Brihuega achieved importance under Charles III. Its circular cloth factory, built in 1787, is an excellent example of early industrial architecture. It stands on a cliff and is surrounded by unexpectedly attractive gardens. The factory looks over the neo-Classical town with the pretty **Plaza del Coso**, the two Gothic churches San Miguel and San Felipe and the old Arabic town wall, that has a bullfighting arena built into it. Perched regally on a red cliff is the **Castillo de Piedra Ber-**

meja, a summer residence already used by the Emir of Toledo.

Cifuentes, sporting an attractively located fortress, and **Sacédon** are the main centers of summer tourism along the "Castilian Sea", as the reservoirs of Entrepeñas, Buendía and Bolarque are called.

To the east the **Alto Tajo National Park** stretches as far as Molina de Aragón and offers breath-taking views of the Tajo valley gorges and its tributaries, walks along quiet mountain paths, and the chance to see the rich flora and fauna in a natural habitat.

The National Park can be reached on a number of different routes, from Cifuentes via Villanueva de Alorcón and Armallón to the Hundido de Armmallones or via Ocentejo; from Huertapelayo via Zaorejas to the Barranco de las Piedras de Hoz; from Molina de Aragón via Corduente to the Barranco de la Virgen de Hoz through Peralejos de las Truchas and Poveda de la Sierra with the mountain lake, the **Laguna de Taravilla**.

Molina de Aragón itself has a Arabic fort, a reminder of its turbulent history. The town changed hands many times between Aragón and Castile, and its name changed according to which province owned it at any given time. Today it is named after Aragón, but is part of Castile. It was destroyed by its own inhabitants in the War of Independence in the 19th century at the end of a siege by Napoleonic troops. Today only some old façades and a Roman bridge remain from the past in the midst of the meanwhile modern, commercial town.

The next mountain region, the **Serranía de Cuenca**, begins at **Priego**, where the fields of red rushes provide material for the local basket industry. The little town is crowded on the slopes of the Río Escabas and produces pottery as well as basketwork. In the north of the mountains the road leads through the pic-

turesque gorge of **Hoz de Beteta** to the town of the same name, a good starting point for a trip to the Laguna del Tobar, to the reservoir of La Tosca, or to the spa town of **Solán de Cabras**.

Close to **Las Majadas** are strange limestone formations called the **Callejones**, which are similar to those of the Ciudad Encantada, but less advertised. 10 km further, in an attractive valley, is the worth seeing wildlife reservation **Parque del Hosquillo** where you may be lucky enough to spot a deer, roe or even mouflon.

The river Cuervo, that tumbles over mossy stones and down falls, springs in the park-like forests of **Sierra de los Barrancos**. This area is popular amongst the locals for day-trips in summer, and has a number of bars and restaurants. In autumn it is a quiet retreat for solitary walkers or mushroom-pickers. Another popular local beauty spot is **Lake Toba** and the famous **Ciudad Ancantada**, the enchanted city, where rain has washed out "streets" in the karstic rock.

Above: In Cuenca the houses hang precariously on the edge of the cliffs. Right: The Museum of Abstract Arts is located inside.

CUENCA

The first impression of **Cuenca** is unforgettable: the town rises on a narrow crag between two deep valleys, the gorge of the gently flowing river Júcar, and that of its livelier brother, the Huécar. Packed tightly on the rock there is hardly room for more than two parallel streets and the houses, the "casas colgades" are built so close to the edge of the cliff with their balconies overhanging, that they seem suspended in mid air.

On the other side of the gorges, in the flatter section of the town, are the shops and hotels of the new town. From here you can begin the steep, memorable climb up to old Cuenca. Beyond the churches of San Felipe and San Salvador you enter the **Plaza Mayor** through the Baroque archway of the old town hall. A number of restaurants have settled on the plaza, to participate economically in the bustle.

The façade of the **cathedral** rises on one side. Little of the its original exterior is left – the Gothic front collapsed in 1902 – but the interior is still impressive, particularly the apse area with the double chancel, the crossing tower, the shortened nave, the numerous chapels and the Renaissance cloister. The altars designed by Ventura Rodríguez and Churriguera are also worth closer inspection.

From the Plaza Mayor, the Calle de San Pedro leads up to the church of the same name. A side road takes you to the legendary **Eremita de la Virgen de las Angustias**, set in the breath-taking rocky landscape, while down the Posada de San José, the only hotel in the old town boasts a fine view of the sheer drop into the Huécar valley. The houses stretch all the way to the **castle**, perched on the highest point of the old town. The area beyond is uninhabited. The road to the left leads to the Church of San Isidora, which presides over a spectacular view of the whole Júcar valley. Next to the church is a small cemetery which was decorated by an early attendant in his own unique and naive way.

211

Together with the towns of Alarcón, Uclés, Huete and Consuegra, Cuenca was part of Princess Zaida's dowry on her marriage to Alfonso VI in the 11th century. After being the object of many desires during the Reconquista, like Sleeping Beauty, Cuenca fell into a centuries-long sleep, awakening only in the 1960s when it established itself as a center of abstract art and alternative culture following the donation of the *casas colgadas* to the group of artists around Fernando Zóbel. He had come to the region to seek a center for his work and had had little luck in Toledo where the authorities were more interested in the tourist trade than abstract art. But Cuenca placed the *casas*, a row of houses overlooking the gorge built in typical 15 century style, at his and his fellow artists' disposal. Together they renovated the houses, living, working and holding exhibitions there. Today the **Museo de Arte Abstracto Es-**

Above: Castilian landscape near Teruel during cherry blossom.

pañol displays works by Zóbel, Chillida, Canogar, Millares, Torne, Tapíes, Saura and other masters of Spanish art who have made a name for themselves in recent decades.

The museum is unique both for its art and its architecture and for the highly original use of space and light. Its excellent restaurant adds the final touch. Nearby are the **provincial museum** in an old granary and the **diocesan museum** in the bishop's palace. The former houses an archaeological collection including many prehistoric finds and Roman remains from Segóbriga. The latter includes Gobelin tapestries and paintings by Ribera and El Greco amongst its most valuable treasures.

The town finally became fashionable when the filmmaker Saura, brother of the artist, chose Cuenca as the setting and background of his films. As a result of its new popularity, a whole new industry producing paper and artists' materials sprang up in Cuenca. The town became extremely popular with weekend visitors.

A large auditorium for open-air concerts has also now been built in the valley. The town also rediscovered its traditional cuisine. In its countless restaurants the menues always include some of the local specialities such as *zarajas*, a kind of lamb dumpling, *morteruelo*, a hot liver paté, and for dessert, providing you still have room, *alajú*, Arabian honey cake with almonds.

West of Cuenca are the **Torcas de los Palanceres**, another impressive natural phenomenon. It consists of around thirty strange indentations in the karstic landscape, weakened for centuries by underwater streams until they finally collapsed. The largest is 700 m in diameter and 80 m deep. 25 km further along the road to Teruel there are similar formations, but most of these have been filled with water. At **Lagunas de Cañada del Hoyo** there are small round lakes where you can enjoy some pleasant swimming in the shade of pine forests.

TERUEL

Cañete, whose houses are built up around the town wall, gives a foretaste of Albarracín. The road first carves its way through the valley of the Turia and through **Teruel**, the smallest provincial capital of Spain. According to a legend, Teruel was founded by the leader of Alfonso II's army who had been sent to defend this small strip of land against the Moors. During the battle the Arabs released bulls with flaming brands tied to their horns. The sight of one of these bulls standing alone on the summit of a hill was interpreted as a divine sign by the Christians. For their leader had dreamed that he should found a town on the spot where a bull with a star would appear. The locals still commemorate the fire bull, the *toro de fuego*. It is found on the town's coat-of-arms, pottery bulls are made locally as gifts and souvenirs, and on the **Plaza del Torico** you can see a

memorial to the bull on a pillar which is revered by the locals despite its puzzlingly diminutive size.

Teruel is a quiet little town with little industry, set in the middle of an agricultural area. But it is busy on market days when people traditionally gather in the numerous bars and restaurants over a glass of heavy red wine or enjoy a bowl of garlic soup and some of the fine locally produced ham. It is also famous for its Mudéjar towers and each of them has its own legend. The towers of **San Salvador** and **San Martín**, called the twins by the locals, were built by two Arabic architects in a contest for the hand of a beautiful lady called Zoraida. San Martín was the first to be finished, but when the architect saw that it was slightly crooked he flung himself in despair from the top of the tower, convinced he had lost all hope of winning his bride.

The **cathedral** which also has a Mudéjar tower, is of Romanesque origin and was rebuilt in the 16th and 17th centuries and restored once again after the Civil War. The Moorish ceiling decoration, the artesonado, must not be missed. The fourth Mudéjar tower is attached, the splendid Gothic church of **San Pedro**, with its beautiful cloister and Renaissance altar in which the mummies of the legendary lovers of Teruel can be seen: "*Los amantes de Teruel, tonta ella y tonto el*", or the lovers of Teruel, she as mad as he. This is another tale of love and woe, of course: The families of Isabel de Segura and Diego Marcilla were eager to prevent their match, as often happened in the Spain of that day. Isabel's family thought Diego was not good enough for their daughter and he was sent abroad to cool his heals. Through no fault of his own he returned later than the date of his planned betrothal and found Isabel married that very day to a member of the Azagra family from Albarracín. Diego collapsed and died of a broken heart and the despairing Isabel soon followed him

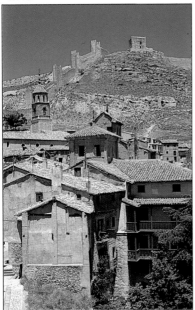

stone and red loam. At the time of the Visigoths it was still called Sta. María de Oriente, but in the 11th century it gained its independence under the Almoravids and took the name of its Moorish ruler. It was in his reign that the broad **city wall** encircling the town was built. Later it became the property of the Azagra family, who ruled it for a while as an independent kingdom. This explains why the Seguras of Teruel considered the heir to the Azagra fortune to be a better suitor for their daughter.

The town does not have a great many monuments to attract the visitor, but its architecture is particularly interesting. The doors, windows and balconies of the houses have been crafted with care. There is also a Gothic **cathedral** which has a number of Flemish tapestries. Many prehistoric cave paintings have been discovered near the town at **Barranco del Navazo** and **Cueva de Doña Clotilde**.

Before finally leaving northern Spain for the Mediterranean or heading for the border on the motorway, you might like to take the road to Alcañiz through **Calanda**, birthplace of Luis Buñuel. Alcañiz, just beyond Calanda, has a castle of the Order of Calatrava (12th/13th century), now a *parador*. It is worth at least stopping for a cup of coffee here. The square with the Renaissance town hall and Gothic market form the center of the small town. The façades of the Gothic and Baroque churches reflect their warm colors onto the streets and squares and are the background to a solemn and mournful Good Friday procession.

The Mediterranean can be reached in the south via **Morella** which is built on terraces on the slopes of the **Maestrazgo Mountains** and has an old town wall. Local crafts are sold here. The route to the west makes a detour through **Valderrobres** in the shadow of its huge castle (14th/15th century). Valderrobres also has a Gothic cathedral with an attractive rose window.

to the shades. Their tragic story is part of local folklore and has been used by Tirso de Molina and Hartzenbusch in their plays. An alabaster sculpture of the pair, reunited in death, decorates their grave and the story is told in pictorial form along the neo-Mudéjar steps that lead through the town gardens to the station.

In Teruel there is a Renaissance aqueduct, Los Arcos and two museums, one in the former bishop's palace and one in the *Casa de la Comunidad*. The latter has an excellent exhibition documenting the development of Mudéjar culture.

The Final Stretch

The town of **Albarracín** lies high above the Guadalaviar gorge in the desolate, rocky mountain region, the **Montes Universales**. The whole town, now a national monument, has steep alleys, squares and typical houses of natural

Above: The Arab wall once formed a protective wall for Albarracín.

ALCALÁ DE HENARES
Accommodation
MODERATE: **Hostal El Torero**, Puerta de Madrid, 18, Tel: 91-8890373.
Museums / Sightseeing
Casa Natal de Cervantes, C/ Imagen 2, 10 a.m.–2 p.m. und 4–7 p.m., Sat and Sun 10 a.m.–2 p.m., closed Mon. **Museo Arqueológico**, Paseo del Juncal, Fri 4–8p.m., Sat 10 a.m.–2 p.m..

PROVINCE GUADALAJARA
(Telephone area code: 911-)
Accommodation
GUADALAJARA: *BUDGET:* **España**, C/ Teniente Figueroa 3, Tel: 211303.
COGOLLUDO: Palacio; Tel: 855411.
SIGÜENZA: *LUXURY:* **Parador Castillo de Siguenza**, Pl. del Castillo, Tel: 390100.
MODERATE: **Hostal El Doncel**, C/ General Mola 1, Tel: 391090.
MEDINACELI, SORIA: *MODERATE:* **Medinaceli**, C/ Portillo 1, Tel: 975-326102.
BRIHUEGA: *MODERATE:* **Pension El Torreón**, Paseo María Cristina 6, Tel: 280300. **CIFUENTES:** *BUDGET:* **Las Secuollas**, Pl. Gen. Franco, Tel: 810037. **SACEDÓN: Mari Blanca**, C/ Maritres 2, Tel: 350044.
Tourist Information
GUADALAJARA: Oficina de Turismo, Pl. Mayor 7, Tel: 220698, 10 a.m.–2 p.m., 4–6 p.m. Inform. on **trail riding** in the Alcarria: Madrid, Pl. de Gabriel Miró 1, 4°C, Tel: 91-2655375.
Museums / Sightseeing
GUADALAJARA: Museo de Guadalajara with departments of archaeology, ethnography and art: 10 a.m.–2 p.m. and 4–6.30, Sundays and public holidays 10 a.m.–2 p.m., closed Mon. **PASTRANA: Museo Parroquial**, 10 a.m.–1 p.m., 5–7 p.m., Sundays and public holidays 10 a.m.–2 p.m., 4–7 p.m.

PROVINCE CUENCA
(Telephone area code: 966-)
Accommodation
PRIEGO: *BUDGET:* **Hostal Los Claveles**, C/ General Mola 15, Tel: 311029. **CUENCA:** *LUXURY:* **Torremangana**, C/ San Ignacio de Loyolo 9, Tel: 223351. *MODERATE:* **Posada San José**; Bar, C/ Julian Romero 4, Tel: 214325 (old town). *BUDGET:* **Hospedería San Isidro**, C/ Ramón y Cajal 33, Tel: 211163. **UÑA: Agua-Riscas**, C/ Egido 17, Tel: 281332. **TRAGACETE:** *BUDGET:* **El Gamo**, Pl. de los Caídos 2, Tel: 289008. **BETETA:** *MODERATE:* **Hotel Los Tilos** Tel: 318098. **CAÑETE:** *MODERATE:* **Hostería de Cañete**, Extraradio; Tel: 346045.

Tourist Information
CUENCA: Oficina de Turismo: Plaza Mayor, in the city hall and C/ Dalmacio García Izcara 8, Tel: 222231.
Museums / Sightseeing
CUENCA: Cathedral, 9 a.m.–1.30 p.m., 4.30–7.30 p.m. in summer, until 6.30 p.m. in winter. **Museo de Arte Abstracto Español and Museo Diocesano**, Tue–Fri 11 a.m.–2 p.m., 4–6 p.m., Sat 11 a.m.–2 p.m., 4–8 p.m., Sun 11 a.m.–2.30 p.m., closed Mon. **Museo de Cuenca**: 10 a.m.–2 p.m., 4–7 p.m., Sundays and public holidays 10 a.m.–2 p.m., closed Mon.
EL TOBAR: Museo Etnológico, 6–9 p.m.

PROVINCE ZARAGOZA
(Telephone area code: 976-)
Accommodation
CALATAYUD: *MODERATE:* **Hostal Fornos**, Paseo Calvo Sotelo 5, Tel: 881300.
NUÉVALOS: *LUXURY:* **Monasterio de Piedra**; Tel: 849011. **DAROCA:** *MODERATE:* **Daroca**, C/ Mayor 42, Tel: 800000.
ZARAGOZA: *LUXURY:* **Goya**, C/ Cinco de Marzo 5, Tel: 229331. **Gran Hotel**, Costa 5, Tel: 221901. *MODERATE:* **Ramiro I**, Coso 123, Tel: 298200. *BUDGET:* **Posada de las Almas**, C/ San Pablo 22, Tel: 439700.
Tourist Information
ZARAGOZA: Oficina de Turismo: Glorieta Pio XII; Tel: 393537; Pl. Jaime I 6, Tel: 297582, 9 –1.30 p.m. 5–7.30 p.m., Sun 9 a.m.–1.30 p.m.
Museums / Sightseeing
ZARAGOZA: Na. Sen. del Pilar, Museums: 9 a.m.–2 p.m., 4–6 p.m.
ALJAFERÍA: Palacio de la Lonja, 10 a.m.–2 p.m., 4–8 p.m., Sundays and public holidays 10 a.m.–2 p.m., closed Mon. **Museo de Bellas Artes**, 9 a.m.–2 p.m., Sun 10 a.m.–2 p.m., cl. Mon and public holidays. **Museo de Camón Aznar**, 10 a.m.–2 p.m., Sat 10 a.m.–1 p.m., Sun 11 a.m.–2 p.m., closed in August. **Museo Pablo Gargallo**, 10 a.m.–1 p.m., 5–9 p.m., Sundays and public holidays 11 a.m.–2 p.m., closed Mon.

PROVINCE TERUEL
(Telephone area code: 974-)
Accommodation
TERUEL: *LUXURY:* **Parador de Teruel** (outside of town); Tel: 601800. *MODERATE:* **Civera**, Av. De Sagunto 37, Tel: 602300. *BUDGET:* **Goya**, C/ Tomás Nogués 4, Tel: 601450.
ALBARRACÍN: *LUXURY:* **Albarracín**, C/ Azagra, Tel: 710011. *MODERATE:* **Arabia**, C/ Bernardo Zapater 2, Tel: 710212.

PETRIFIED PAST

The topography of the Iberian Peninsula is ideal for building castles and
fortresses on crags protruding from
towering table mountains, the mountains
on the islands, and above the cliffs lining
the river valleys. From the earliest civili-
zations, fortifications incorporated natural defenses. The Romans built *oppida*
and *castra* in Spain, often on the conquered defenses erected by the Spaniards
(in Gerona, Ibros, Tarrahona and Numancia). Ruins of buildings from this time
still exist, but the city walls of Lugo,
Coca, Astorga and Leon have been almost perfectly preserved. During the
Roman Empire the first *castellae* were
built as well as the system of walls.

The Visigoths strengthened what the
Romans had left behind, but little is left
of their work, since they were mostly
built out of wood. The Arabs brought a
more sophisticated kind of military technique with them and built their defenses
accordingly. These were not actual buildings, but involved a walled in area gird-
ing the soldiers' camps and the artillery's
machinery. In addition they constructed a
so-called *albarrana* look-out tower either
within or on the wall. The walls had
special gates, called *coraza*, with entrances shaped like elbows, designed to
hold up the enemy; an example of this is
the Puerta de los doce Cantos in Toledo.
Inside there was a stream, the *aljibe,*
which provided water in times of siege. A
castle included in the defenses was described as an *Alcazaba*; fortified residential palaces, on the other hand, were
called *Alcázar*, like the Alcázar in
Segovia or the one in Toledo, which was
later further enlarged by the Trastamaras
and the Habsburgs respectively to look

*Preceding pages: Encierro in Pamplona in
honor of the San Fermines festival. The
fortress of Valencia de Don Juan (15th century, León).*

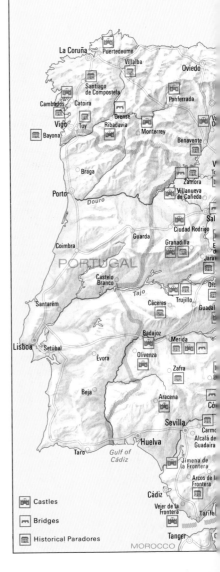

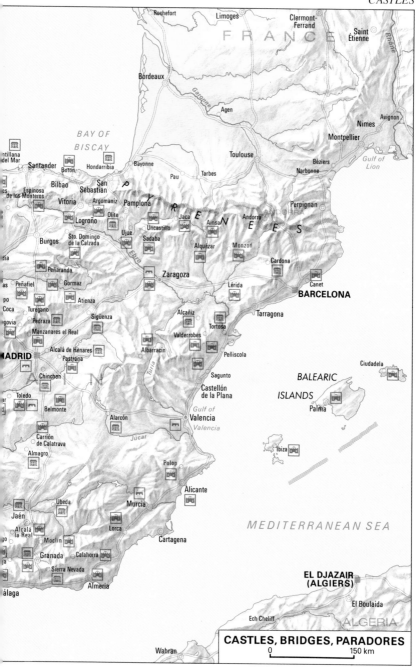

Rochefort
Limoges
Clermont-Ferrand
Saint Étienne
FRANCE
Bordeaux
Garonne
Rhône
Agen
Nimes
Avignon
Montpellier
BAY OF
BISCAY
Toulouse
Béziers
Gulf of Lion
Narbonne
Santillana del Mar
Santander
Buton
Hondarribia
Bayonne
Pau
Tarbes
Perpignan
Espinosa de los Monteros
Bilbao
San Sebastian
Argomaniz
Pamplona
PYRENEES
ANDORRA
Vitoria
Logroño
Olite
Jaca
Ainsa
Andorra
Burgos
Sto. Domingo de la Calzada
Ujué
Uncastillo
Sádaba
Alquézar
Monzón
Cardona
dia
Peñaranda
Ebro
Zaragoza
Lérida
Canet
as
Peñafiel
Gormaz
Atienza
BARCELONA
po
Coca
Turégano
Pedraza
Sigüenza
Alcañiz
Tarragona
egovia
Manzanares el Real
Alcalá de Henares
Albarracín
Valderrobes
Tortosa
MADRID
Pastrana
Chinchón
Turia
Peñiscola
SPAIN
Toledo
Belmonte
Alarcón
Sagunto
Ciudadela
BALEARIC
ISLANDS
Carrión de Calatrava
Almagro
Júcar
Castellón de la Plana
Gulf of Valencia
Valencia
Palma
Polop
Ibiza
Úbeda
Alicante
Jaén
Murcia
MEDITERRANEAN SEA
Alcalá la Real
Moclín
Lorca
Granada
Calahorra
Cartagena
Sierra Nevada
ja
Almería
álaga
EL DJAZAIR (ALGIERS)
El Boulaida
Ech Cheliff
ALGERIA
Wahran

CASTLES, BRIDGES, PARADORES
0   150 km

more like a palace. There are well preserved examples of Arabic walls and castle buildings in Molina de Aragón and Sigüenza (*parador*), both in the province of Guadalajara, the Aínsa and Monzón (in the province of Huesca), the Castillo de la Zuda of Lerrida, Castilnovo at Sepúlveda (in Segovia), Gormaz (in Soria), Albarracín (in Teruel), the Aljafería of Zaragoza, and the walls of Daroca (in Zaragoza).

During the Reconquista, the Christians built fortresses to defend their front, which moved often according to the course of the wars. For many years one of the most stable fronts was the Duero Valley. The most beautiful examples are: Frías, Peñaranda de Duero (in Burgos); Jadraque, Atienza, Torija (in Guadalajara); Valencia de Don Juan (in Léon); Ampudia and Torremormojón (in Palencia); Villanueva del Cañedo and Ciudad Rodrigo (*parador*) (in Salamanca); Cuellar (in Segovia); Valderrobles, Morella (in Teruel); Mota, Peñafiel, Portillo, Villalba de los Alcores (in Valladolid); Puebla de Sanabria, Benavente (*parador*) and Toro (in Zamora); Cetina, Sádaba, Sós, Uncastillo, Ejea (in Zaragoza); Fuenterrabía (*parador*) (in Guipuzcoa). The walls of Avila and Ciudad were also built at this time.

The military orders such as the Santiago Chivalric Order, the Knights Templar, the Calatrava and the Alcántara were given land in return for defending the new Christian settlements. In Ponferrada, for example, the Knights Templar built a large enclosure with room for all the inhabitants, if necessary. The *parador* of Alcañiz (in Teruel) was a Calatrava castle and the Templar castle of Castro-Urdiales (in Santander) was later converted into a lighthouse.

From the 13th century onwards castle towers were built onto private palaces by the nobility. The later ones were not really intended to serve defensive purposes at all, and were more for show than anything else. Such towers include those of the Velada, Verdugo and the Torreón de los Guzmanes in Avila; in Segovia there is the Torre de los Arias d'Avila, and the Torreón de los Lozoya; in Salamanca, the Torre del Aire and the Torre Clavero; and in Villalba (in Lugo) the Castillo de Andrade.

Many of the castles which have been preserved until today are made up of a mixture of different cultures. There might be a long Arabic wall, for example, often comprising two or three walls, some of which were built on the remains of old Roman walls, and were enlarged on their most exposed side by the addition of a castle after the Christian conquest. When the castle was out of the front line, a tower of homage, *torre de homenaje*, was often built to demonstrate Christian superiority. These are found in Manzanares el Real (in Madrid), for example, and also in Torrelabatón, Castillo de la Mota, Medina del Campe (in Vallodolid) and Guadamur (in Toledo). The religious orders also built fortified church buildings at this time; these included Alquézar and Loarre (in Huesca), Ujué (in Navarra), Tui and La Guardia (in Pontevedra), Turégano (in Segovia), Zorita de los Canes (in Guadalajara); Monterrey (in Orense).

Only few castles were built after the war in Granada in 1492. From this point on cannons were installed and the walls of the castle were considerably thicker, as you can see in Coca (in Segovia). In the 15th century, because of the declining need for defenses, the castles were converted into palaces (see the Alcázars of Segovia, Toledo or the Castillo de Buenamor).

Like the Arabic defenses, the fortifications of later centuries were reduced to rubble. Under the Habsburgs various star-shaped citadels were erected, which

Right: The impressive fortress of Medina del Campo (Valladolid).

may still be seen in Fuenberrabía, Pamplona and Jaca.

There are about 2.500 listed castles in Spain, of which 200 are completely preserved. In 1.500 of them you can still make out the structure in broad outline. Altogether about 10.000 defensive constructions have been counted from the Gothic period; these include bridges, towers, walls and so on.

Many historical bridges have been preserved in Spain; there are elegant but steep Roman bridges, over which the carts had to be pulled by oxen and there are many bridges from the Middle Ages. Some of them are Arabic. The bridges meant security for the pilgrims against the rapids and against fraudulent ferrymen. Some famous bridge-builders including Sto. Domingo de la Calzada, who built the road for the pilgrims to Santiago, were even canonized. To have a bridge was a privilege and many villages are named after their bridge, for example: Puentedeume and Puentearéas, Puente la Reina, Puente de Orbiga and Puente de Arzobispo. There was often a toll to pay on the bridges, which is why several of those built in the Middle Ages also have gates. Others were protected by fortified towers. The Renaissance bridges from the time of the Catholic Monarchs onwards and from the Habsburg era are not as monumental, some even possess an almost Italian elegance. The Baroque bridges inspired by the new Bourbon dynasty already bear witness to newfangled architectural experiments.

Some bridges are escpecially beautiful: the Roman bridges of Cangas de Onís, from which an Asturian cross hangs, and Burgo de Osma; the medieval bridges of Estella and Puente la Reina (in Navarra), Anguiano (in Rioja), San Marcos (in León), Pedrosa del Rey (in León), Yanguas and Garray (in Soria), Lemona (in Vizcaya), San Martín in Toledo; the Renaissance bridges of Ribadavia (in Orense), Ucero (in Soria), León and Madrid and the Baroque bridges of Aranjuez and San Vicente de la Barquera (in Cantabria).

THE WORLD OF FRANCISCO GOYA

The letters Francisco Goya wrote to his friend Zapater from the court of Madrid suggest a man with an almost provincial concern for social and financial comfort. On the other hand, they also reveal how careful he was not to make any comments which might bring him into conflict with the omnipresent, omnipotent Inquisition. It is almost as if he wanted to deny what he had described in his paintings. He writes about his works, about the more expensive ones, and about the cheaper portraits too.

Goya was born in Fuendetodos in 1746 on the day that Philip V died; he started out as an apprentice at the workshop in Zaragoza where the court painter Bayeu had also learnt the artist's trade. His attempts to obtain a grant for a trip to Italy failed, but he was awarded a prize two

Above: The Milk Maid of Bordeaux (Goya).
Right: Bull-fight scene (Goya).

years later. On his return he painted first in Zaragoza, and, equipped with a recommendation, he visited Bayeu in 1775. Here he was employed in the royal carpet-weaving factory, making designs (*cartones*). At this time, Goya painted anecdotal scenes, dances, festivals, dainty noblewomen as young *majas*, and women taken from everyday life dressed up and flirting with young *majos*.

A year after his arrival in Madrid, he had married Josefa Bayeu, a tactical but not terribly happy marriage in which Josefa always took her brother's side in any professional competition between the two – as was the case with the work of the two artists in San Francisco el Grande in Madrid, for example. Goya began doing commissioned work, portraits and religious themes. He was struck down several times by an illness which left him partially deaf. During one period of convalescence he practiced his etching technique by copying the work of Velázquez. By 1780 he had earned himself quite a reputation for this work and gained access to the circle around Prince Don Luis, who had married a member of the bourgeoisie, the Marquise of Chinchón, and lived in the country. Goya spent some time there painting family. His contacts with the aristocracy helped him to become the king's painter in 1786, and painter of the Royal Chamber in 1789. His appointment as head of the Academy signalled the climax of his career.

In 1792, Charles IV suggested that he give up his work at the carpet-weaving factory and devote himself to his other work. He was hindered, however, by serious illness and increasing deafness, and his pictures reflect his inner state of mind. In 1797 he became acquainted with Doña Cayetana, the Countess of Alba. Goya painted two portraits of the countess and traveled with her to her country seat in Sanlúcar, where he worked on the studies for his *Caprichos*. 80 etchings were produced, all of them satirically depicting

Spanish society at the beginning of the 19th century: the stupidity of the nobility and politicians, the corruption of the clerics and judges, the superstition and double standards of the middle classes and the terror of the Inquisition. Goya, who also feared the Inquisition, presented the King in 1803 with the whole collection of these paintings.

At the court he concentrated most of his artistic efforts on painting portraits of the royal family and the nobility: The *Family of Charles IV* and the moving picture of the wife of Godoy, daughter of the Marquise of Chinchón, whom the queen herself had married to her protegé. The fresco in the cupola of the chapel at San Antonio de la Florida, and both the *Majas* were painted at this time. The Countess of Alba died in 1802.

Goya experienced the turmoil of the War of Independence as an eye-witness. He painted the revolt on the square of the Puerta del Sol drowned in blood by the Mamelukes who were fighting on the French side, and the executions of the 3rd May. He allowed Joseph Bonaparte to pay him court and painted his portrait. After the expulsion of the invaders in 1814, who had fanatically transformed churches into barracks and 15th century altars into firewood, he published his *Horrors of War*, in which he also attacked the quibbling between the Liberals and the Monarchists.

His wife Josefa died in 1812. When Fernando VII acceded to the throne, the now 68 year old artist distanced himself from the court and began to paint the *Tauromaquia*, the bull-fighting scenes. A little later the Inquisition took action against Goya for his painting of the naked *Maja*. In 1819, deaf and embittered, Goya moved to the outskirts of the city into the Quinto del Sordo, on whose walls he covered with the sombre visions, of his "black painting". His last series of etchings, the *Follies*, was produced here. After Riego's failed putsch, with which Goya sympathized, he left the country and moved into the exile in Bordeaux, where he died in 1828.

SPAIN'S NATURE

The nature-loving visitor to Spain is often disappointed when first confronted with the results of human interference with nature. Many centuries of tree-felling have produced vast, open spaces and even deserts; the exploitation of natural water courses to create reservoirs for irrigation and for generating energy have turned rivers into little more than streams. The water table all over the country is constantly dropping. Modern intensive farming techniques have involved cutting down hedges and trees and generally exploiting and draining the soil; industry spews huge amounts of waste gases into the air and sewage into the rivers. All the environmental problems which Central Europe has known about for 20 years were late in coming to Spain, just as economic development was. The long-term damage is concentrated especially in dry areas where the fertility of the earth cannot be restored even through slow cultivation.

The government body in charge of nature preservation, ICONA, is dealing with these problems through reforestation and by seeking agricultural advice. The natural tree stock for the Iberian Peninsula, before the Romans built on it and burnt it, before the Habsburgs used it to build their *Armadas* and before the following generations made whole forests into books, mostly consisted of chestnuts, beeches and oaks. ICONA plants chiefly pines, and in the north eucalyptus trees, two very fast-growing species with poor quality wood which is good for making paper. But the eucalyptus acidifies the ground; the roots of pines grow near the surface. Both accelerate the drainage of surface water by densely covering the earth with needles and leaves, which only decompose very slowly into humus and stifle new growth. In the meadows around the rivers poplars are planted, which absorb water faster than other trees and can dry up entire streams. This kind of forestation has aroused widespread criticism. Many villages are angered by the fact that they are not allowed to let their goat herds graze in the newly planted woods. It is a prohibition which is clearly based on sound judgement, because the growing number of goats has led to increasingly severe damage to young trees through grazing. Over the past few centuries it has prevented natural vegetation from spreading. For villages this represents a departure from traditional rights and a restriction of their scarce resources. As a result many woods were burnt down. In Galicia in particular, where in summer 150 forest fires are recorded daily, there are scarcely any tree parks left. After a fire the bushes are the first to grow back again and then these are burnt as well, after which only thorn bushes with extremely strong roots will grow.

National Parks and Nature Reserves

Well-planned nature conservation aims at counteracting this development. Besides several national parks, large open spaces have been declared nature reserves and water preservation areas. Indigenous wild animals are protected by special hunting laws. The autonomous regions, too, are increasingly protecting certain areas, not least because this might help to boost declining tourism.

In the whole of northern Spain there are three national parks, all situated in the high mountainous regions. In the outlying mountains of Cantabria extends the **Covadonga National Park**. It has an area of about 17.000 hectares in the Picos de Europa between Asturias and León, and reaches a height of 2.400 m. The two rivers, the Cares and Dobra, cross the region with their crystal-clear and ice-cold

Right: A hang-glider takes off in the Picos de Europa.

water. The glacial lakes, the Enol and the Ercina, can reached by car from Covodonga. The park has a hotel and several huts or *refugios*. Chestnuts, oaks and yews grow right up to the timber-line. The wildlife is the same as that found in the Central European Alps, although only here can you find the last specimens of the Iberian brown bear. The 20 in this park, and the other 60-70 in the **Somiedo Nature Park**, further to the west, are all that remains of these former lords of the mountains.

Wolves are increasingly found in the northern Cordilleros. You can also see chamois, foxes and little predatory animals and capercaillie more often now. Otters ply the rivers in search of trout. Salmon fishing is strictly regulated. A daily limit on licences granted to anglers is in effect and these determine where angling may and may not take place.

The other two national parks are in the High Pyrenees. The **Ordes**a and **Monte Perdido** park has an area of almost 16.000 hectares. With its height of 3.355 m the Monte Perdido is the highest peak in the park, the eponymous *parador* of the same name is situated on one side. It is only possible to walk here in the summer months once the snow has melted. There are special campsites and huts for walkers. This area lies in the Huesca Province and can also be reached easily from **Torlo**.

Further east, in Catalonia, and north of the Tremp, is the 2.200 hectare **Aigües Tortes** and **Lago de San Mauricio National Park**. It consists basically of two valleys, the Sant Nicolau, which is near Taull and Boí and offers the visitor access to many small glacier lades, and the Escrita, which you can reach from the Espot ski-resort. The San Mauricio reservoir lies at the foot of the awe-inspiring cliff-face of the Encantata Massif. Both parks have similar flora and fauna. Mountain pine and black pines, beeches and fir trees form the basic tree stock, and these are interspersed with hazlenut trees, yews and birches. The bushes are often juniper and box. On the mountain pas-

tures there is even genuine edelweiss that one is stricly prohibited from picking. The world's last mountain goats live on these slopes. Foxes, boars, chamois, wild cats and martens are also common. The birdlife found here includes imperial eagles, bearded vultures, the rare snow grouse, woodpeckers and kingfishers.

In the north, there are several less well protected reserves including the **Cies Islands Park**, whose charm lies in its climate and scenery. It is in the Galician province of Pontevedra and is also home to many sea birds. Other reserves include the **Dunes of Liencres** in Cantabria, the park of **Somiedo** in the mountains between Asturias and León, the magnificent mountain lake **Lago de Sanabria** in Soria and Rioja, the mountain region around **San Juan de la Peña** in Huesca, the **Hoces del Duratón** in Segovia, the **Canyon de Ríos Lobos** in Soria, the beechwoods of **Riofrío, Tefera Negra**

Above: The Medulas (León) were once a gigantic Roman goldmine.

and **Montejo** in the Guadarrama Mountains, the upper course of the Manzanares and the **Ciudad Encantada** in Cuenca.

Besides the especially well-protected areas there are also attractive and unspoilt areas which have remained untouched by human beings on account of their inaccessible location. The mountain areas of Galicia, Asturias and León have beautiful scenery and are suitable for walking. The few inhabitants who still live there are very hospitable. Here are just a few places where you may get a feel for genuine Spain: the **Sierra del Culebra** in Zamora, the **Ancares** in León and Galicia, the **Sierra del Courel** in Lugo, the **Sierra del Teleno** and the **Bierzo** in León, the **Oscos** and the **Sierra de Rañadoiro** in Asturias, the **Peña de Francia** in southern Salamanca, the **Sierra Pobre** of Madrid, the **Sierra de Ayllón** and the **Alcarria** in Guadalajara, the **Serranía de Cuenca** and **Sierra de Urbasa** in Navarra and the **Sierra de Urquilla** in the Basque country.

The more spectacular scenic spots,

some of which, like the Picos de Europa, are well-known and frequently visited, and others which are off the beaten track, have been mentioned above in the relevant tour descriptions. Among them are the **Medulas** in León, the **Arribes del Duero** in Zamora and Salamanca, the natural park of **Alto Tajo** in Guadalajara and **Los Callejones** and the **Torcal de los Palancares** in Cuenca.

There is no tradition of walking, riding or cycling in Spain, apart from along the pilgrims' path to Santiago. The Spaniards see it as part of their daily routine to have to walk many kilometers to work or to reach the shops. They consider it a modern and hare-brained idea, when they see someone volunteering to walk through the countryside with boots and a rucksack when there is no real need to do so. A lot of resourceful tour organizers have found ways round this, however. On the old cattle droving tracks, the *Transhumance*, and the *Cañadas*, riding expeditions are organized, taking people in small organized groups along traffic-free roads for periods of up to four days. Several addresses where you may inquire about these excursions are available in the information section at the back of the book.

Another alternative is the footpath in the southwest of Madrid, which runs along several disused railway lines. You may walk, ride or cycle by mountain bike from Villamanta via Aldea de Fresno and Pelayos to **San Martín de Valdeiglesias**, a journey of 30 kilometers. You might prefer, however, to take the southern route to **Villa del Prado**, which is 20 kilometers long. These routes take you through farmland, along the Alberche river, through evergreen oak and pine forests. The longer of the two trips even encompasses the San Juan reservoir.

The third kind of footpath is on the ancient carriage ways. In **Muros**, Galicia, various cobbled streets laid by the Suebi lead beyond the village to the hills on the

peninsula. Carriages have carved deep tracks in the stone. Even the old Roman roads still exist. A really fascinating route connects Burgos and Santander. From the village of **Valdelateja,** situated on this road, there is a round trip of about six hours hiking to the east to the deep river valley of the Ebro. The way back begins in **Pesquera** on the plateau above the river. The path takes you through the ghost village of **Cortiguera**, where the beautiful old houses have become overgrown with weeds. The path then follows the ancient Roman road above-mentioned. A steep climb brings you back to your point of departure.

Hunting and Fishing

Hunting and fishing rights are strictly regulated and restricted everywhere in Spain. Signs bearing the words *coto privado de caza, caza vedado*, or simply a square sign cut diagonally in two, one triangle painted black and the other white, show that this is an area where hunting is prohibited. In all cases a licence is required for hunting. The most convenient thing for a foreigner to do is to obtain a licence through an agent. The hunting season is, though, outside the holiday period, and depending on the kind of animal and the region comes somewhere between October and February. Fishing is controlled by each *Comunidad Autónoma*, and it is mainly the bodies responsible for agriculture who grant licences. For the whole of Spain the trout fishing season begins on the 3rd Sunday in March. In Asturias this date applies for salmon fishing as well. In every village the local bells are rung when the first salmon of the season are caught. On many rivers there is a restriction on the number of licences granted per day, and on the number of fish one may catch. On others fishing is only permitted if the fish are thrown back in again.

SPANISH FILM

On an old building of the Carrera de San Jerónimo in Madrid hangs a plaque with the words: "The first film was shown in this room." On that day a film operator from the *Lumière* filmed schoolgirls leaving school and people coming out of the Pilar Church in Zaragoza after mass. These two films were the first steps on a journey that was to lead Spanish cinema into a major, debilitating dilemma between chastity and the church. In addition, failing internal organization, and depending on the government for financial assistance, one can safely state that Spanish film industry is a mess. Here is a brief account of its history to date.

After the Civil War in 1939, the Spanish film industry was used by the government for propaganda purposes. Franco, who himself loved film and who had once even published a filmscript under the pseudonym of Jaime de Andrade (*Race*, 1941), had the film media thoroughly investigated for its propaganda potential. The Ministry of the Economy decreed that foreign films could only be shown if they were dubbed "so that the Spanish language could be preserved". This policy favored the Hollywood film industry and German and Italian propaganda films. Censorship standards were established and the dubbing helped to see that these were maintained. The Spaniards would sit crunching sunflower seeds in the cinema as a way of combatting both hunger and the cold. It was also forbidden to kiss in public at this time. The Spanish people must have had a strange idea of life abroad, since divorce and sin were censored, and the dubbing distorted things so much that a couple might be portrayed as brother and sister, so that the appearance of a

Right: At the weekends the large Gran Via cinemas in Madrid are overcrowded.

blonde in the husband's life would not seem to be immoral. Spanish films were bursting with nationalistic pathos. Only occasionally did one slip by the censor and cause a scandal as, for example, Berlanga's *Bienvenido Mr. Marshall* of 1952.

In 1955 various authors gathered in Salamanca and declared contemporary Spanish cinema to be politically ineffective, socially inaccurate, intellectually inferior and commercially useless. Names like Bardem came to the fore, and the Italian, Ferreri, brought the influence of Italian Neo- Realism to Spain (*El Pisito*, Ferreri, 1958). Films on social issues were released and enjoyed great popularity (*Muerte de un Ciclista*, Bardem, 1955). The satirical portrayal of social reality, extending back through the whole Spanish cultural tradition, was stylized. (*Plácido*, Berlanga, 1961). The same types found in the works of Cervantes, Quevedo, Velázquez and Goya re-emerge in Berlanga's *Verdugo* (1964), Bardem's *Calle Mayor* (1956) and Buñuel's *Viridiana* (1961).

In 1962 the national director of cinematography, who happened to be an army colonel as well as a film-maker, issued new laws for the protection of Spanish films. An official film school, the EOC, began producing new names. Picazo (*La Tía Tula*, 1964), Martin Patino (*Nueve Cartas a Berta*, 1965) and Fons (*La Busca*, 1966) are some of those still known as the "new Spanish films" of that era. At the same time the first of Saura's socially critical films (*Los Golfos*, 1960) were made.

Hollywood had already discovered how cheap and spectacular the Spanish scenery was. The gigantic co-productions of the 1960s were released: *El Cid, 55 Days in Peking*, *King of Kings*, *The Fall of the Roman Empire*. The Spanish actors took on the parts of heroes and spoke their lines in Spanish, since they could not speak any other language. Almería was transformed into a Texan suburb, and

in cooperation with the Italians gave birth to a large number of spaghetti westerns.

Dissatisfaction at these developments prompted the establishment of the so-called Barcelona School in 1966, an antedote to Madrid, which was equated with centralized power. A series of symbolist films were released: *Ditirambo* (Suárez, 1967), *Nocturno 29* (Portabella, 1969), which never drew very large audiences.

A Basque cinéast living in Madrid, Elías Querejeta, replied to the new initiatives from Catalonia by producing films with higher social and intellectual standards. Since 1966 almost 99% of the Spanish films which have won awards or been box-office hits, have come out of the Querejeta factory, such as the film which has been declared the greatest film in Spanish cinema history, *El Espíritu de la Colmena*, made by V. Erice (1973).

During the last years of the Franco era, it was customary for many Spaniards to go to Perpignan or St. Jean de Luz on weekends to see a Bertolucci, Pasolini, Oshima, or Kubrick film, since the works of all these directors were forbidden in Spain. At this time in Spain films with titillating titles were made in two versions: one would have explicit nude scenes and was targeted at the Latin American market, while the other would show the actors clad in modestly cut underwear, and was meant for the home market. That is why it is quite understandable that the cinema screens filled with soft porn after the death of Franco and the end of censorship in 1977.

The film industry has overall changed very little. No schools have developed. Individual directors make films from time to time, chiefly for television; among these are Gonzalo Suarez, García Sánchez and Gutierrez de Aragon. A few, such as Saura or Camús, have become famous outside Spain. Over the last few years, however, one person has hit the news as the enfant terrible of Spanish cinema: Pedro Almodóvar, whose satirical depictions of modern Madrid often use the picaresque novel for source material.

MULTI-CULTURAL SPAIN

Over the last fifteen years it has become fashionable in the outer provinces of Spain to declare oneself a special national group in opposition to centralized power. The phenomenon has been a historical norm since the times when the Catholic Monarchs first pursued a policy of national unity in the 15th century. From 1701 onwards the absolutist Bourbon monarchy, the various military regimes of the 19th century, and finally the Franco dictatorship brought about a number of popular uprisings in the country. The historical and cultural basis for the various nationalist groups was the different languages spoken in the peninsula. There were the three romance languages: Galician Portuguese, Castilian and Catalan, and the ancient Basque language; the historical development of Spain as a collection of independent kingdoms has also played a major part in the development of nationalism.

It was usually during times of crisis in central government that the "historical nationalities", principally those in the Basque country and Catalonia, claimed their special rights and privileges, the *fueros*, and made their demands for independence; gradually various requests emerged from across the entire spectrum, ranging from forceful autonomy to radical demands for complete independence. Since 1977, when the present form of government was given its constitutional basis, the legislators had to decide between acknowledging separate nationalities on the one hand, whilst integrating them into a federal system on the other. Besides the radical alternatives which were put forward by Basque and Catalan extremists in particular, Galicia and Valencia were also proposing more moderate solutions to the problem. While

Right: The Basques' long struggle for independence becomes apparent in this graffiti.

Spain is already firmly part of the European Community, the details of autonomous status for various groups have still not yet been fully ascertained. Whether Spain can or cannot bring terrorism under control will be the test of how well it does in the EC.

Catalonia: Catalan nationalism draws its support from among the wealthy protectionist bourgeoisie and the *Renaixença* movements of the end of the 19th century, the *Renaixença* being the name usually given to the strong cultural retrospective view of the heyday of Catalonia in the Gothic era. The strongest influence on the Catalan movement came from Prat de la Riba. In 1892 he founded the *Unió Catalanista* and assembled a league about him, which hammered out a general constitution for Catalonia. Together with Muntaniola he published a *Compendium of Catalan Doctrine*. It was in the form of questions and answers, and soon became a real Catalan catechism. It began:

What is the most fundamental political duty?
To serve the homeland.
What is the homeland of the Catalans?
Catalonia.
So Spain is not the homeland of the Catalans?
No, it's no more than the state or political grouping to which we belong.

There were various factions within the movement. While Prat took the bourgeois line, Pi i Margall pursued the interests of the proletariat and wanted to turn the movement into a social rather than a Catalan one.

During the Franco period industrial development and Catalonia's desire to be more involved in Europe resulted in a resurgence of Catalan tradition and language. The Terra Lliure terrorist movement occasionally raised its head, but the strongest political support went to the Convergencia i Unió which at that time represented the regional government.

In Valencia, Catalan culture was encouraged by the recent resettlement of the coastal areas of Catalonia under Jaime I, the interior became populated by the Aragonese. The bourgeoisie in the capital had always been sympathetic to Catalonia since the time of Charles V, with the result that the conflict between town and country also continues to echo the old nationalist tendencies or toward a centralized governmental system.

Galicia: With the festival plays of 1875 and the writers Rosalia de Castro and Curros Enriquez, the Galician language and culture was revived. No political goals were involved until after Franco, as the industrial bourgeoisie maintained close relations with the central government. High emigration figures and heavy dependence on fishing and agriculture prevented a proletariat from ever growing up in the region. Today there is a strongly nationalist conservative party and a left-wing terrorist group which emerges sporadically, the *Grupo do Guerilleiro Pobo Galego*.

Basque Country: The Basque nation has always occupied a special position in history, because it has its own language and culture. With its *fueros* it also gained a certain political independence from central power. The present form of Basque nationalism dates back to Sabino Arana and his race doctrine at the end of the 19th century. During the Republican era the first statute concerning autonomy came into effect, whose advocates went into exile after Franco's victory. After the ensuing democratization two very different strands of Basque nationalism emerged. The Basque National Party, PNV, which got most of its support from among the bourgeoisie and sought dialogue with the central powers, and the *Abertzales*, the separatists, who were from Herri Batasuma's party and were supported chiefly by the industrial proletariat and small-holders. Their armed subsidiary, which broke from the youth organization, is called the militant ETA. Today it continues to try to make headline news by terror, as it always has done.

FOOD AND DRINK

Spain's good wines come from firmly established wine-growing areas, *Denominación de Origen* (D. O.). There are strong regulations governing these regions; depending on the kind of grape, the harvests are fixed at between 60 and 90 hectoliters, and nothing is allowed to be mixed with this wine. There are five quality categories, which may vary according to the place the wine is kept and how long it matures. This period always refers to the time the wine spends in the barrel and in the bottle. The longer the latter, the better the wine.

1. *Sin crianza* (no vintage, but place of origin given).

2. *CVC, conjunto de varias cosechas* (different harvests).

3. *Crianza*, 3 years maturation, 1 of which is in the barrel, 1/2 in the bottle.

4. *Reserva*, 4 years maturation, 2 in the barrel and 1 in the bottle.

5. *Gran Reserva*, 5 years maturation, 3 in the barrel and 1 in the bottle.

Northern Spain's most famous wines come from the Rioja regions: Rioja Alta, Rioja Baja and Rioja Alavesa, and from the adjacent Navarrese regions. The wines of the Duero Valley are as good. It is here that you will find the most famous Castilian vineyards: Cigales, the wine-growing area on the Rió Pisuerga in the Valladolid province with its light rosé wines, the *clarete*; Ribera Del Duero – a vast area on the bank of the Duero as it runs eastward out of Valladolid. Rueda produces all varieties of white wine; they are young, light and pale and with age they gain a golden color and a strong taste. Heavy, good quality wines are produced in Toro.

In the mountainous regions it is the isolated *tallgen* (valleys) with their mild mountain climate which are known for

Right: Fresh fish is to be had at every market throughout Spain.

their special wines. In addition there is the *Bierzo* of León, near Villafranca and Ponferrada, the *Ribeiro* wine grown on the steep banks of the Río Miño in the Orense province; the *Albaniño* wines are grown all over Galicia, especially along the lower course of the Miño. These are delicious pale white wines which are best with Galician and seafood dishes.

Apart from those from the area classed as *Rioja* in the southern Alavas, Basque wines are very light and not recommended by wine connoisseurs. They are good if all you want is a quick gulp, and are popularly known as chacolí.

On hot summer days the most refreshing drink is the sparkling Asturian apple wine, *sidra*, which is also found in northern León and parts of Galicia. It should not be confused with the sweet cider, famous outside Spain. Good *sidra* should be dry and a little cloudy. Its alcohol content is no higher than that of beer. In the Asturian pubs it is poured over the shoulder into paper-thin glasses so that it foams properly in the glass. The wooden floors of the old *chigres* are completely soaked with delicious drink.

There are several typical kinds of spirits and liqueurs in northern Spain, which come into their own on cold autumn days. The so-called *licor de Ribadeo* is a kind of Kümmel brought back to Galicia from Riga by sailors. In Navarra they drink the sloe "gin" *pacharán*; Anís comes from Chinchón; the local Grappa is called *ornjo* and the Schnapps here is called *aguardiente*.

Northern Spanish Cookery

Spanish cuisine is traditionally a rural one. The basic ingredients of many dishes are long-lasting leguminous vegetables and chick-peas (*garbanzos*), smoked sausage spiced with paprika, known as *chorizos*, and salted fish or *bacalao*. The dishes are heavy and as they contain a lot of meat, vegetables and po-

tatoes, they are rather hard work to eat; they would also disgust any champion of nouvelle cuisine, since they are always over-cooked. Although the individual regions produce their varied specialities, similar dishes and ingredients are found throughout Spain: olive oil is used in almost every dish. One of the few spices used is the paprika-like *pimento*. Garlic is only used in certain dishes, however.

Every region of Spain has its own special kind of cheese. They range from the mild buttery cheese of Galicia which is called *tetas* because of its shape, to the very immature white *queso de Burgos* and the sharp goats' cheese made in Soria, as well as the *queso de Cabrales*, from the Picos de Europa and mature sheeps' milk cheese from the Mancha.

The beloved *tapas* are well-known throughout Spain. These are delicacies displayed on the counters of countless bars and you can sometimes order them in small quantities. With the advent of microwaves, it has been possible to get them hot almost everywhere. Besides

tapas there is, of course, the *tortilla Española*, the potato omelette, of which you can easily order yourself a *pincho*.

The meat specialities of Castile include the oven-baked *horno*, roast kid, *cabrito*, lamb, *cordero* and sucking pig, called *cochinillo*.

Fish and seafood are abundant in the sea off the Spanish coast, but there are also fresh fish to be found all over Spain. The *pulpo Gallego*, the Galician octopus, and shell-fish are eaten in the small Galician coastal villages. In the Basque country, where French cookery has become well-established, you will find the best fish dishes in the whole of Spain: the *merluza*, sea pike, the *besugo*, gray perch, or *rape*, devil-fish, are favorite delicacies here.

There are also delicious stews which are prepared in the traditional rural way in many areas: the *fabada Asturiana*, made with fat white beans, *cocido Madrileño*, chick-peas, cabbage and different types of meat and *pote Gallego*, which tastes quite similar.

235

FIESTAS

Every Spanish village immerses itself in a festival at least once a year; lasting anywhere from a day to two weeks. It is dedicated to the patron saint of the village, the *patrón* or *patrona*, who is paraded around the village in a procession. The rest of the festival is spent dancing, playing music, and enjoying oneself with gallons of wine and hell-raising merriment. Any village of more than 1500 inhabitants usually includes two or three bull-fighting events in its festival, if it is to be a real *fiesta*. The smaller villages usually put on *novilladas*, fights with young bulls; one of the fights is for the village lads, the second involves a type of circus act with dwarfs as *matadors*, and the third is a genuine bull-fight.

In South America, southern France, Portugal and outlying parts of Spain,

Left: The banderillero's eyes are fixed on the bull. Right: The bull's eyes are fixed on the banderillero.

bull-fighting is more and more becoming extremely popular, and it is wrong to imagine that bull-fighting is restricted to the large arenas of the cities. A journey through some of the villages performing bull-fights in their festivals is enough to show the visitor that this is clearly not the case. From San Isidro in Madrid to San Fermín in Pamplona and the Semana Grande in Bilbao, the bull is always the center of the festival's attention.

The History of Bull-fighting

The roots of bull-fighting go back a long way. The *toros bravos*, wild bulls, were native to most parts of southern Europe. They were tamed, killed, or castrated to make them useful or harmless. In the almost 700 year long Reconquista, the *caballeros* also developed; they were a combination of knight and nobleman, who rode around armed with lances, fought the Moors, and trained with wild bulls. The most famous bullfighter of this military phase was El Cid, known as the *campeador*. Even the bull was given a special name, *toro bravo* meaning brave, courageous and untameable. Only in the 16th century was the knight's lance replaced by a special instrument, the *rejón*, but the fight was still carried out on horseback. In the 17th century bull-fighting was a favorite pastime among the court nobility, especially in Madrid, and for the Habsburg kings, Philip III and IV, it became an addiction. The Plaza Mayor had enough space for 42.000 spectators and thus became a bull-fighting arena.

The Bourbon kings did not, however, share the national euphoria. King Philip V only permitted bull-fighting in special circumstances, and he forbade his noblemen to get themselves killed or wounded for the sake of such a nonsensical activity. Only later the common people were also allowed to fight; the first *matadors* emerged and the first fights not on horse

back were staged. At the turn of the 18th and 19th centuries, there were already some heroes of bull-fighting; names like Pedro Romero and Pepe Hillo, whose gruesome death was captured by Goya in his *Tauromaquia*. The figure of the matador gained stature in the 19th century. Rafael Guerra was the first to minimize the number of steps which the matador takes between each figure he makes with his *capa*. Finally, the end of the century and the period before the Civil War in the 20th century, are considered to be the Golden Age of the *matador*. Names like Rafael Gomez, called *El Gallo*, Vicente Pastor, or the Mexican Rodolfo Gaona made bull-fighting history. In the past few years, though, the big names have disappeared, and even the quality of the bulls often leaves a lot to be desired.

The Ritual of the Bull-fight

During a bull-fight (*lidia*), lasting about two hours, two bulls are killed by three *matadors* each. (These fine animals are especially reared for the arena, and are thus extremely well treated for the first years of their life.) The order is worked out beforehand and the *matadors* perform in order of seniority, the least experienced going third and sixth. Every matador has his helpers, his *quadrilla*, consisting of three *banderilos* and two *picadores*; the latter are on horses.

Three is the magic number in bull-fighting. There are also three parts (*tercios*) to each fight. In the first of these, the *tercio de varas*, the bull and horse meet. This is the test for the bull. His behavior when it meets the horse and the *picador's* lance, the *vara*, allows one to judge whether this is a brave or cowardly representative of the breed. An unaggressive bull prefers to look for the way out, and this earns him a loud boo from the crowd. The rules state that the bull may attack the horse three times, during which he is stabbed in the neck with the point of the *picador's* lance. The president of the bull-fight gives the sign for the end of one *tercio* and the beginning of the next. In the meantime the *matador* performs a few brilliant parries with his *capa*, and demonstrates the various figures he uses in the fight: the *veronicas*, *chicuelinas* or *gaoneras*, which are often named after their originators.

The *tercio de banderillas* tests the whole team. The six brightly-colored sticks with their barbed ends have to be aimed two at a time straight at the bull so that they land properly, and the *banderilleros* must retreat just when the bull sets on with an angry movement of its head. The *matador's* crew is always close at hand just in case they need to distract the animal's attention with a *capa*.

In the last *tercio* the *matador* finally stands alone in front of the bull with just the *muleta*, a stick with a cloth attached to it. The more talented the matador, the better he can dominate the animal's move. His ability becomes all the more convincing when he turns his back on the bull and calmly walks away. All the beauty, drama and triumph of the bull-fight are captured in these few minutes. The secret lies in the composure of the *matador*. The bull must not detect any movement in his body. Nor must the *matador* ever show the bull his profile, because the bull would then see his chest moving as he breathes. This is the only way he can concentrate all the bull's attention on the *muleta*. If the *matador* steps forward or waves the *muleta*, he will encourage the bull to attack.

When the sign comes from the president's seat for the coup-de-grace, the arena becomes absolutely silent. With the *muleta* in one hand and the sword in the other, the matador stands between 1 and 1 1/2 m away from the bull's head. He forces him almost to the ground with the cloth, so that the bull has to drop his head down low, and only now can the sword

Right: A friendly chat at the La Paloma folk festival in Madrid.

be inserted between the cervical vertebra, and bring about the immediate and bloodless death of the animal. If, once this is done, the animal is still not dead, then it may be stabbed again with a dagger, neither of which action is enjoyed at all by the crowd.

The spectators play a very important part in assessing the fight; not just because women throw red carnations to their favorite *matadors*. The number of white handkerchiefs waved by the audience also demonstrate to the president the audience's opinion of the fight. He then decides whether the *matador* should be awarded a prize. This might be an ear or two, and the tail of the killed animal. These trophies are then presented to the (presumably) beaming *matador*.

Bull-related Festivals

The Navarrese festivals, of which the most famous are the San Fermines of Pamplona, are characterized by their bull-fighting and dancing. All along the Duero and Ebro valleys there are *peñas taurinas*, youth clubs organized solely around these festivals. The festivals go on day and night for a long weekend. People sleep in the morning, and anyone who has no hotel room to stay in, or who simply cannot find their way home, generally find a comfortable nook on the street, or resort to a park bench, if any are available. For the children there are *gigantes* and *cabezudos*, huge paper maché figures to amuse themselves.

In Soria the five festival days of San Juan are devoted to the bull and its uses. It is driven into the town, fought, killed, carved up, auctioned off in tiny parts and eaten by the locals. In the evening, the *peñas* gather in the park, and walk, singing and dancing, to the town center, where they dance until the early hours of the morning.

Other festivals which have the bull as their theme are the *el toro enmaromado*

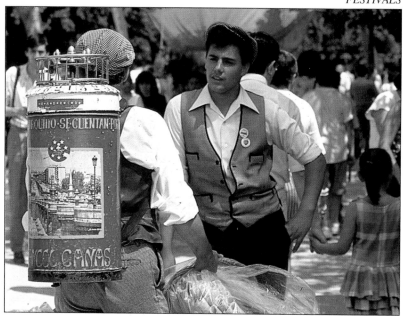

of Benavente, where the bull is tied up by its horns; while in the *toro de la vega* in Tordesillas the bull is chased out of town rather than into it; in Coco they celebrate the *toro del alba*; in Teruel the *toro de fuego*, and in Candás, in Asturias, the beach is turned into a bull-fighting arena.

Village Festivals with Special Themes

The **saints** celebrated everywhere in Spain include the Virgen del Carmen, San Juan, San Pedro and San Pablo, Santiago and the Virgen del Septiembre (on 19 September). These dates coincide with the end of the farming calendar and are similar to May Day festivities.

Festivals at sea have a special atmosphere. They are mostly pilgrimages, on which the *patrón* is carried over the sea in a procession of boats. If you are very persistent you may be allowed to join one of them. Recently there have also been performances of popular works on these pilgrimages, of the naval battle at Malpica, for example, or the Viking pilgri-

mage from Catoira. These pilgrimages are mostly made for the Virgen del Carmen, patron saint of sea-travel.

A pilgrimage often begins at the road to the chapel (*ermita*) of the saint. The pilgrims eat and dance on the nearby meadow, a mass is held, everyone is blessed, and the procession starts up again. In Galicia there are a lot of these, since for many of the young people in villages this was the only way to find a husband or wife. The pilgrimage of Pobla de Caramiñal is always joined by people who have come very close to losing their life in the past year, and they bring a shroud or a coffin with them.

Many festivals end with eating and drinking, but some are exclusively based on food. The most famous of these is that of the *bollu* of Oviedo. Everyone gathers in a big meadow to eat a *bollu preñau*, a loaf of bread with a sausage baked in it. The *bollu* takes place wherever there are Asturians. Those who left their homeland used to take this bread as provision for their whole journey. Other festivals are held to celebrate rural food, like bread and cheese, *pan y queso* in Quel, Galician octopus, *pulpo* or the *empanada*.

Wine festivals are really very special events. Originally they were held by the wine-growers to celebrate the end of the harvest, but have now turned into huge drinking festivals. The wine surplus means there is always lots of wine around, for the "wine battle" in Rioja or the "wine fountain" on the Duero. At festivals like these people usually wear white, but no one expects their clothes to stay clean the whole night through. So don't wear your best clothes if you are thinking of joining in the fun and celebrations!

Performances: In many villages old literary or mystery plays, like the *Misterio de Obanos* or the *Morisma* of Aínsa are performed. These festivals are more passive; you just have to wander around and watch the proceedings. Professional actors are hired in Hita, and it is a special sort of pleasure to hear beautiful classical verse performed in the open air.

In Anguiano young men called *zancos* dance on stilts and in the cobbled back streets here and in San Pedro de Manrique people walk bare-foot over red-hot coals.

There are very few folkloric festivals. Folklore is kept alive in the smaller villages, thanks often to the sentimentality of Spain's many emigrés. At the festival of Jaca you can also see folkloric performances from other countries.

The *fiestas vaqueiras* are held in Asturias. They originated amongst marginal ethnic groups in the Asturian mountains. There are almost no *vaqueiras* left now, and the festivals have been turned into tourist events, which does not mean that they are not worth taking part in. They usually mean a good folk performance and you can here some lovely singing.

At the festival of the Virgen del Pilar in Zaragoza, when the Spanish bull-fighting season has just finished and the South American one has just begun, the Festival of the Jotas is a popular folk dance in Castile and Aragón.

The wild horse chase often has a festival to go with it. The horses are chased, to be branded and to have their long manes and tails trimmed in the rape. There are very few places in Asturias and Galicia where wild horses may still be found, however. Finally, every year in Cangas de Onís a centuries-old and funny shepherd competition takes place.

Sport: Some of the rivers in the north are the site of canooing competitions that are both fun and serious at the same time. These events sometimes attract hundreds of contestants. There is a great tradition of rowing regattas on the coast of Santander; even Oxford and Cambridge have sent crews to participate. In Basque country all sorts of competitive games have been made up by the Basque people themselves, ranging from tug-of-war to wood-chopping, stone-lifting and *pelota*.

Religion: As can be expected from such a deeply and practicing Catholic country as Spain, religious celebrations and festivities take up a major portion on the calendar of events. The festivals of Corpus Christi consist of a solemn procession and a bull-fight. In some villages, Puentearéas for example, the streets are covered with a bright carpet of flowers. In Oñate, special dances are performed, and in Toledo, the streets are decked with canopies and are festively decorated.

The Holy Week is celebrated everywhere in processions. The most unusual customs are those of the area between Cuenca and Teruel, where melancholy drum-rolls echo through the streets from Good Friday until Easter Sunday, until people's hands and ear-drums cannot stand it any more. In Zamora and Valladolid the processions take the form of a walking art-exhibition, in the freezing Castilian cold. The *pasos*, the various scenes from the story of Christ's Passion are displayed in museums.

Festival Calendar

May Festivals: Pontevedra, May 1. Tafalla, Nav. April 30–May 1. Briviesca, Burgos: *Romería* May 2. Andoain, Guip: *Sta Cruz* May 1–5. Jaca, Huesca, 1st Friday in May; Fuentepelayo, Seg.: *San Miguel* May 3. Lérida, San Anastasio, May 11. Sto. Domingo de la Calzada, Rioja May 10.–15.

Festivals with Horse Shows: Oya, Pont. 2nd Sun in May; Cedeira near La Estrada: *Rapa*, 1st Sun in July; Viveiro, Lugo: *Curro de Candaoso* 1st Sun in July; Loredo near Ribamontán, Cant.: *Derby*, August; Reinosa, Cant.: *San Mateo*, Sept 21. Atienza, Guad.: *Caballada*, Whitsunday.

Gastronomic Festivals: Cervo, Lugo: *Fiesta de la empanada*, end of May; Briviesca, Burgos: *La Tabera*, Tue before Ascension Day; Oviedo: *Martes del Bollu*, Whitsun Tuesday; Logroño: *Fiestas Bernabeas* June 11; Pola de Lena, Cant.: *F. del Cordero* 1st Sun in July; Catoira, Pont: *Día de la Solla*, 2nd Sat in July; Quel, Rioja: *Fiestas del Pan y Queso* August 6. Carballino, Orense: *Festa do Pulpo* August 15. El Grove, Pontevedra: *Marisco-Festival* 1st Sun in Oct.

Wine Festivals: Haro, Rioja: *Wine Battle* June 29. Cambados, Pont.: *Viño Albariño* 1st Sun in August; Ribadumia, Pont.: *Viño Tinto del Salnés* June 1. Salvaterra, Pont.: *Viño do Condado* 1st Sun in August. Toro, Zamora: *Fuente del Vino* August 28. Logroño: *Wine Festival Riojana* Sept 21.

Folkloric Events: Benabarre, Huesca: *Pastorada* June 8.Cudillero, Ast: *La Amuravela*, 1st Sun in July; Roncal, Nav: *Tributo de las tres vacas* July 13. Cangas de Onís, Ast: *Fiesta del Pastor* July 25. Luarca, Ast: *Vaqueiros*, last Sun in July; Jaca, Huesca: *Festival Folklórico*, last week in July, in years ending with an uneven number; La Alberca, Salam: *La Loa*, August 15; Obanos, Nav: *Misterio* August 20. Miranda del Castañar, Salam, Sept 8. Anguiano, Rioja: *Los Zancos*, last Sat in Sept. Ainsa, Huesca: *La Morisma* Sept 15, every 2nd year.

Pilgrimages: *La Lama*, Pont. August 5. Sotomayor, Pont. August 5. Segovia, *San Frutos de Duratón* Oct 25.Ribadeo, Lugo: *Santa Cruz*, 1st Sun in August. San Andrés de Teixido, near Cedeira, La Cor: *Romería de las ánimas* Sept 8. Pobla do Caramiñal, La Cor: *Procesión de mortajas* 3rd Sun in Sept. Alcalá de la Selva, Teruel: *Virgen de la Vega* Sept 8.

Bullfighting Festivals: Alfaro, La Rioja August 16. Sahagún, León August 12. Benavente, Zam: *Toro enmaromado*; Wed before Corpus Christi Day; Ayerbe, Huesca: Santa Leticia, *Toro de fuego* Sept 9. Fuentesaúco, Zam: *Encierros de Toros*, Sat/Sun after July 2. Tudela, Nav: *Santa Ana* July 26. Vitoria: *Virgen Blanca* Aug 5. Coca, Seg: *Toro del Alba* Aug 15. Pasajes, Guip: *San Fermín*July 7. Portillo, Vall. Aug 15, Sept 8. Calahorra, Rioja, last week in August; Pamplona and Lesaca, Nav: *San Fermín*July 7. Nogueruelas, Teruel: *Toro de fuego* Aug 14–18. Arévalo, Av: *San Victorino* 1st Sun in July; Ter: *Vaquilla del Angel* 2nd Sun in July; Cantavieja and San Agustín, Ter., end of August. Lodosa, Nav: *San Emeterio, San Celedonio*July . Tordesillas, Vall.: *Toro de la Vega*, Sat after Sept 8. Ciudad Rodrigo, Salam: *Carnaval del Toro*; Candas near Carreño, Ast: *Toros en el mar* Sept 14.

Maritime Festivals: Santurce, Viz. Sept 9. Catoira, Pont: *Vikings' Pilgrimage* Aug 5. Laredo, Cant: *San Antonio de Padua* June 13. Burela, Lugo, beginning of June; Pont: *San Benitiño de Lérez* July 11. Lekeitio, Viz: *Fiesta de los Gansos*Sept 2. Bermeo, Viz: *Gira marítima* July 22. Luarca, Ast: *Procesión del Rosario* Aug 15. Betanzos, La Cor: *Rio Mandeo* Aug 16. Ares, La Cor. 2nd or 3rd Sun in August. Malpica de Bergantiños, La Cor: *Procession and Sea Battle*, last full moon in August; Santoña, Cant: *Virgen del Puerto* Sept 8. Corcubión, La Cor. July 16.

Corpus Christi Day: Toledo; Redondela, Pont; Paloteos de Fuentepelayo, Seg; Castrillo de Murcia, Burgos: *El Colaccho*; Oñate, Guip: *Korpus-Dantzak*; Pontearéas, Pont: flower decorations.

San Juan, June 24: Arbizu, Nav; Seg; Andoain, Guip; Medina de Rioseco, Vall; Soria, Thur–Mon after April 23. San Pedro Manrique, Soria: *Paso del Fuego.*

San Pedro, June 29: Zarauz, Guip: *San Pelayo*; Burgos; Lekeitio, Viz; Pasajes, Guip. Sestao and Sopelana, Viz.

Santiago, July 25: Santiago de Compostela; Puente la Reina and Valcarlos, Nav; Sabiñánigo, Huesca; Padrón, La Co; Clavijo, Rioja.

Virgen de Agosto, August 15: Amurrio, Alava; Alar del Rey, Pal: *downstream canoe race on the river Pisuerga*, 2nd Sun in August. Cabezón de la Sal, Cant: *Mountain Day*; La Guardia, Pont: *Pilgrimage to Sta Tecla*; Bilbao: *Semana Grande* (Festival Week); Deva, Guip; Burgo de Osma, Soria; Ondárroa: *Día del Arrantzale*; Sada, La Cor.

San Ronque, August 16: Barro-Llanes, Ast; Bronchales, Ter; Carasa, Cant.

Others: Oviedo: *Fiesta del Emigrante* Sept 21. Sorzano, Rioja: *Tribute of the 100 Virgins*; May 20. León: *Fiesta de las Cantaderas*1rst Sun in Oct. Marquina, Vizcaya: *San Miguel* Sept 26–29. Huesca and Foz, Lugo: *San Lorenzo*, August 10.

Nelles Maps ...the maps, that get you going.

   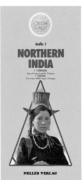

Nelles Map Series

- Afghanistan
- Australia
- Burma
- Caribbean Islands 1/
  Bermuda, Bahamas,
  Greater Antilles
- Caribbean Islands 2/
  Lesser Antilles
- China 1/
  North-Eastern China
- China 2/
  Northern China
- China 3/
  Central China
- China 4/
  Southern China
- Crete
- Hawaiian Islands
- Hawaiian Islands 1/Kauai
- Hawaiian Islands 2/
  Honolulu, Oahu

- Hawaiian Islands 3/
  Maui, Molokai, Lanai
- Hawaiian Islands 4/Hawaii
- Himalaya
- Hong Kong
- Indian Subcontinent
- India 1/Northern India
- India 2/Western India
- India 3/Eastern India
- India 4/Southern India
- India 5/North-Eastern India
- Indonesia
- Indonesia 1/Sumatra
- Indonesia 2/
  Java + Nusa Tenggara
- Indonesia 3/Bali
- Indonesia 4/Kalimantan

- Indonesia 5/Java + Bali
- Indonesia 6/Sulawesi
- Indonesia 7/
  Irian Jaya + Maluku
- Jakarta
- Japan
- Kenya
- Korea
- Malaysia
- West Malaysia
- Nepal
- New Zealand
- Pakistan
- Philippines
- Singapore
- South East Asia
- Sri Lanka
- Taiwan
- Thailand
- Vietnam, Laos
  Kampuchea

SPAIN-NORTH
©Nelles Verlag GmbH, München 45
  All rights reserved
  ISBN 3-88618-378-5

First Edition 1991
Co-Publisher for U.K.:
Robertson McCarta, London
ISBN 1-85365-254-7 (for U.K.)

Publisher:	Günter Nelles		Freytag & Bernd,Wien
			Ravenstein Verlag,
Chief Editor:	Dr. Heinz Vestner		License Nr. 1/139
Project Editor:	Dr. S. Tzschaschel	**DTP-Exposure:**	Printshop Schimann,
Editor:	Marton Radkai		Pfaffenhofen
Translation:	Ch. Banerji,	**Color**	
	F. Cushley, L. Rhodes,	**Separation:**	Priegnitz, München
	B. Woodroffe	**Printed by:**	Gorenjski Tisk, Kranj,
Cartography:	Nelles Verlag GmbH		Yugoslavia

  - 01 -

TABLE OF CONTENTS

TRAVEL PREPARATIONS

Spanish Tourist Offices

USA, Water Tower Place, Suite 955 East, 845 North Michigan Ave., Chicago, ILL 60611, Tel. (312)642-98-17.

USA, 8383 Wilshire Blvd., Suite 960, Los Angeles, CA 90211, Tel. (213)658-71-88.

USA, 1221 Brickell Ave., Miami, FLA 33131, Tel. (305)358-19-92.

USA, 665 Fifth Ave., New York, NY 10022, Tel. (212)759-88-22.

GREAT BRITAIN, 57-58 St. James Str., London SW1A1LD, Tel. 499-11-69.

CANADA, 102 Bloor Street West, Toronto, Ontario M5S 1M8, Tel. (416)96131-31.

AUSTRALIA, 203 Castlereagh Street, Suite 21, NSW 2000, Sidney South, Tel. (612)264-79-66.

Climate/Best Time to Travel

Average daily temperatures in May, July, September, and maximum temperatures in August (°C):

	May	July	Sept	Max
North coast	14	19	17	29
Galicia, inland	16	21	19	38
Basque region, Vitoria	12	18	17	34
Pamplona, Huesca	15	23	19	35
Zaragoza, Lérida	17	24	20	35
León	12	20	19	34
Burgos	11	18	15	32
Ávila, Salamanca	14	22	18	34
Madrid	16	24	20	38
Cuenca, Teruel	14	21	18	34
Toledo	17	26	21	41

Midday temperatures are relatively high and night temperatures are low throughout the interior. On the coast the climate is damper, midday temperatures are less extreme and the nights are mild.

Clothing

Whilst you can be guaranteed of summer weather throughout Spain in July and August, the months of May/June and September/October are the best for traveling, but the most changeable. In all areas you should take rainwear with you, in mountain areas and on the north coast take a jacket or pullover. The high summer temperatures sometimes make even a bikini too much to wear, but it is customary throughout the country to be properly dressed. Only on the beach can you go into a restaurants wearing shorts or an airy top without attracting attention.

Currency/Foreign Exchange

The Spanish Peseta has been a relatively stable currency since Spain joined the EC. You can change money at home or take travelers checks with you. Because of the considerable danger of theft it is inadvisable to carry large amounts of cash with you. A check card with a secret number is the best form of getting money. Many banks which have signs outside saying "Foreign exchange" will not accept travelers checks. You will always need your passport when changing money. Exchange offices have good rates but often take large commissions. Most of the larger hotels will change money for their guests without difficulties and without charges. The Post Office Bank, the *Caja Postal* building, is not always the same as the Post Office. You can withdraw money there from European accounts.

There are 1000, 2000, 5000 and 10 000 Peseta notes, and rarely 500 Peseta notes too. Coins are to the value of 1, 5, 10, 25, 50, 100 200 and 500 Pesetas. New coins have recently been introduced and so there are usually two types of coins worth the same amount. Foreign visitors often have trouble with the 100 Peseta coin which has no numbers on it *(cien)*.

Entering the Country

Spain has no visa regulations, but is soon to introduce them for some African

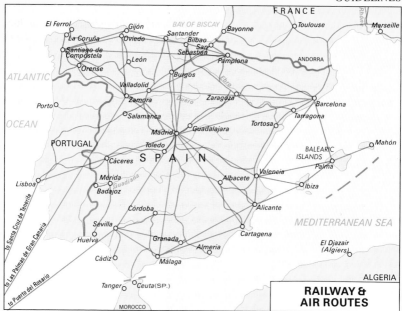

El Ferrol · Gijón · *BAY OF BISCAY* · Bayonne · Toulouse · Marseille
La Coruña · Oviedo · Santander · Bilbao · San Sebastián · ANDORRA
Santiago de Compostela · León · Pamplona
Orense · Burgos
ATLANTIC · Valladolid
Porto · Zamora · Zaragoza · Barcelona
OCEAN · Salamanca · Tarragona
Madrid · Guadalajara · Tortosa
PORTUGAL · Toledo · BALEARIC ISLANDS · Mahón
Cáceres · S P A I N · Palma
Mérida · Albacete · Valencia
Lisboa · Badajoz · Ibiza
Córdoba · Alicante · *MEDITERRANEAN SEA*
Sevilla · Cartagena
Huelva · Granada · Almería · El Djazair (Algiers)
Cádiz · Málaga
ALGERIA
Tanger · Ceuta(SP.)
MOROCCO

RAILWAY & AIR ROUTES

countries. All you need to enter the country is a valid passport. Members of an European Community country can enter with their identity card.

Getting there

The easiest way to get there is by plane, but Spain's public transport network is not the best. For a holiday in a city the plane is recommended, for it is extremely hard to find somewhere to park a car in most towns. You can always hire a car for excursions. If you come by car you can come from England or Italy by ferry or via France. The quickest routes are the motorways on both coasts around the Pyrenees, but the Pyrenean mountain chain is not so great that you can't cross it using one of the passes or the tunnel of Vella in one day.

Health

No vaccinations or health precautions need to be taken. You can drink the water in Spain everywhere, even from public fountains.

TRAVELING AROUND SPAIN

By Car: There are main roads, regional roads and communal roads. The conditions are usually good, but in the first half of the '90s you should allow for increased work crews on the roads because the entire road network is being extended with EC money.

Autopistas (motorways) are toll roads *(peaje)* and therefore usually free of traffic jams. *Autovías* are not.

Traveling by car is the natural way of traveling in Spain. The large overland roads, numbered N I to N VI radiate like a star from Madrid and have in some places been extended to *Autovías*. They are almost always packed. Lorry traffic leaves the cities in the morning to arrive by the afternoon, so if you are following these roads make sure you leave before the lorries or a long time after them.

By Bicycle: It is becoming more and more popular to travel Europe by bike. But note that a higher percentage of Spain is as mountainous as Switzerland!

There are no bicycle routes, but there are many hardly used provincial roads. Arriving by train with a bike is possible, although not on all trains. This variation is still better than taking your bike in the car, because you should never park and leave a packed car in Spain.

By Air: The national airline IBERIA flies from Barcelona and Madrid daily to 20 inland airports. There is a shuttle service operating between the two large cities which leaves at least once an hour, which you cannot book in advance. AVIACO offers further inland flights.

By Train:Spain's railway connections suffer from the ageing broad-gauge railway tracks and the many mountains. The network does not cover all parts of the country and is not well served. There are good connections within the densely populated areas of Catalonia and the Basque provinces. There are three categories of long distance trains: *Interurbano, Talgo* and *Express.* The latter cost more. A high speed track between Madrid and Sevilla is currently being built. It will be finished in 1992. Further routes from Madrid to the Basque region and to Catalonia are planned which will join the country to the European network. The railway companies are *Renfe* and *Feve*. Tickets for longer journeys should be bought with seat reservations in advance at travel agents, for in the high season trains are often overcrowded and the queues at the station counters only move forward at a snail's pace.

There are weekend special offers on journeys from Madrid, the so-called *trenes lince,* cheap return tickets to León, Albacete, Jaén, Puertollano and Caceres. There is also a series of package trips, *trenes turisticos,* which include accommodation in very good hotels and tours: Al-Andalus-trips through Andalusia lasting a few days, weekend trips including accommodation from Madrid to Salamanca, to the Extremadura, to Cuenca, Burgos or la Mancha. There are also day-trips to Ávila, Aranjuez and Sigüenza. From Barcelona there are day-trips to Gerona. You can book these trips from abroad IBER-RAIL C/Capitán Haya, 55-Madrid, Tel: 91- 2793605/3793200.

By Buses: Public transport between small villages and cities is usually covered by bus. You need to inquire about these buses at travel agencies or the bus companies. As a rule, in smaller towns buses go to the nearest town from the main square twice a day.

PRACTICAL ADVICE

Accommodation

The information boxes of this travel guide to Spain contain only a small selection of the huge choice of accommodation in Spain. For the larger towns we have recommended accommodation in all available categories. We have tried to choose centrally situated and architecturally attractive accommodation.

The official classification is from 1 to 5 stars in the following categories:

H . . . . hotel
HR . . Hotel Residencia (holiday hotel
for a longer stay)
HA . . . . Hotel Apartamentos
RA . . . . . . Residencia Apartamentos
M . . . . Motel
Hs . . . . Hostal (simple hotel)
OP . . . . . guest-house (in cities, often
long-stay accomodation)
HsR . . . . Hostal Residencia
(often long-stay accomodation)
F . . . . Fonda (the most simple
type of guest-house)

All hotels, regardless of category, are usually clean, but the beds are often bad, even in the very good hotels. Noise is not cause for complaint, and windows overlooking the inner courtyard from which you cannot see the sky are treasured throughout Spain.

Paradores nacionales are state-run hotels in the upper price brackets and almost always in a nice setting. The map on page 221 shows where these *paradores* are and whether they are in a historical building. Illustrated catalogs of the *paradores* can be obtained from any tourist office. In the high season it is recommended to reserve a room, which you can do from abroad. The central reservation headquarters for the *paradores nacionales* in Spain is C/ Velasquez, 18, 28001 Madrid, Tel: 4359700, 4359744, Fax 4359944.

Breakdown Services
The Royal Automobile Club, the RACE, helps in breakdowns and accidents. It has agreements with the following foreign automobile clubs: ADAC, DTC, AvD, AA, RAC, ACI, TCI.

The national emergency tow service can be reached in Madrid on Tel: 91 - 5933333.

Car Hire
The easiest way to hire a car is by credit card. Without one you will need to leave a deposit of around $ 850. You will need to show your passport and a drivers license which is more than one year old. There are special rates on weekends.

Cinema
There are cinemas in the cities which show foreign films with subtitles *(versión subtitulada).*

Daily Schedule
The day begins slowly and late in Spain. You have breakfast in a bar with a coffee and something to dunk in it, preferably *churros*. Office and shop hours are from 10 to 2 o'clock. Whatever you don't manage to do during official hours will usually have to wait for the next day, especially in summer.

In Spain the main meal of the day is eaten between 2 and 4 o'clock. At lunch time the cheapest meals are offered in the restaurants and cafés. Almost all of them

have a good lunch menu which includes bread and wine. Wherever you find low prices and menus just written on a piece of paper you can be sure of simple, but good home cooking.

Electricity
The voltage throughout the country is 220 volts and 50 Hz. Most hotels have europlugs, but if not you can buy an adapter in every electric shop.

Etiquette
Spain is European, but there are some details which are different from Central Europe or North America. There is a polite form of address *(usted),* but most people use the informal *tu* in shops and restaurants. It is normal to throw your rubbish on the floor in restaurants and cafés – they are swept often enough to maintain hygiene. Central European customs of speaking more quietly after 10 at night or turning down noise are unknown in Spain. The course of the day is according to the sun: about 2 hours later than northern countries, and you will have to get used to not eating lunch before 2 or your evening meal before 9 o'clock.

Festivals
Every town has a local fiesta once or twice a year which can last for anything from a long weekend to two weeks. Normal business operates on the back burner during this time, the whole town takes part in the processions and dances and no one gets up early in the mornings. Visitors will have to put up with more noise. Complaints will only meet with lack of understanding. The only thing to do is join in!

Guides
Spanish tour guides have to study for three years and are usually well-qualified. But in the strongholds of tourism you may find tour guides who take you into shops where they get a commission

instead of showing you the sights. In such cases you can complain to the tourist office. In most towns you can book English, French or German guides from the tourist office, but prices are high and it is only worthwhile if you are in a large group. Smaller groups have to rely on printed guides. They often have misleading opening times. Tourist offices are not informed of current events such as concerts. In the cities of Madrid and Barcelona you can buy weekly events calendars from newspaper kiosks, which contain the most reliable information. It is often possible to still get tickets on the same day of the event.

Holidays
The national holidays are:

January 1, New Year's Day; January 6, The Epiphany; Easter: Maundy Thursday, Good Friday and Easter Monday; May 1, May Day; August 15, The Assumption; October 12, Virgen del Pilar and Columbus's Day; November 1, All Saints' Day; December 6, Constitution Day; December 8, Day of the Immaculate Conception; December 25, Christmas Day.

Each region also has its own holidays and local holidays in the town.

Horseback riding
Asociación de Marchas da Caballo de Cataluña (in the Catalonian Pyrenees and Andorra), Tel: Barcelona 93/2118448; Pirineos sin fronteras (Pyrenees), Tel: Huesca 974/551385; Alcarria al Caballo (in Alcarria), Tel: Madrid 91/2655375. Caballotour (in Gredos mountains), Tel: Madrid 91/5634904; Centro de Recursos de Montaña (in the Sierra Norte de Madrid), Tel: Madrid 91/8697058; Trastur (in the valleys of Asturias), Tel: Oviedo 985/806036; Equitour (Gerona, Castile), Tel: Barcelona 93/4196272; Jesús Manuel Berna (Gredos, Castile), Tel: Madrid 91/5192644.

Hunting
Federación Española de Caza, Av. Reina Victoria, 72, 1º, Madrid 28003.

Museums and Art Galleries
Private art galleries follow the market and are often even open on Sundays. Public museums and galleries are almost always closed on Sundays and Mondays. There is often a day during the week when EC nationals get in free.

Opening Times
Shops usually open between 9 and 10 in the morning and have a break between 2 and 5 pm, which might be half an hour earlier in the winter and in the north. In the evenings they close around 8 o'clock. Shops are open on Saturdays, sometimes in the afternoon too. Department stores and shops in the city centers are often open in the afternoons and close a little later in the evenings. Museums and monuments usually follow the same plan, but are open on Sunday afternoons and almost always closed on Mondays.

Opening times vary from year to year and are considerably longer in summer than winter. Sights outside the towns are often closed completely outside the high season. You can always inquire after the key holder to churches and have the church unlocked.

Pharmacies
Farmacias are to be found everywhere. They are well stocked and sell many medicines without prescriptions. Opening times are as for shops. If you are lucky you will find information on the emergency duty pharmacy *(urgencia)* in the window.

Photographing
You are allowed to take photos at most monuments, but often video cameras are prohibited. Flash bulbs are almost always forbidden.

Postal Services

The Post Offices *(correos)* are often only open in the mornings. But you can buy stamps in every *estanco,* the state tobacco shops. Letters and postcards to EC countries cost the same. National inland rates are different for local and long distance letters. Within Europe it is not necessary to send letters by air mail.

Press

In cities and holiday resorts on the Mediterranean there is always a good selection of national and international daily newspapers. Spanish papers are also printed on Sundays.

In summer French and English news is broadcast at lunch time. At 3 o'clock the most important Spanish news is shown. From then until 5 o'clock is *siesta.* Evening events, restaurants etc do not begin before 9 o'clock. Normal families do not go to bed before 1 in the morning, and that includes the children in summer too.

Telecommunication

You can make international calls from all telephone boxes. Dial 07 for the international network and wait for the tone. Then dial the national code (Germany 49, Austria 43, England 44, Sweden 46, Switzerland 41, France 33, Canada and USA 1, Holland 31, Ireland 35, Norway 47 and Italy 49). The German town dialing code is dialed without the first 0. Dial 004 for national information, 008 for European information, and 005 for international information. In most towns there are offices of the telephone company *Telefonica* with long distance phone boxes in the *locutorio*.

Theft

Even a well-disguised tourist is obviously a tourist. In cities, never carry a handbag on the streets, keep your wallet in your trouser pocket. The busier the pavement, the surer you can be that someone will be trying to steal someone else's purse. Your passport, tickets, travelers checks etc. are safer locked in your suitcase in the hotel than on your person. Foreign cars are pre- destined to be broken into, especially if they contain anything. Usually the small window on the pavement side is smashed with a stone. You cannot safely leave a car with a radio on any Spanish street, not even for a quarter of an hour in broad daylight in a good area. Guarded underground garages take no responsibility for the contents of your car, but offer certain protection.

If your nerves are good you can try to "buy back" your stolen goods on the same or the next day on the black market of Madrid (Rastro) and Barcelona (Plaza Real).

Time

Although geographically Spain lies in another time zone it follows Central European time, including summer time, when the clocks are changed with the countries of Central Europe. The Canary Islands are 1 hour behind.

Tips

In cafés and restaurants tips are usually included in the price. The additional sum on the bill is IVA, value added tax. Tips are still usually welcomed. It is not advisable to offer traffic police or *Guardia Civiles* tips to try to get them to change their minds about violations of traffic regulations!

Tourist Information

In every provincial capital and in many tourist centers there are tourist information offices (i=*informacíon,* or *oficina de turismo)* which will provide you with printed information and maps. They follow normal opening times. Only in the more important tourist areas are they open on Sunday mornings in summer. There are also *Comunidades Autónomas* offices in some towns.

Weights and Measures

Weights, measures and clothing sizes are the same as in most Central European countries.

EMBASSIES / CONSULATES

(Madrid local code: 91)
Canada: C/ Nuñez de Balboa, 35; 4314300
Ireland: C/ Claudio Coello, 73; Tel: 5763500
USA: C/ Serrano, 75; Tel: 5763400
Great Britain: C/ Fernando el Santo, 16; Tel: 3190200.

GLOSSARY

good morning	buenos días
(after 2 p.m.)	buenas tardes
good night	buenas noches
hello	hola
please	por favor
thank you	gracias
yes	si
no	no
goodbye	adiós
excuse me	perdón
How are you?	Que tal?
good	bién
What time is it?	Qué hora es?
How much is it?	Cuánto cuesta ésto?
Where is ..?	Dónde está ...?
right	a la derecha
left	a la izquierda
one	uno, un
two	dos
three	tres
four	cuatro
five	cinco
six	seis
seven	siete
eight	ocho
nine	nueve
ten	diez
eleven	once
twelve	doce
twenty	veinte
hundred	cien
thousand	mil
today	hoy
tomorrow	mañana
yesterday	ayer
minute	minuto
hour	hora
day	día
week	semana
month	mes
year	año
Monday	Lunes
Tuesday	Martes
Wednesday	Miércoles
Thursday	Jueves
Friday	Viernes
Saturday	Sábado
Sunday	Domingo
Holiday	Festivo
Do you have a room?	Hay habitación libre?
double room	habitación doble
single room	habitación sencilla
with breakfast	con desayuno
quiet	tranquilo
today's menu	menú del día
dessert	postre
bread	pan
drink	bebida
wine	vino
beer	cerveza
mineral water	agua mineral
carbonated/uncarbonated	con/sin gas
black coffee	café solo
coffee with a little milk	cortado
milk coffee	café con leche
breakfast	doughnutschurros
omelette	tortilla
potato omelette	tortilla española
fish	pescado
soup	sopa
meat	carne
pork	cerdo
veal	ternera
chicken	pollo

lamb	cordero
steam	edguisado
fried	frito
grill	eda la plancha
bake	dasado
batter	edempanado
salad	ensalada
vegetables	verdura
peas and beans	legumbres
bill please	La cuenta, por favor!

sea pike	merluza
trout	trucha
salmon	salmón
tuna fish	bonito
sword fish	emperador
herring	gallo
gray perch	besugo
devil-fish	rape

AUTHORS

Maria Reyes Agudo is an expert on Romanesque and Gothic monuments. Her favorites are the isolated Pyrenean villages with their forgotten treasures in small, unprepossessing churches.

Orcha Folch is an architect and genuine Catalan. He is also a freelance journalist. He knows Barcelona like the back of his hand: you can rely on his bar and restaurant tips.

Gabriel Calvo Lopez-Guerrero is a language and literature lecturer, journalist and filmscript writer. He observed Spain from Germany for ten years. He now lives and writes in Madrid.

José Ramón Monleón from Valencia is a doctor and radio play writer. If he has any time left between his two professions, he loves to travel around remote mountain areas.

José Manuel Riancho tries to earn a living from short films and documentaries. His research has led him to the outermost corners of Castile. He comes from Santander and lives in Madrid.

Dr. Sabine Tzschaschel from Munich has toured the world as a geographer. Studies of Spain have taken her all over the country.

Alfredo Marqués Correa, a Madrileño, is an enthusiastic bullfight fan.

PHOTOGRAPHERS

INDEX